Index Annuities

A Suitable Approach

Jack Marrion

&

John Olsen, CLU, ChFC, AEP

Published by Olsen & Marrion, LLC.

Printed in the United States of America

First Printing, January 2011

ISBN 0-9728251-4-2

Olsen & Marrion, LLC
2187 Butterfield Court
St. Louis MO 63043

(314) 255-6531

info@indexannuitybook.com

Index Annuities: A Suitable Approach

The Authors

Jack Marrion is president of a research consultancy that publishes the **Index Compendium** newsletter and the **Advantage Compendium** research studies. He is frequently referenced by regulators and in SEC rule filings relating to annuities, and often appears as an expert witness. His first index annuity book ***Index Annuities – Power & Protection*** was regarded as **the** ultimate text on index annuities.

In 2006 the National Association of Insurance Commissioners asked him to address their annual meeting and teach regulators the realities of index annuities. He was invited back in 2009 to talk to the NAIC about the effects of aging on senior decision-making. Best's Review said he was likely to affect the course of the industry. He holds an MBA from the University of Missouri and his doctoral studies in the area of cognitive bias in decision-making represent a new paradigm in the marketing and development of retirement income products.

John L. Olsen, CLU, ChFC, AEP is an insurance agent and financial advisor practicing in St. Louis County, MO. John is a past president of the St. Louis chapter of NAIFA, a past board member of the St. Louis chapter of the Society of Financial Service Professionals, and a current board member of the St. Louis Estate Planning Council. He has written numerous articles on annuities, insurance, and estate and retirement planning and is co-author (with Michael Kitces of *The Annuity Advisor* (National Underwriter Co., 2nd ed., 2009). In addition to serving his own clients, John consults to other advisors on advanced cases and provides expert witness services in cases involving annuities and other retirement income products. He is also a sought-after speaker who has given presentations to numerous industry groups.

Introduction

Welcome. This is a book about index annuities. The authors have written about them before. John Olsen's book ***The Annuity Advisor*** (which he co-authored with Michael Kitces) provided an in-depth look at how annuities work, their uses and misuses, and extensive discussion of annuity taxation. Jack Marrion's book ***Index Annuities – Power & Protection*** covered index annuity basics, crediting methods and sales tips. The book you hold in your hand was written for the new index annuity world – a world where one needs to understand, not only how index annuities work, but where they fit and don't fit, and when they are suitable or unsuitable.

After you read this book you will know how to compare different crediting methods and understand when lifetime benefit riders make sense (and when they don't). You'll have seen the "real world" returns index annuities have generated and be able to recognize some common and dangerous "tax traps" that can cause problems in annuity planning. You'll have a better appreciation of what "suitability" really means, and a better understanding of the kinds of advice you can, should, cannot, and must never give in your dealings with prospects and clients.

If you'd like to jump start your learning, begin with Chapter 1 – Annuity Basics, and Chapter 2 – Annuity Interest, and then use the index in the back to investigate future topics as needed. We've arranged it so that you don't need to read every single word to make this book work for you. Key points of each chapter are highlighted in blue and the back of each chapter contains a cheat sheet summarizing the important ideas.

This book attempts to give you the facts about index annuities and where they fit. We once said that index annuities are a wonderfully simple concept made complicated. We hope this book makes everything clearer. We would like to thank Tonia Cronin and Yvonne de Brazil for their suggestions on readability.

Chapter 1 – Annuity Basics

The first index annuity was purchased 15 February 1995 by a 60 year old from Massachusetts. Over the next five years his $21,000 premium placed in a *Keyport KeyIndex* annuity grew to $51,779. The index annuity era had begun.

Cumulative Index Annuity Sales (in Billions)

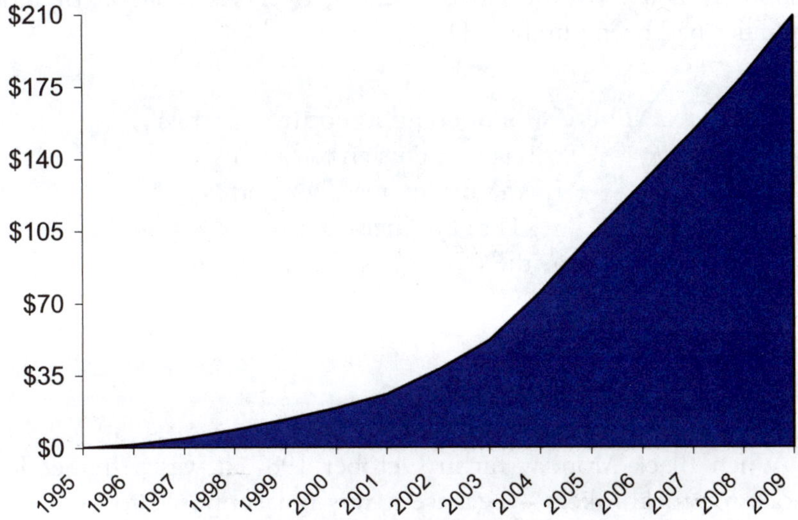

Data Source: 1995-2006 Advantage Compendium, Beacon Research, Fixed Annuity Premium Study: 2007-2009

As the financial tools to create index annuities had been around for several years, why were index annuities introduced only in the mid '90s? One big reason for that is that the psychology of the times was right. It had been a rocky 1994 – bond fund returns were poor, the S&P 500 ended the year on a down note, and many stock funds and variable annuities had marginal or negative returns. In addition, the 8% and 9% rates consumers had realized on traditional fixed annuities in the previous decade appeared to be over. Interest rates were on a long downward slope, from a historic point of view, and insurers were looking for an annuity that had the potential to deliver respectable returns. It was time to announce a new annuity that would provide the principal protection from market losses enjoyed by all fixed annuity owners, but given them the potential for higher interest.

Index annuity sales were barely over $100 million that first year, but grew to $1.5 billion in 1996, $3.0 billion in 1997 and $4.0 billion in 1998. Growth slowed down over the next few years, but with memories of the millennium bear market still fresh, index annuity sales exploded to over $23 billion in 2004 and reached over $27 billion by 2005. By the close of 2009, over $200 billion of index annuities had been purchased.

There was once an agent from Ames
That gave clients annuity gains
It isn't his interest they said
That put them ahead
T'was the risk of loss that he tames

A Tool For Uncertain Times

When Black Monday hit in October 1987, it was a tremendous shock to stockbrokers – because it was not supposed to be able to happen. They had been told, and believed, that a sudden drop of that magnitude was impossible.

The bear markets of the last decade have cut much deeper than the one 20 years ago. People near retirement may need to work for more years to be able to retire and current retirees may need to cut back their standard of living to try to ensure that their money does not run out. But perhaps the most long-lasting outcome is that the risk/return paradigm guiding consumer financial habits has changed.

The 1920s were a time of irrational exuberance where the "little people" invested in the stock market – many for the first time. The resultant crash soured investors of the day and their children were repeatedly told to stay away from the stock market. It wasn't until the

1960s that interest in investing began to rise and the general press again spoke positively of the stock market. The 1960s attitude then became that investing in blue chips or the "nifty 50" would make you a lot of money. However, in the crash of 1973-1974, the market dropped by half – and then it failed to recover. The stock market limped along for several years and the tone of the media changed once again – this time, to "investing in the stock market is a sucker's game."

1982 began the greatest bull market of the century, with fortunes being made by professional investors. There were a couple of bumps along the way – a severe one in 1987 and a minor one in 1990 – but the market quickly recovered. After 15 years or so of a rising market, the small investor once again entered the market en masse in the late 1990s. The millennium bear market tested their faith, but was followed by 5 straight up years. By 2008, it was obvious to many that the market would trend up forever.

Then came the crash of 2008-2009; it was a generation killer. The damage to investor's psyches may well be similar to that caused by the Great Depression and the '70s bear markets. It may keep individual investors leery of investing for decades. However, they probably won't be able to flee to the bank and earn high safe yields, as they could in the 1970s. Index annuities are one of the few instruments that still offer the potential for higher yields and that protect principal and credited interest from market loss.

Real World Returns

We will explore actual index annuity returns in depth in Chapter 5, but the following chart provides an overview of index annual performance during volatile times. The average index annuity return reported beat the index for five of the eight periods since 1997. How is that possible?

Let's look at a specific example. The annualized average index annuity return of the carriers providing policy returns for the five years ending 30 September 2008 was 6.05%. The annualized return

Annualized 5-Year Returns

Periods	S&P 500 Return	Index Annuity Average Return
1997-2002	9.39%	9.19%
1998-2003	-0.42%	5.46%
1999-2004	-2.77%	4.69%
2000-2005	-3.08%	4.33%
2001-2006	5.11%	4.36%
2002-2007	13.37%	6.12%
2003-2008	3.18%	6.05%
2004-2009	-1.05%	4.19%
2005-2010	-1.47%	3.89%

for an S&P 500 index fund with a 0.15% expense ratio for the same period was 5.05% (the annualized return for the index alone - that is, without considering dividends - was 3.18% and that is the return shown in the chart). Even though the index annuity returns did not include reinvested dividends and were generally tempered by caps, the average index annuity returned more than a fully participating dividend yielding index fund. Why? Because during that final year when the index went down, the index annuity owners kept their credited interest earned in previous years.

Staying On Message

Here is how three carriers defined their index annuities when introduced in the mid '90s:

"You enjoy the safety and security that a traditional fixed annuity guarantees, combined with the potential of interest earnings linked to the S&P 500 Index"

Interstate Assurance Company, Freedom 500 Index Annuity, 3158-D, 7/96

"You will only share in the increases in the index. Your index annuity value will never decline due to decreases in the index and previous increases once earned are locked in and guaranteed"

Community National Assurance Co., Money$Worth Indexed Annuity, P-AN7, 8/95

"Excess interest is determined annually and is based on your contract's participation rates, which are a percentage of the performance of the S&P 500".

Unity Life. SPIDA, #9521, 1996

The message of index annuities has stayed amazingly on target over the years. Index annuities are still marketed as fixed annuity with higher interest potential due to an index link.

Index Annuity Safety

Insurance companies are regulated by the state governments of the individual states where they are licensed. Every state (plus Puerto Rico) provides a minimum of $100,000 in withdrawal and guaranteed cash values for all fixed annuities (California covers 80% of annuity contractual value to a maximum payout of $100,000). This doesn't mean that everyone that ever owned a fixed annuity has been fully protected.

We have found four carriers where fixed annuity owners with values not covered by a state guaranty fund limit did not receive 100 cents on the unprotected dollars when the carrier failed. Inter-American Companies (an employee benefits carrier that issued some annuities) got into trouble in the '80s and was liquidated in 1991, too early to be completely covered by guarantee funds. Consumers that purchased fixed annuities issued by London Pacific Life, National American Life Insurance Company of Pennsylvania, and Summit National Life Insurance did receive up to state guaranty limits, but account values in excess of those limits may never be fully paid. It appears that holders of these annuity contracts received a little over 90 cents on the dollar on account values in excess of state guaranty limits, but that, in all cases, amounts up to state guaranty fund limits were protected. There may be other carriers out there that have not returned a hundred cents on the annuity dollar, but we have been unable to find them.

During the last sixteen years, customers of roughly three dozen life & health carriers received help from state guarantee funds. When state insurance regulators step in they will often attempt rehabilitation of the insurer and there are many insurers that have entered state receivership, been rehabilitated, and emerged from state care. If rehabilitation does not work, every state guaranty fund will cover up to $100,000 of cash value in the event of final carrier insolvency. But as stated previously, annuity values not protected by these funds have not always been covered.

What about Executive Life?

The case most often cited as an example of fixed annuity holders getting back less than their principal is Executive Life. After going through more court briefs and decade-old reports than anyone would want to, we can safely say that people that *surrendered* their annuities when Aurora National Life Assurance Company took over Executive Life's business did take a hit to principal – those opting out of the reorganization process were only promised 56% of their account value, and even those annuity owners who stayed with the new carrier did not receive 100% of their *accumulated account value*. However, we cannot find any evidence that would support the contention that fixed annuity owners that stayed the course ultimately got back less than 100% of their *original principal.*

So, Can I Lose Principal In A Fixed Annuity?

Absolutely! If you do not follow the rules you agreed to when you bought the annuity, you could lose money. Getting out of a fixed annuity early can trigger penalties that may eat into principal, but if you leave early and incur a loss, that loss will be a result of your decision. The real question is what is the likelihood of losing your money because the issuer goes under? Even though there have been annuity customers that have lost money due to company failure the reality is this: While it is *possible* that the purchaser of a fixed annuity may lose some principal, due to insurer insolvency, that result is *extremely unlikely.*

Why An Index Annuity Isn't A Variable Annuity

Index annuities are separate and distinct from variable annuities. A fixed rate annuity pays a stated rate of interest that can be no less than the minimum guaranteed rate of interest. An index annuity pays a minimum rate of interest and credits "excess" interest based on the movement of, and the annuity's participation in, an external index. In any index annuity policy year, the rate of participation in the index for the crediting period is fixed and known; the only unknown is how the index will move. Neither fixed rate nor index annuities can lose either principal or credited interest based on market risk.

► Variable annuity principal is subject to market risk (unless placed in the fixed account). Index annuity principal is not subject to market risk.

► Variable annuity returns may be lost due to market risk. Index annuity credited interest cannot be lost due to market risk.

► Variable annuities do not pay minimum interest rates. Index annuities do credit minimum guaranteed interest rates.

Fixed index annuities provide a guaranteed minimum interest rate and a guarantee of principal. Variable annuities provide these guarantees only with respect to amounts invested in the "fixed account"; the value of the "variable" accounts can and will vary with the investment performance of those accounts. Moreover, variable annuities are *securities*, regulated by the Securities and Exchange Commission (SEC), and are sold as securities. All annuities (both fixed and variable) are issued by insurance companies, are not government or bank obligations, and are not FDIC insured.

Let's Get The Terms Straight

Strictly speaking the term "annuity" means "a series of payments over time". However, when most people use the word, they're referring to a *commercial annuity* – a contract for income between an issuing insurance company and a purchaser, as opposed to a *private annuity* – a contract for income between two individuals. There are different kinds of commercial annuities. It is possible to say that there are "two kinds of annuities" but in two dimensions:

When income payments must commence. An *immediate annuity* is one in which income payments will (and must) commence within one year of purchase. A *deferred annuity* is one in which income payments may be deferred for more than a year (often, to a maximum age or, in some cases, indefinitely).

How the cash value will be invested. A fixed annuity is one in which all contract values will be invested in the general account of the issuing insurer. All fixed annuities guarantee the principal against loss (unless caused by surrender charges) and a minimum rate of interest that will be credited to the contract.

By contrast, a *variable annuity* is a contract where the value is expressed in *units*. During the *accumulation phase* of the contract (that is, prior to the *annuity starting date* – the point at which income payments commence under the contract), its value is expressed in *accumulation units*. The value of each accumulation unit can, and generally will, vary each day, according to the market value of the separate investment accounts selected by the purchaser.

Index annuities are generally fixed annuities. As with all fixed annuities, their value is expressed in fixed dollars; moreover, they guarantee principal (subject to surrender charges) and a minimum rate of interest. However, the manner in which they credit additional, non-guaranteed interest is different. Traditional fixed annuities credit such "excess" interest as declared by the issuing insurer, at whatever rate that insurer decides, at that time, is appropriate. We will call such contracts 'fixed rate annuities" (because the rate is fixed by the issuing insurer (always for at least one year).

Index annuities credit non-guaranteed interest based upon the performance of an underlying *index* (hence, the name). This is most often the S&P 500® Index.

Statements about "annuities" that do not make clear what kind of annuities are being described, can be confusing or misleading. A statement that is true of a deferred annuity may be false when applied to an immediate one, and vice versa. And a true statement about a fixed annuity may be false when applied to a variable annuity, and vice versa.

Tax Treatment of Annuities

All deferred annuities generally enjoy "tax deferred" treatment. The cash value growth is not subject to tax as earned, but, instead, is taxed only when distributed. This tax-deferral applies only to annuities owned by "natural persons" (human beings). [IRC § 72(u)]. Cash value growth in deferred annuities owned by "non-natural persons" such as corporations or trusts will be taxed as earned, unless the owning entity is acting as the "agent of a natural person" [IRC §72(u)(1)]. All distributions from annuities are either (a) "amounts received as an annuity" or "amounts not received as an annuity".

(a) "***Amounts received as an annuity***" includes both the payments from an immediate annuity and payments made under a regular "annuity payout option" from a deferred annuity (i.e.: a deferred annuity that has been "annuitized"). These income amounts are taxed as part interest and part non-taxable "return of principal", according to an "exclusion ratio". The ratio depends upon the length of the payout period and, for *life-contingent payouts* (where annuity payments will persist for the entire life of the annuitant), whether a *refund feature* (a guarantee of payment if the annuitant dies before all of the money placed under that life payout options has been received as annuity payments) was elected.

(b) "***Amounts not received as an annuity***" are any other distributions (actual or "deemed") from a deferred annuity. Such amounts are taxable to the extent of "gain" (or earnings) and the tax treatment depends upon when the contract was issued.

Contracts issued before August 14, 1982 are taxed under the "FIFO" ("first in, first out") regime. All distributions will be considered nontaxable returns of principal until all principal has been received.

Contracts issued after August 13, 1982 are taxed under the "LIFO" ("last in, first out") regime. All distributions are considered "gain", and taxed as Ordinary Income until all gain has been distributed.

An ***Early Distribution Penalty*** is assessed upon the taxable portion of all distributions unless an exception applies. The exceptions are distributions –

"(A) made on or after the date on which the taxpayer attains age 59 1/2,

(B) made on or after the death of the holder (or, where the holder is not an individual, the death of the primary annuitant (as defined in subsection (s)(6)(B))),

(C) attributable to the taxpayer's becoming disabled within the meaning of subsection (m)(7),

(D) which is a part of a series of substantially equal periodic payments (not less frequently than annually) made for the life (or life expectancy) of the taxpayer or the joint lives (or joint life expectancies) of such taxpayer and his designated beneficiary,

(E) from a plan, contract, account, trust, or annuity described in subsection (e)(5)(D),"

(F) allocable to investment in the contract before August 14, 1982, or

(G) under a qualified funding asset (within the meaning of section 130(d), but without regard to whether there is a qualified assignment),

(H) to which subsection (t) applies (without regard to paragraph (2) thereof),

(I) under an immediate annuity contract (within the meaning of section 72(u)(4)), or

(J) which is purchased by an employer upon the termination of a plan described in section 401(a) or 403(a) and which is held by the employer until such time as the employee separates from service" [IRC §72(q)(2)]. "

The tax treatment of annuities is much more complex than the general rules given here and we talk more about taxes in Chapters 7 and 9. For an even more detailed description, see Olsen & Kitces, *The Annuity Advisor,* National Underwriter Co., 2nd ed., 2009.

Liquidity & Penalties – Surrender Charges

Surrender charges are probably responsible for more annuity sales complaints than any other factor. Partly, this is because they are not properly disclosed by some annuity representatives; but even when they are fully explained, surrender charges are perceived as a disadvantage by most buyers – and many sellers. Buyers will often prefer a deferred annuity with surrender charges to one without them, once they understand the alternatives.

An insurance company incurs *acquisition costs* when it issues an annuity. These costs (including printing & issue costs, commission expense, annuity guarantee expense, and mandated *reserve* requirements) exceed the initial premium received. The insurer will invest those premium dollars and profit thereby, but only if it retains them long enough; this usually takes several years. If the annuity is surrendered prior to that time, the insurer will lose money.

One way for insurers to offset that loss is to impose *surrender charges* – a "percentage of contract value" charge on early surrenders which usually declines over time to zero at the point where the insurer has earned back the acquisition costs. Another way is for the insurer to impose a "front end" sales charge. The question becomes "which loss prevention method do I want the issuer of my annuity to use?"

Market Value Adjustment (MVA)

An MVA feature means changes in the interest environment are taken into account if the annuity is cashed in before the end of the surrender charge period. What this can mean is if interest rates have risen since the annuity was issued, the penalties for cashing out could be higher than the schedule stated in the policy, and if rates have fallen since issued the penalties could be lower or even zero.

Why is a Market Value Adjustment even necessary? It's because the issuer of a fixed rate or index annuity invests most of the buyer's premium in *bonds*. The market value of bonds varies *inversely* with current interest rates. Thus, a $1,000 bond paying 5% interest ($50 per year) is worth $1,000 when prevailing interest rates are around 5%. But if interest rates have risen to, say, 6%, the market value of that 5% bond will be less – perhaps $833.33 (at which price, the $50 annual income from that bond will represent a 6% yield).

Why Do Bond Values Fall When Interest Rates Rise?

You own a $1000 bond paying $50 a year (5%) in interest. If rates on new bonds increase to 6% this means new bonds pay $60 per $1000. Why would a buyer pay you $1000 to get $50 when a new bond will give them $60? They wouldn't, they'd pay less for your $50 interest bond, and this is why existing bond values fall when interest rates go up.

When the owner of an annuity surrenders it for its cash value, the issuing insurer may need to sell bonds to raise that cash. If the bonds it sells are worth less, at that time, than the insurer paid for them, the insurer suffers a loss. The Market Value Adjustment compensates the insurer for that loss. But an MVA can also work in the annuity owner's favor. If interest rates have *declined* since annuity purchase, the bonds the insurer bought will be worth *more*. In that situation, the MVA adjustment will be *positive*. It will *increase* the annuity surrender value.

Because the MVA allows the insurer to share the risk of interest rate changes with the annuity buyer, the insurer may credit a higher interest rate to contracts with this feature than it credits to those without it. This fact is recognized in the *Buyer's Guide To Fixed Deferred Annuities* produced by the National Association of Insurance Commissioners, which states, "Since you and the insurance company share the risk, an annuity with an MVA feature may credit a higher rate than an annuity without that feature."

It is worth noting that the MVA only applies during the surrender charge period). If you do not surrender the policy during the period when the MVA is applicable, you never pay the MVA and might get a little better rate.

Death Benefit

In the event of death, the vast majority of fixed rate and index annuities pay the full account value to the named beneficiary and no penalties are charged. Some annuities do assess surrender penalties at death while a few others require the account value to be paid out over time. A substantial benefit, available in nearly all deferred annuities, is the *spousal continuation* option. If the annuity owner names his or her spouse as primary beneficiary, that surviving spouse can, at the owner's death, treat the annuity as though the surviving spouse/beneficiary was the original purchaser and continue the annuity (and enjoy its tax-deferral benefit), *as owner,* to the maturity date (which, in some contracts, may be deferred indefinitely).

Most variable annuities and some fixed annuities offer a *guaranteed minimum death benefit* that may be greater than the account value. It may be payable upon the death of the *annuitant* or of the *owner.* This is an issue only when the annuitant and owner are two different individuals – a situation that should be avoided whenever possible.

Annual Fees & Charges

All financial instruments assess charges, either explicitly or implicitly. A bank that issues a CD hopes to credit interest to the depositor at less than it earns by investing that depositor's dollars. The difference, often called the *interest rate spread*, is not a contractual charge, but is more in the nature of a retailer's markup. A *fixed rate* annuity works the same way. Your interest rate is what the insurance company pays you, not what it earns on your money.

By contrast, a variable annuity levies expenses directly, both in the form of *separate account expenses* (which vary with the investment accounts chosen) and as *contract charges*. The former are *investment charges.* The latter, including the *Mortality and Expense (M&E)* charge and any charges for a *guaranteed death benefit* and *guaranteed living benefits* are insurance charges, designed to reimburse the insurer for the risks it incurs by offering those guarantees.

The charges and expenses in an index annuity are generally modifications in the amount of indexed interest that will be recognized (for purposes of crediting) or actually credited. There are no direct charges for insurance risks (such as the M&E charge in a variable annuity.

A fixed rate or index annuity may charge a separate fee for additional annuity benefits (there may be a fee if a guaranteed lifetime withdrawal benefit rider is chosen, for example), but it is generally incorrect to try to equate a 1% index annuity yield spread with a 1% investment fee because the index annuity insurer does not generally receive the spread (as the issuer of a variable annuity does).

Maturity Date

Not to be confused with the surrender period, the maturity date is the date by which the policy owner must take distributions. Thus, the period from the date of issue to the maturity date is the longest period in which annuity interest can be earned but not yet taxed. Maturity dates are usually the annuitant's 80th to 90th birthday, but some new policies may be kept even after age 100. (The annuitant is the person upon whose age and sex the annuitization life income is based).

Safety of Principal

Fixed rate and fixed index annuities do not subject principal and credited interest to market risk. They are as safe as the insurance company issuing the annuity and annuity companies have an exceptional record of safety.

Some Questions To Ask About Fixed Annuities

- What is the initial interest rate or index participation rate and how long is it guaranteed?
- Does the initial rate include a bonus?
- Are there any special requirements to receive the bonus or to cash out the annuity?
- What is the guaranteed minimum return?
- What are the surrender or withdrawal penalties or charges?
- Is there a Market Value (MVA) Adjustment?
- Do the surrender costs still apply at death?
- What rate is being credited on similar annuities issued in the past?

Cheat Sheet

- Index annuities are the latest stage in the evolution of the annuity

- Deferred annuities offer tax-deferral, lifetime income options, and may avoid probate. Money withdrawn is always taxed as ordinary income (to the extent that it is includible in income) and may be subject to IRS "Under Age 59½" Premature Distribution Rules.

- The major difference between fixed and variable annuities is that a variable annuity owner bears the investment risk, while fixed rate and fixed index annuities protect principal and credited interest from investment risk and guarantee a minimum interest return.

- The major difference between fixed rate and fixed index annuities is the crediting of interest earned above and beyond the minimum guarantee.

- Fixed index annuities are insurance products; not securities.

P.S. – A Little Annuity History

It all began with Caesar. As a sign of fidelity spoils of war were given to the Roman Emperor who was then supposed to give most of it back to the soldiers that earned it. However, the Emperor changed this by only giving half of the booty back to the soldiers, and giving the other half to the army *signiferi* with the understanding that this money would be used to provide a pension for the soldier upon retirement. No interest was earned on this mandatory pension plan, but it did provide an income for life and is viewed as the first annuity.

In the 700s the Catholic Church began issuing life annuities whereby a life income would be paid for large contributions. The Catholic Church also offered a type of variable annuity based on *societas sacri officii*. These were church offices sold by the Pope that had the authority to do business on behalf of the church. These offices could be very profitable and thus very expensive to purchase, so office seekers would form syndicates and offer people life annuities for their contribution. Many of these paid out a portion of the income received by the church office, so that the income stream was variable.

Beginning in Germany in the 1200s landowners would solicit money and promise to pay an income for as long as the lender lived – some of these "life rents" could be passed along to heirs so the annuity was essentially forever. Also around this time merchant gilds began selling true private annuities and competing with the church. Unlike early church annuities these private annuities were often age-weighted, meaning older people got a higher annual income than younger people (and a higher income than the church paid).

Annuity transactions did not always run smoothly. In 1308 a French Archbishop paid the Abbey of Paris 2400 *livres* in exchange for a life annuity of 400 *livres* a year. The Abbey accepted, apparently believing the Archbishop was in poor health. Fifteen years later, with the Archbishop still alive, the Abbey sued to have the contract stopped claiming so much had been paid out that the annuity was "usurious." The court refused to hear the case and the Archbishop collected a total of 7600 *livres* before he died in 1327 earning an effective annual return of 15.6%.

Annuities were used as a way to get around the religious bans against usury – the charging of interest. This concern began to fade as governments began borrowing money and paying out amounts that looked amazingly similar to interest payments. The first government borrower was Venice in the 1100s, but by the 1500s many countries took money from individuals, paid interest on the money, and occasionally were set up to pay back the principal at a later date, but so that these wouldn't technically be loans and subject to accusations of usury, the interest paid was never referred to as interest but as "rents."

Even as usury became less of an issue, some governments increasingly offered life annuities to fund operations because they felt they were less expensive than issuing bonds. In the 1690s England authorized the issuance of a million pounds (roughly equal to $500 million today) of life annuities at a payout rate of 14%. France and Holland were also big issuers of annuities to fund government expenses.

One of the problems with determining how large the life annuity payment should be is there was little data on how long people lived. In 211 A. D. the Roman scientist Domitius Ulpianus created the first mortality tables and may be rightfully considered the first actuary. However, after the empire fell the Catholic Church ignored age and simply paid the same amount regardless of age.

In 1725 Abraham de Moivre published a tract on annuity valuation taking an educated guess at the matter. After this, better records were kept on mortality and more accurate actuarial tables were developed by the middle of the 18th century.

Friendly societies were formed in the 1700s for the purpose of collecting voluntary subscriptions (premiums) from members that paid out either a future annuity income or death benefit. As these societies grew professional managers were hired, and the collection of premiums and payouts of life annuities and death benefits became a business. The Equitable Society in England, formed in 1756, was the first modern life insurance company.

In 1759, and for a decade thereafter, New Jersey, New York and Pennsylvania chartered church corporations that provided a type of annuity benefit to "distressed ministers and their widows" but these were more charities than real insurance companies. The first true U.S. insurance company was chartered in Pennsylvania in 1794, but soon went out of business. However, in 1809 a domestic venture began called the Pennsylvania Company that did stay around. It was followed by New York Life in 1830 and New England Mutual Life in 1835 – thirty years later there were 110 life insurance and annuity companies in the U.S.

Annuity growth was slow in America. In 1910 annuity premiums totaled only $6 million, and were only $11 million by 1920. These were single premium annuities; the first flexible premium deferred annuity was marketed in 1921. However, by 1930 annuity premiums had increased almost tenfold to $108 million. By 1932 they doubled to over $200 million, and by 1939 annuity premiums were almost $400 million and represented more than 10% of all life/annuity sales.

Why the explosion of annuity sales in the 1930s? In their seminal annuity study published in 1944 Dickinson & Elliott summed it up simply by saying, "in the period of financial stress of the early 1930's, many people turned to annuities as a safe form of investment."

As the number of companies providing pension plans grew in number in the '50s and '60s so too did the purchase of group life annuities to fund the payout. Individual annuity sales also grew, albeit slowly. Deferred annuity sales began to take off in the mid '70s as Wall Street brokerage firms began offering high interest paying annuities and variable annuities become widely available. Annuity sales reached $22.5 billion by 1980, but were still viewed as a sideline by the insurance industry. Indeed, it was not until 1980 that *Best's Review* finally published an article dedicated exclusively to annuities

The start of the '80s had some prophesizing the death of annuities. The first blow was when the tax law changed requiring annuity withdrawals to be first taxed as interest instead of principal, thus ending the availability of early tax-free withdrawals. Then interest rates plummeted making other financial vehicles appear more attractive. Finally, the bankruptcy of Baldwin-United in 1983 cast doubt as to the safety of annuities – it should be noted that when it was all over not only did every Baldwin-United annuityowner get all of their principal back, but earned yields of 4%-7%

The 1990s were a time of innovation. Variable annuities began offering more flexibility, more investment choices and more benefits that emphasized the insurance side of this product. Fixed carriers competed more directly with banks by expanding the availability of multiple year annuities that matched interest rate guarantees with surrender period length, and in 1995 index annuities were introduced allowing consumers to realize the protection of a fixed annuity and benefit from increases in an equity index.

As the new millennium got under way annuities began offering a broad array of living benefits, once again placing the annuity focus on providing a secure income. Deferred annuity sales took off and by the end of the decade U.S. annuity sales were around a quarter trillion dollars a year. A long and successful run for a financial instrument created 2000 years ago.

Chapter 2 – Annuity Interest

How Do Fixed Rate Annuities Pay Interest?

When you place your money with the bank they invest this money, earn a return, and after subtracting their costs pay you a stated interest rate for a stated period of time. Your principal does not fluctuate, but the interest you receive can, and usually does, fluctuate from period to period.

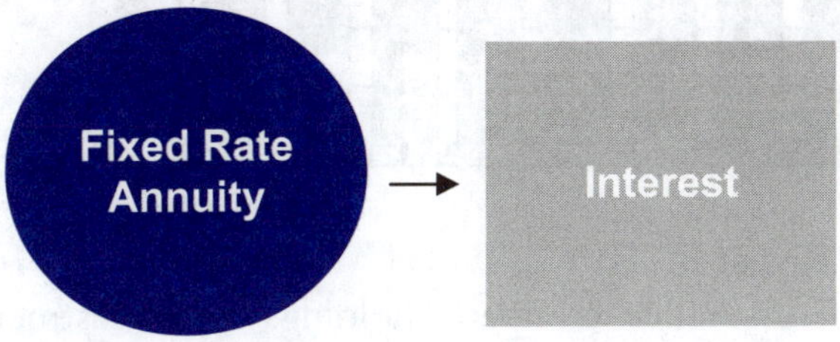

A fixed rate annuity operates in a similar way, except you place your money with an insurance company instead of a bank. When you place your money with the insurance company they invest this money, earn a return, and after subtracting their costs pay you stated interest.

Minimum Rate

A fixed rate annuity guarantees to credit a minimum yield and that is what makes a fixed annuity a fixed annuity instead of an investment. The minimum rate typically ranges from 1% to 3% – but it may be linked to movements of an external interest indicator – such as U.S. Treasury Notes.

One Year or Multiple Year Rates

All fixed annuities guarantee the interest rate for at least the coming policy year (or guarantee the rate of participation in the case of an index annuity). Typically the annuity will guarantee the rate for one year at a time and declare a new interest rate on the policy anniversary for the next year. But the new rate can never be less than the minimum guaranteed interest rate.

Annuity Annual Interest Credited

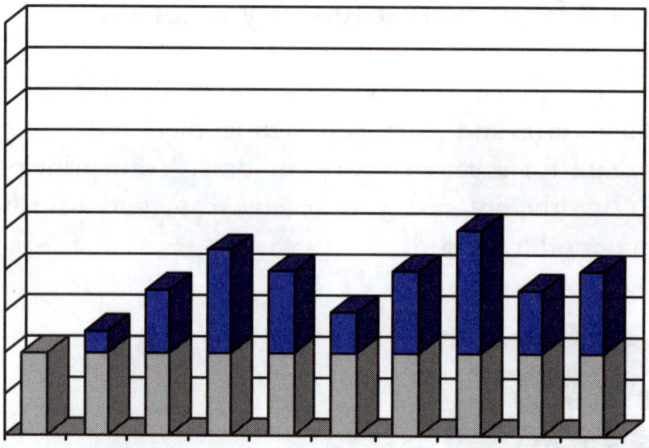

What do they invest in?

The bulk of insurance company holdings are investment grade bonds. They may own a smattering of direct loans, possibly some preferred stocks and perhaps some real estate, but by and large they buy bonds because of the predictability of the income.

Fixed rate annuities provide a minimum guaranteed interest rate. If the insurance company believes that it can pay extra interest from their general account, above and beyond this minimum guarantee, it will declare a fixed rate of interest and pay the annuity owner a stated interest rate for a period.

How Do Index Annuities Pay Interest?

In a fixed rate annuity you place your money with an insurance company, and they invest this money, earn a return, and after subtracting their costs, pay you stated interest.

The difference between the fixed rate annuity and the index annuity is that the return earned above the minimum guarantee is used to buy an index-link tied to the performance of an external index. This index-link permits you to share in the potential increase in the index during the period without losing interest already credited if the index declines.

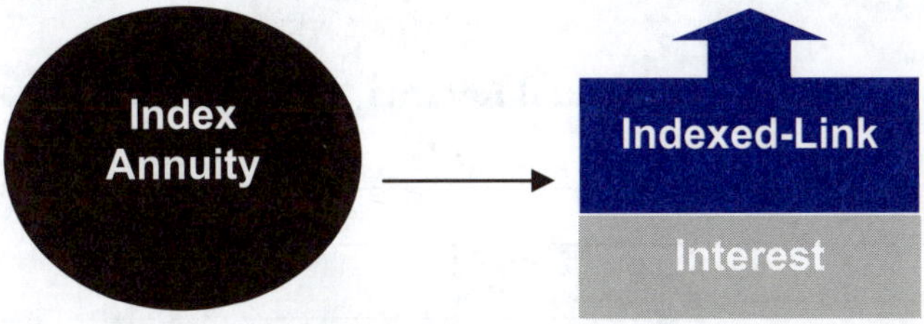

Basing excess interest earned on an external index gives you the potential for more interest if the index cooperates. If the index goes down instead of up, you earn no index-linked interest for the period, *but you do not lose what you already have.*

The Key Difference Between An Index Annuity And An Index Investment

The owner of an index annuity does not invest in the securities of the index, but merely stands to receive excess interest if the movement of the interest benchmark is positive. Because you are not investing in the market, you will lose neither principal nor credited interest if the index drops. From an interest earning point of view, the worst thing that can happen in an index annuity is that the index will not go up and you will not earn any additional index-linked interest.

However, because *an index return typically does not include reinvested dividends*, the return of the index annuity does not reflect reinvested dividends. And because it costs the insurer to provide the minimum guaranteed return, the index annuity owner typically will not participate in 100% of index increases.

A rise from 1000 to 1100 in an index represents a 10% increase in that index. If an index annuity participated in, say, 60% of the period increase, the annuity would credit 6% interest. What if you owned a portfolio made up of the securities in the index and these securities paid a 2% dividend? Your return would be the 10% increase in the index plus the 2% dividends earned for a total return of 12% (versus 6% for the index annuity owner).

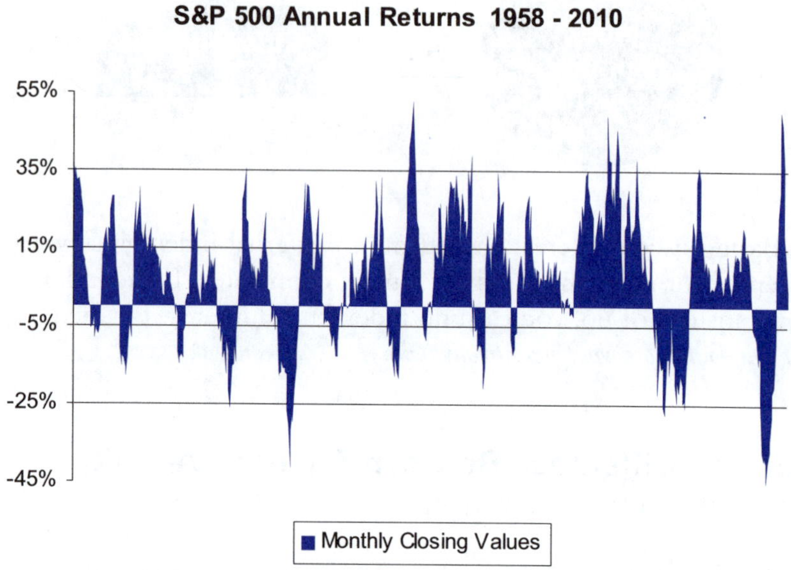

Since index annuities were introduced, the actual effective annual index annuity participation has ranged from 10% to over 100% of actual index gains for positive index periods (index participation over 100% usually involves averaging, which will be discussed in the next chapter). However, the index does not always go up.

Index Annuities Provide A Fresh Start (Reset)

Let's look at the difference between investing in the index and owning an index annuity. Say the index was at a level of 1000 today, but by the end of the period it has declined to 800. If you own the index, you will have a 20% loss. But because the index annuity is not an investment, the index annuity owner simply sees no index-linked interest earned for the period.

Suppose in the next period the index rose to 900. The index investor still has a loss because 900 is less than the initial level 1000.

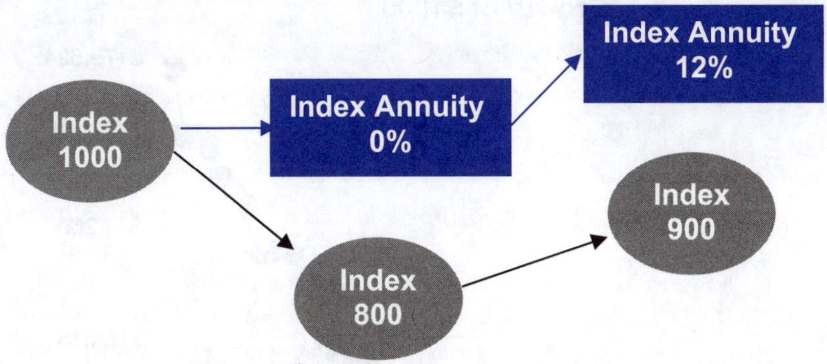

But the index annuity provides a fresh start to take advantage of index declines. The index annuity calculates index-based interest for the next period based on where the old period ended. The index annuity would *reset* and use the level of 800 as a base, so if the index increases to 900, the index annuity owner's interest will be based on this growth, even though the index is still lower than when it all began.

Reinvested Dividends versus an Annual Reset

If you could have placed $1,000 in the S&P 500 Index on 1 January 1960 it would have grown to $18,615 by 1 January 2010. If your S&P 500 included reinvested dividends (and no fees) it would have grown to $84,260. But if your S&P 500 used a fresh start *annual reset* approach – meaning no dividends are included but years with losses are treated as zeros – your $1,000 would have grown to $179,624. Turning losses into years of zero gain more than offset the advantage of reinvested dividends over this period.

This chart is not saying that if you could have bought an index annuity in 1960, you would have had achieved this growth. What it does show, however, is that dismissing index annuities as uncompetitive – simply because their interest earnings don't reflect reinvested dividends – is wrong.

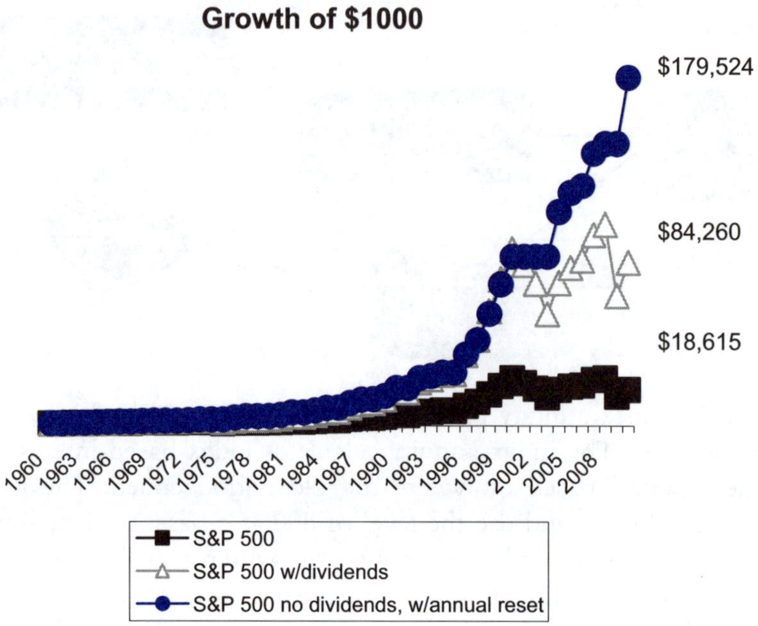

How Much Interest?

The highest index annuity interest rate ever credited for a single year was over 40%, in both 1998 and 2010. On the other hand, in 2001, 2002, and 2008, the major stock market indices declined, and index annuities linked to these indices credited 0% for the year - but no previous interest was lost.

Index annuities are designed to provide the potential for long-term yields above those of other safe money places – while always protecting principal and credited interest from market risk - and they have performed as intended.

Minimum Guarantee

A fixed annuity guarantees the crediting of a minimum rate of interest – which is what makes it a fixed annuity. In the case of an index annuity, the minimum guarantee is usually structured to protect principal and, perhaps, pay back a few extra bucks by the end of the surrender period, rather than crediting a minimum interest amount each year.

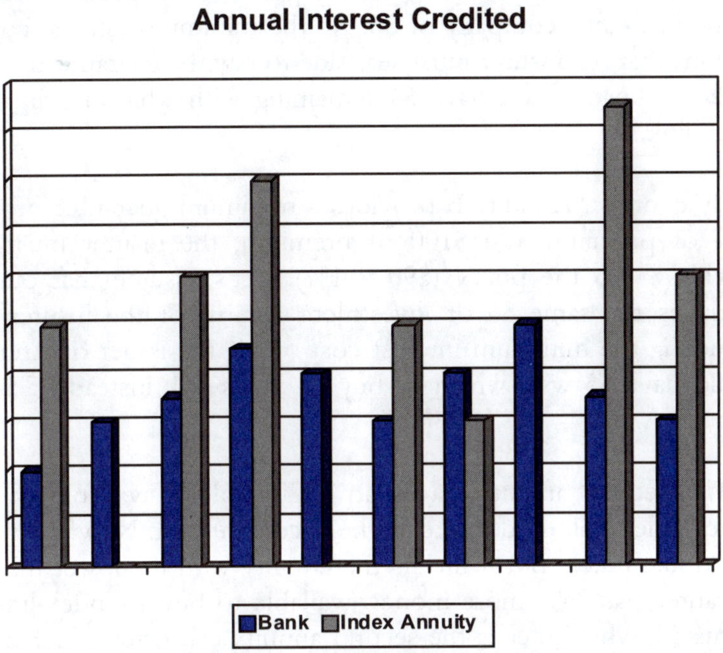

For example, an index annuity might guarantee to return a minimum of $110 for each original $100 of premium by the end of a ten year surrender charge period. If the index does not produce at least this minimum index-linked return, the insurance company will credit, retroactively, enough interest to bring the annuity value to $110. Actual minimum guarantees may be higher or lower than this example, depending on the annuity.

Comparison

If a guaranteed return of, say, 2% is calculated on less than the full amount invested, then the minimum effective annual return is less than 2%. But why would one accept a minimum return calculated on less than 100% of the premium? *Because it may provide the potential for a higher overall return.*

For example, Annuity A provides a minimum guarantee of 2% on 100% of premium. On $100 of premium, the insurer would thus guarantee a minimum interest credit of $2 to the policy ($100 x 2%) this year. Let's suppose that our $100 premium produces a net return to the insurance company of $6. As the minimum interest cost (the amount that the insurer must set aside to pay the guaranteed interest) is $2, the insurer will have $4 remaining with which it can buy an index-link.

By contrast, Annuity B provides a minimum guarantee of 1% on 90% of premium. On $100 of premium, the insurer must credit roughly $1 to the policy ($90 x 1%). Let's assume that our $100 produces the same $6 of investment return for the insurer. After deducting the minimum interest cost of $1, the issuer of Annuity B would have $5 with which to buy an index-link instead of $4 with Annuity A.

The second annuity leaves an additional $1 available to buy a bigger index-link used to create the excess interest. Now, $1 may not sound like much, but it means the annuity with the lower minimum guarantee has 25% more money available to buy an index-link – $5 versus $4, which means the second annuity can offer a higher index participation rate, providing the opportunity for more interest.

The trade-off is this: Annuity B gives us the opportunity for more index-linked interest (because its issuer can buy more index links with our $100 premium). Thus, Annuity B will perform better in a "best case" scenario. But "best case" doesn't always happen. If the index remains flat, or even declines, over our entire annuity crediting period Annuity A, with a 2% minimum guarantee, will be worth $122 ($100, compounded at 2% for ten years, while Annuity B, with its 1% on 90% guarantee, will be worth only $100 ($90, compounded at 1% for 10 years).

<u>Which Is Better – A High Or Low Minimum Guarantee?</u>

The preferred guarantee depends on your comfort level and the way index-linked interest is credited. If an annuity calculates and credits index-linked interest annually, it would take a very prolonged bad market, and a very poor annuity pricing environment, for that contract to produce an average return under 2% or 3% a year in index-linked interest. But index annuities that do not credit interest until the end of a multiple year term are more likely to credit only the minimum guarantee in a bad patch. From a pricing model viewpoint, you gain a little more possible upside in the index if you accept a lower minimum, or you can trade for a little higher minimum return if you accept a little less index participation.

> The sizzle behind the Index Annuity Guarantee side is not the minimum return; it is the protection of premium and credited interest from market risk.

How Is The Minimum Interest Credited To The Policy?

A 2% interest rate paid on 90% of the premium would be worth 103% in seven years. If you began with a premium of $100 and the index steadily dropped for seven years the minimum guaranteed part of the annuity statement would look like the example above.

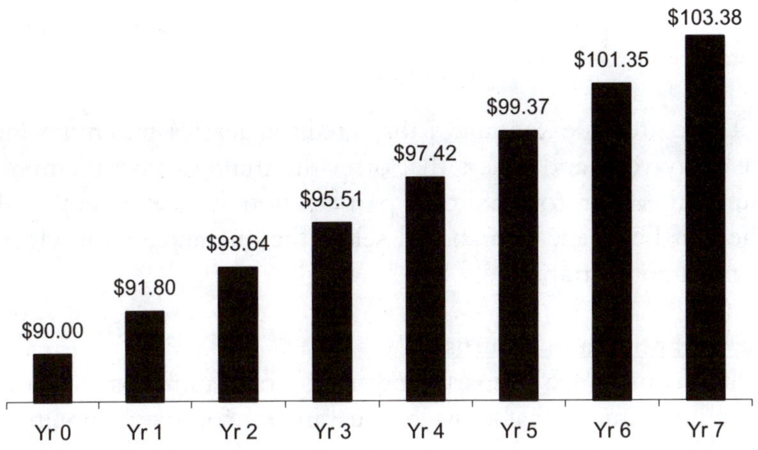

Ignoring surrender charges, the minimum guaranteed value exceeds the original premium by the end of year 6 in this example. (It's worth noting that, if you die, the annuities will almost always give your beneficiaries *the greater of* the original premium or the guaranteed value).

Let's be very clear on this. If the calculated index-linked gain for any year is positive, the annuity owner will receive the interest earned. If the calculated index gain is zero in any year, the typical index annuity will not credit the minimum guaranteed interest to the accumulated value in that same year; instead the typical contract will record 0% interest. Guaranteed interest is normally calculated *over the entire term* and is credited *only if it exceeds the total index-linked interest for the entire period.* So, if the index annuity crediting formula produced returns of zero in year one, zero in year two, and ten percent in year three, the annuity contract would not credit 2%, 2%, 10%; instead it would show 0%, 0%, 10%.

The minimum guarantee almost becomes irrelevant from a protection point of view, once the calculated index-linked gain exceeds it. For example, if the annuity, purchased for $100, credits 4% in index-linked interest at the end of the first year, it will have an accumulated value of $104. If that contract guarantees a minimum accumulated value of $103 at the end of the interest crediting period, that $4 of interest earned has already exceeded the minimum guaranteed for the entire surrender penalty period so the minimum guarantee doesn't matter.

There are index annuities that credit at least a minimum interest rate every year, and others that offer the thinnest possible minimum return (in order to maximize participation in the index), and still others in between. You should select the guarantee with which you are most comfortable.

<u>The Real Minimum Returns</u>

State insurance department rules on annuities specify the minimum returns that must be guaranteed for fixed annuities. For many years, the guaranteed benefit for single premium annuities had to be at least 3% interest, credited to 90% of premiums. (A lower premium percentage was permissible for flexible premium annuities). The rules then changed to permit a lower guarantee, reflecting the lower interest rate environment at the time. The rules will probably change again.

Actual index-linked interest usually exceeds the minimum

Today, there are a variety of minimum rates. However, the reality is that, under most crediting method assumptions, the actual index-linked interest credited for a surrender period term will be higher than the minimum required benefit.

Although there have been 5 year periods where the index ended lower than it started, there have never been 5 consecutive down years in either the S&P 500, Dow, Russell 2000, or Nasdaq.

This suggests that a strong minimum guarantee is not really needed for many index annuity designs, because the structure of the product will very likely produce better than minimum results even in bad times. It also suggests that money saved by reducing the guarantee to state required minimums can be better spent to enhance index-link performance.

The Index-Linked Part

After covering expenses, the remainder of a premium paid for *a fixed* rate annuity is placed in the insurer's general account where it is invested in bonds and other instruments. If the insurer's net investment return, in a given period, is higher than the annuity's minimum guaranteed return, the insurer declares and credits a fixed rate of interest for that period.

An index annuity works the same way, but with one important exception. If the insurer's net investment return is higher than the annuity's minimum guaranteed return, the additional return over the minimum guarantee is invested in an index link, enabling the earning of excess interest, linked to the movements of that index.

So, both fixed rate and index annuities have costs that are deducted from the premium. Both fixed rate and index annuities guarantee a minimum return; the difference is simply in how any remaining cash is used. In a fixed rate annuity, any extra cash left over, after covering expenses and the minimum guarantee, is used to buy more bonds, and the insurer announces a stated interest rate. In an index annuity, any extra cash is used to provide *index-linked interest*, and the insurer announces a stated degree of index participation.

How It Is Usually Done

One of the objections sometimes raised when the index annuity story is told is that it seems too good to be true. How can the insurance company provide both potential and protection? Let's look at how the index-link concept usually works.

If you have ever given a car seller $50 to hold a car for you at a certain price, you have participated in *options*. When you put $50 on the table to hold a car and the car seller agrees to accept your $50, that seller is obligated to sell you the car at the agreed upon price. But as the option buyer you are not obligated to buy the car; you simply have a right to buy it at that price. You can walk away and the most you can lose is your $50.

Equity options work the same way. Here is a real world example to show how the index annuity approach often utilizes options to provide the potential for higher annuity interest. For the sake of clarity, we will ignore transactions costs, and use a fictitious name for our real world example.

Cereals & Calls

Let's suppose that we have $50, and that the price of one share of common stock of a fictional cereal company, Admiral Mills, is currently trading, at just under $50. Let's further suppose that we know that we can purchase, from Competitive Bank, a nine-month certificate of deposit that will produce 2.8% interest on our deposit).

We know that if we buy the CD, it will return 2.8% in nine months. What will be the return on the common stock of Admiral Mills over the same period? We do not know. It could be greater or less than 2.8% - or we could lose some (or, conceivably, *all*) of the money we invested.

There is a third choice. Let's suppose that a *stock exchange listed call option,* giving the purchaser the right to buy one share of Admiral Mills common stock at $50 at any time within the next nine months, is trading at $2.05. If we buy the call option – or equity-link – we have the right to buy Admiral Mills at $50 a share and this right costs $2.05.

CD $48.63	+	Option $1.37	= $50

Let's say our first requirement is to ensure that we will still have $50 in our hands nine months from now. If we put $48.63 in the CD it will grow back to $50 at the end of nine months ($48.63 x 2.8% interest). This leaves us $1.37 left, out of our original $50. A full option, giving us 100% participation in any growth in Admiral Mills stock, costs $2.05. But we do not have $2.05. No problem. The option seller says we can buy two-thirds of the option for our $1.37, ($1.37/$2.05 = 66.8%) and he will keep the rest.

It is now nine months later. What if Admiral Mills stock is at $56 a share? We would exercise our option, buy the stock at $50, sell it at $56, and make $6. Our "participation rate" in this increase is two-thirds or 67%, so our share of the gain is $4 with the index seller keeping the other $2.

CD $50.00	+	Option $4.00	= $54

The CD is now, nine months after we bought it for $48.63, worth $50. If we add the value of our CD ($50) to the $4 we realized from our equity-link we find that we've ended up with $54, or an 8% return on our $50.

But what if the price of Admiral Mills stock had been $50 or less? We would not have used our option (because we could have bought that stock more cheaply without it) and the $1.37 spent on it is gone. However, because most of our money was placed in thc CD, we still have $50, and if we feel "bullish" about Admiral Mills stock, but want to guarantee at least the return of our entire principal, we can always try this option/CD combo again.

That's how an index annuity works. The primary differences are the insurer uses bonds instead of CDs, index options instead of stock options, and an annual period instead of nine months.

Stock Options & Index Options

The previous example employed an option on a specific stock. The options purchased by the insurance company to generate index-linked interest are usually for the entire index and are called *index options*. Index options are a bit more complicated because there are not specific stocks backing the option, but the basic concepts are the same. In either case, the index annuity buyer is not buying options, but, rather, an annuity contract that derives its ability to pay excess interest from the return on options on the option purchased by the insurance company.

For example, the ABC Insurance Company's index annuity credits interest based on movements of our imaginary Federal Stock Index. If the index is currently at 100, ABC can purchase an option giving it the right to buy the index at a level of 100 at any time during the next year.

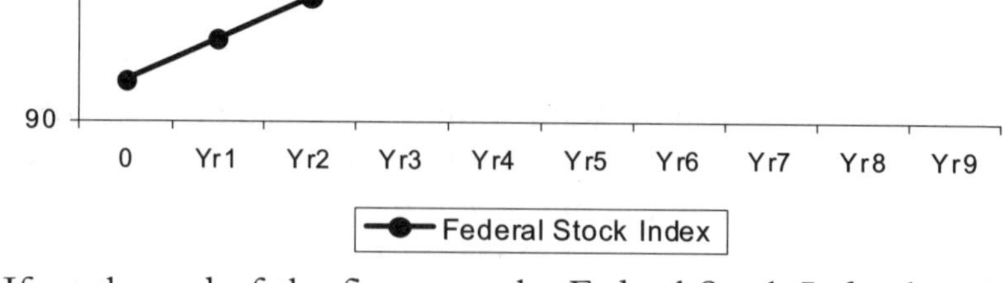

If, at the end of the first year, the Federal Stock Index has risen above 100, ABC will use (or *exercise*) the option. If the index rises to 110, it would make a gain of 10% [(110-100)/100 = .10]. It can then use that profit to pay excess interest to the owners of the ABC Index Annuity. Of course, if the index does not rise above 100, it would let the worthless option expire. But all it will lose is the cost of the option.

This is how most index annuities participate in the index. Option prices are more volatile than direct equity prices. If the index closes lower than 100, the option will be worthless (although, of course, the index itself would still have value.) But owning both the option and the bonds means that the insurance company can pay the guaranteed minimum return to the policyowners – because it bought enough bonds to back that guarantee.

Why Would The Seller Sell Us The Option?

If buying an option gives the buyer rights to potential gains and the ability to walk away if the index is down, why do sellers sell? Perhaps the seller feels that the index is not heading up during the term of the option. While the option is outstanding (not yet *exercised*), the seller will continue to receive any dividends that may be paid. Moreover, it has the money the buyer paid, in exchange for the option. In a flat market environment a seller could essentially sell the same option over and over again.

Time Value & Cost Of An Index-Link

An option is a right to buy or sell something in the future. A major aspect of the cost of that option is *duration* – how long a future. If I want the right to be able to buy stock you own at today's price, but the option will expire tomorrow, you probably would not charge me much for that option – after all, the price should not move much in a day. However, what if I want to be able to buy your stock at today's price at any time in the next five years? A lot can happen over five years, so you would certainly charge more for that right to buy – because that extra time has a value.

The *time value aspect* of an option's price reflects the fact that the uncertainty, as to what the stock's price will be at any point during the option period increases with the length of that option period. This means that an option good for five years will command a higher price than an option with a one year life. But the option cost does not vary *directly* with duration. A two-year option will not cost twice as much as a one-year option.

Option Cost (¢ out of a Premium $)

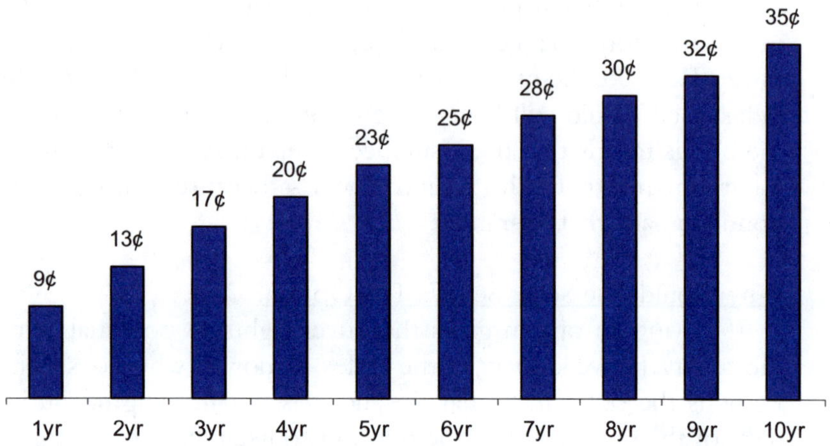

Longer period designs can offer higher index participation

The bottom line is this: Because it costs less to buy one long-term option instead of many one-year options, using the longer term option allows the annuity to offer a higher participation rate. The big difference, however, is that term end point methods generally do not lock in index gains until the end and if the index is not higher at the finish, no index-linked interest will be earned.

Where's The Risk?

Most index annuities use options to link index movement to the potential crediting of excess interest above the minimum guarantee. What risks does this present to the buyers of these products?

Although both stocks and mutual funds offer the potential for gains, and although long-term investors in these vehicles have historically realized average returns higher than those on safer alternatives, stocks and mutual funds present market risk. The stock market goes up and down – often steeply. It offers upside potential, but no assurance of a minimum return or that the investor will not lose some or possibly all of the money invested. Index annuities eliminate this market risk to principal.

When a consumer buys an index annuity, the principal is backed by, and is as safe as, the insurance company that issued the annuity. States and rating agencies examine insurance company books on a regular basis, and you rarely hear of an insurance company going bust. What if a company does go belly up? An annuity contract is an asset of the insurer, and, historically, another insurer has simply bought the annuity contracts of the troubled company and life has gone on; moreover, every state has a guarantee mechanism to protect annuity contract owners up to a maximum account value if a company tanks. It is possible to lose money in an insurance product if an insurance company fails, but based on history, it is unlikely.

Many index annuities impose steep surrender charges in the early contract years, and an annuity owner cashing in during those years could receive less than the original principal. This is a risk that must be fully discussed with annuity buyers. When it isn't, bad things can be expected. "Principal loss", due to surrender charges, is probably the single most frequently cited factor in annuity complaint cases.

As with all fixed rate insurance products, index annuities provide a minimum guaranteed return. Excess interest beyond this minimum guarantee is calculated based on movements on an external index, but the customer is not directly or indirectly involved in buying the index.

The insurance company is also insulated from risk when they buy options on the index and not the underlying securities. Buying an option gives you the right – not the obligation, to buy or sell something. This is how options work. If the index were worth less at the end of period than the insurer paid at the beginning, it would simply let the option expire. The insurance company would be out the money it spent on the option – a predetermined and known expense – but that is the limit to its risk.

Index Annuities – Talking About Risks

- The index annuity owner does not directly or indirectly own the index or any stocks
- Both credited interest and principal of the index annuity are protected from market risk
- The index annuity is backed by the insurance company (but not by any government agency such as the FDIC)
- The insurance company usually provides the potential for index-linked interest through the purchase of options. Buying options gives you rights, not obligations
- Most of the premium is used to buy bonds to protect the minimum guarantee and only a little is used to buy the options.
- One risk index annuity owners face is that they might have earned a higher return in another vehicle (but then again, hindsight's always 20-20)
- Although all fixed annuities provide a guarantee of principal, this guarantee is usually conditioned upon the annuity owner leaving his money in the annuity for at least a certain number of years

How Much Of The Index Upside Do You Get?

Index annuity owners get the opportunity to earn index-linked excess interest. If the index goes up 10% or 100% or 1000%, how much of the upside could they get? It depends on a number of factors. There are two basic fundamentals affecting how much index participation you get – interest rates (that affect the minimum guaranteed side) and option prices (affecting the index-linked side).

When interest rates are rising and/or option prices are falling, insurance companies can buy more options, which let them offer increased index participation. When interest rates are falling and/or option prices are rising, insurers have less money available for options, so index participation falls.

<u>Interest Rates Affect Index Participation</u>

In the earlier minimum guarantee example we assumed the insurance company had available, after expenses, $6 (or 6%) on $100 of premium, and that it required $2 to cover the 2% on 100% of premium minimum guarantee, leaving $4 remaining to buy the index-link. We also said that it cost $5 to buy an index-link that would allow us to participate in 100% of any potential increase in the index. If we have $4, we could buy 80% ($4/$5) of the index-link giving our annuity an 80% participation rate.

We have said most of an insurance company's portfolio is invested in bonds. What if bond yields had risen and the insurance company had available $7 after expenses on every $100 of premium? The minimum guarantee would still cost $2, and so this would now leave $5 available to buy an index-link. If a "full" index-link still costs $5, and we have $5, we could buy 100% ($5/$5) of the index-link, giving our annuity a 100% participation rate. Rising rates mean more money is available for index participation.

What if bond yields had fallen and the insurance company had only $5 left from that $100 of premium? The minimum guarantee would still cost $2, which would leave $3 available to buy an index-link. If a "full" index-link still cost $5, and we have $3, we could buy 60% ($3/$5) of the index-link giving our annuity a 60% participation rate. Falling rates mean less money is available for index participation.

Bond Yield ↑ = Increased Participation

Bond Yield ↓ = Decreased Participation

When interest rates are lower, you need to allocate more cents out of each dollar to invest in bonds to provide the minimum guaranteed return. More money spent on bonds leaves less money available to buy options. When rates are higher you need to allocate less money for the bonds, which leaves more money available to buy options.

Option Prices Affect Index Participation

We said that the cost of a "full" index-link or option to cover $100 of premium was $5. If we had $3 remaining after covering the minimum guarantee we could buy 60% ($3/$5) of the index-link giving our annuity a 60% participation rate.

Option Prices ↑ = Decreased Participation

Option Prices ↓ = Increased Participation

What if the index is expected to soar next year? The option seller would probably want more money because it believes the probability of having to pay off on the option is greater. The index option might cost $6. If we still have $3 remaining after covering the minimum guarantee, we could now buy 50% ($3/$6) of the index-link giving our annuity a 50% participation rate.

What if the index is expected to drop next year? The option seller would probably accept less money because it believes that the probability of having to pay off on the option is less. The index option might cost $4. If we still have $3 remaining after covering the minimum guarantee we could now buy 75% ($3/$4) of the index-link giving our annuity a 75% participation rate. Assumptions about where the stock market is heading greatly impact option prices.

In addition, big option buyers get quantity pricing breaks. A carrier buying $25 million of options usually gets a better price than one buying $1 million of options. This means the big buyer gets more options for each dollar spent, which can translate into higher caps or rates.

Finally, a carrier can forgo buying options entirely by using a process called *dynamic hedging*, which attempts to mimic the option's behavior by building a small portfolio of other equity instruments. Explaining the mechanics of dynamic hedging would require writing a separate book. In a nutshell, dynamic hedging gives the potential for higher returns, but the risk is also higher than simply buying the options outright.

Other Factors Affect Index Annuity Participation

Although interest rates and option prices are the two primary factors in determining index participation, they are not the only ones. We already talked about how the strength of the minimum guarantee affects the money leftover to buy options. Other areas are expenses and pricing assumptions.

If one insurance company's expenses are higher than another's, it will have less money available after paying those expenses and, consequently, will offer less participation. (Expenses include overhead, commission, direct policy costs and premium bonuses).

Pricing assumptions include things like assumptions as to how long the annuity will remain in force. For example, if one annuity has a longer surrender period than another its issuer will typically earn a somewhat higher rate of interest on the bonds it buys, because it buys bonds with longer durations, which means more money is available for buying options. Pricing assumptions also incorporate the return the insurance company will accept and how conservatively or aggressively it tries to predict the future.

Finally, if the degree of index participation in one index annuity can be changed to reflect changes in the market while another annuity locks in index participation, the annuity with the flexibility to change should offer more index participation.

One Year or Multiple Year Rate Lock-Ins

Typically, an index annuity will determine how much of any index-linked annuity interest you will earn for one year at a time, and will declare, on the policy anniversary, the new level of participation for the following year. Some index annuities lock in all of the initial participation elements for two years, three years, or even for the entire penalty period of the annuity.

How Can You Get More Than 100% Participation?

At times index annuities have offered more than 100% direct participation in possible index growth. We have heard folks say this is impossible – how can you pour five quarts of milk into a four quart container? The reason is simple: financial markets are not milk.

Let's say we have $5 left over to buy an index-link on $100 of premium. Let's also say that a seller charges $4 for a "full" index-link. Our $5 would enable us to buy 125% of the "full" link ($5/$4). If the index rose 10% we would earn 12.5%! The reason this can be done is that the option seller is using the extra $1 it receives to buy an additional 25% of another different option on the index. The seller can give 125% participation because there is 125% of hedged index behind it. The seller is still selling 100% of what it owns (125%/1.25).

The Term Of The Annuity

You may hear an index annuity described as having a five year or ten year term. In our experience, when people talk about the term of an annuity, they are usually referring to the length of time during which surrender penalties may be charged (the "surrender charge period"). Thus, an annuity with surrender penalties for the first five contract years is often referred to as having a five-year term; an annuity with a ten year penalty period is said to have a ten year term.

But this understanding of "annuity term" is both inaccurate and misleading. The real "term" of an annuity is from the date of purchase until the contract maturity date. At maturity, the accumulated value of an annuity must be paid out – either in a lump sum or in the form of regular income payments. The typical annuity maturity date usually occurs at age 85 or 90 or 100. In effect, the actual "term" of the annuity could be 20, 30 or 50 years depending upon how old the annuity buyer is at time of purchase. *But this does not mean the annuity owner is locked into the contract for that entire time!* Although the insurer is required to meet the terms of the annuity until the maturity date, the annuity owner can almost always walk away at any time, after paying any applicable surrender charges. Moreover, it is almost never *true* that the owner must wait until the maturity date to annuitize the contract. Most deferred annuities allow annuitization after one year (though some require a wait of up to five years).

Surrender Charges

All index annuities charge a penalty if the policy is cashed in prior to the end of the surrender period. Depending on the policy selected, surrender periods vary in length from one to eighteen years, and penalties can be as high as 25% of initial premium (although very high penalties are usually offset by a "premium bonus". (Typically large up-front bonuses are actually the main cause of very high surrender charge schedules).

Surrender penalties do not usually apply if the policy is paid out due to death of the owner (and *all* deferred annuities issued since January 18, 1985 *must* pay out upon the death of the owner) or if the policy is annuitized. A typical surrender charge is expressed either as a percentage of the accumulated value of the annuity or as a percentage of the original premium. *Although index annuity principal is protected from market risk, most index annuities would return less than the original premium if surrendered too early.*

A few index annuities do not state a specific surrender charge, but instead base the net surrender value on the minimum guaranteed value. Although this calculation may not be called a surrender charge, it has the same effect. For example, if the minimum guaranteed surrender value is based on 3% interest compounding on 90% of the premium, then the cash received upon surrender would be 90% during the first contract year, 92.7% during the second, 95.5% during the third and 98.3% during the fourth year. This is really a *de facto* declining penalty of 10%, 7.3%, 4.5% and 1.7% for the first four years of the contract.

What Happens After The Surrender Period Is Over?

In most index annuities, nothing happens when the surrender period ends, except there are no more charges on withdrawals. A few annuities may begin a multiple year period with new surrender charges.

Cheat Sheet

- Although every index annuity has a minimum guaranteed interest rate, the interest is usually calculated on less than 100% of the premium received.

- Most insurance companies provide the potential for index-linked interest by buying options on the underlying index. An option gives you the right - not the obligation, to buy or sell something within a period of time.

- Index annuities provide a fresh start in that they begin calculating new index gain from where the previous period ended. This resetting of index values gives index annuities the potential to credit interest even during volatile market times.

Chapter 3 – Crediting Methods

In the last six years only ONE completely new structure has been created, the r*ainbow method.* Every other crediting method on the market today had its genesis in a structure used in the past, and this includes the *balanced allocation* method (earlier called *the equity kicker* method), *hurdle*, and *low water mark* designs. The truly new development in the index annuity world is the lifetime income withdrawal benefit and this is discussed at length in Chapter 6.

There are still really only two ways to credit index-linked interest to an annuity. One can either measure index movement over a year or two – an *annual reset* method, or one can measure index movement over a period of years – *a term end point* method. And yet, over four dozen variations on these methods have floated around since index annuities were introduced.

The first index annuity offered a term end point method variation that used the higher of the index value at the end of the surrender period or the index value on any policy anniversary. This *term high point method*, also known as a *high water mark* design, was consumer-friendly but expensive to offer, and has not been available for the last five years (although variations of this design are still available they are not the same thing). We've decided to include brief descriptions of crediting methods that are not currently offered because they may resurface.

This chapter illustrates how all of the major index crediting methods work by using the fictional Federal Stock Index. In the next chapter we will examine the good and bad points of the different methods.

Term End Point (Term Point-to-Point)

Our definition of a *term end point* structure was one that measured index movements over a period greater than a year or two.

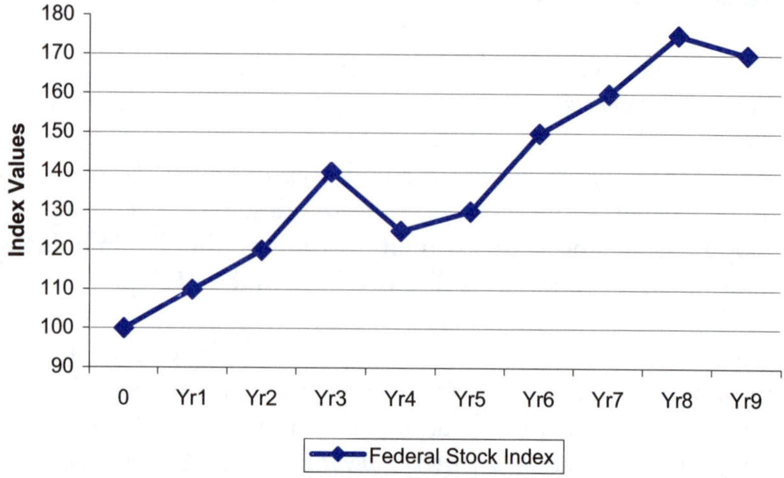

Example: You have decided to buy an index annuity. You will earn index-linked interest based on the performance of the fictional Federal Stock Index, which is currently at an index level of 100. The insurance company says that at the end of nine years they will credit the greater of the minimum guarantee or 100% of any index-linked interest earned calculated by dividing the ending index value by the beginning index value

How Term End Point Interest Is Calculated

(170 /100) - 1 = 70% Index Gain
70% x 100% participation = 70%
70% = Total Interest Earned

It is now the end of year nine and the Federal Stock Index is at a level of 170. The index annuity divides the current index level by the starting index level and multiples the gain by our original premium. You earned a total of 70% interest for the nine years.

What if the index difference had been negative because the ending index was at a lower level than when you began? The index annuity would credit the minimum guaranteed return.

A typical term end point index annuity only credits interest realized from index movements at the end of the term. Interest is not calculated and credited annually. Therefore, if the annuity owner surrendered the contract prior to the end of the term they would not usually receive any interest based on positive index movements.

In the chart on the previous page the Federal Stock Index has reached a level of 140 by the end of year 3 representing a 40% increase in the index from the day the annuity was purchased. If the annuity is then surrendered, how much of this gain does the typical annuity share in? The almost always answer if the annuity used a term end point crediting structure would be zero (but almost every index annuity will treat death as the end of the period and calculate any index gain at that point.).

Term end point methods do not calculate and credit gain until the end of the period. However, some annuities using the equity kicker design (Balanced Allocation Method) did allow the annuityowner to lock in the realized gain prior to the term end point.

Participation Rate

The degree to which one participates in any calculated index gains may be expressed as a percentage. In our Term End Point example you received 100% of the calculated interest movement. Another way of saying this is that the participation rate was 100%. The participation rate reflects the cost of linking index gains to the annuity and may be more or less than 100%.

A term end point method calculates index movement from a start point to an end point some years away, but it is rare to find a pure, stand-alone term end point product. A few of the products marry a term end point with a fixed account (e.g.: the Balanced Allocation Method mentioned). A few of the products use the summed index movement of several indices and use this composite to compute index gain or loss.

Actual Index Movement = 70%

If Participation Rate	Then Credited Interest
120%	84%
100%	70%
80%	56%
60%	42%

Term Yield Spread (Term Asset Fee)

Term yield spread calculates the total gain for the index over the period, determines the annualized return, deducts a spread from the annualized return to find the index annuity annualized return, then compounds the annualized return to determine the index annuity credited interest.

Example: The Federal Stock Index began at a level of 100 and was at 170 nine years later for a total gain of 70%. A nine-year gain of 70% represents an annualized gain of 6.07%. If there was a 1% yield spread, the carrier would deduct 1% from the index annualized gain of 6.07% and credit an annual interest rate of 5.07%. If you compound 5.07% for nine years, *the cumulative interest* equals 56.11%.

An index annuity interest crediting asset fee or yield spread is in not the same as a variable annuity asset fee or mutual fund asset fee because the "spread" can never result in a negative value; the lowest interest credited to an index annuity is zero. The index annuity "spread" or "fee" is simply another way of saying participation rate.

Multiple (Blended) Indices

The method adds up the returns from different indices and applies a participation rate to the overall index gain or loss. The index annuity performance over multiple years uses a percentage of the gains or losses of the different indices.

The credited interest for the term might be based on 35% of the Federal Stock Index gain or loss over, say, five years, 35% of the Federal Bond Index movement, 20% of the Foreign Index and 10% of the Medium Federal Index. If the respective gains or losses for the term were, 60%, 20%, 40%, and -50%, the blended gain or loss would be:

How Blended Interest Is Calculated

Federal Stock Index	60%	x	35%	= 21%
Federal Bond Index	20%	x	35%	= 7%
Foreign Index	40%	x	20%	= 8%
Medium Foreign Index	-50%	x	10%	= - 5%
Blended Index Movement				31%

If the gain participation rate was 100% the index annuity would be credited with 31% index-linked interest. At the end of the term a new participation rate is determined for the next term.

This method may also allow for at least some participation if the blended movement was negative. Say that the blended index movement was a loss of 31%. A preset participation rate of 5%, 10%, or more would be applied. At a 10% participation rate the policy would credit 3.1% index-linked interest even though the actual index performance was negative.

This is not a *rainbow method* (described later in the chapter) because the allocation of the indices is fixed and does not change based on index performance.

Term Two-Step (Stepped Participation)

Although this term end point variation is no longer offered it was an intriguing method. The *term two-step* credits a higher participation rate on initial index movement and a lower rate on any additional movements.

The Federal Stock Index began at a level of 100 and was at 170 nine years later for a total gain of 70%. A term two-step method might offer a participation rate of 100% on the first 50% of positive index movement and 50% thereafter. Therefore, this annuity would take the first 50% of the gain times the 100% participation rate for a first step subtotal of 50%. The annuity would then multiply any remaining gain – in this case 20% (70%-50%) by the second step participation rate of 50% (20% x 50%) to get a second step sub total of 10%. The first step subtotal (50%) is added to the second step subtotal (10%) to determine total interest credited.

Why was a two-step approach used? It was a way for the insurer to lower exposure to a large increase in the index and keep costs down, without resorting to caps or lower participation rates. The approach maximizes returns in fair or good markets.

High Point Term (High Water Mark)

The first successful index annuity used a high point term crediting method, also known as *high water mark*. We consider a high point term structure as a type of term end point method with one very important difference. The difference is the ending index number is the higher of the end of the period value or the highest previous annual unaveraged anniversary value.

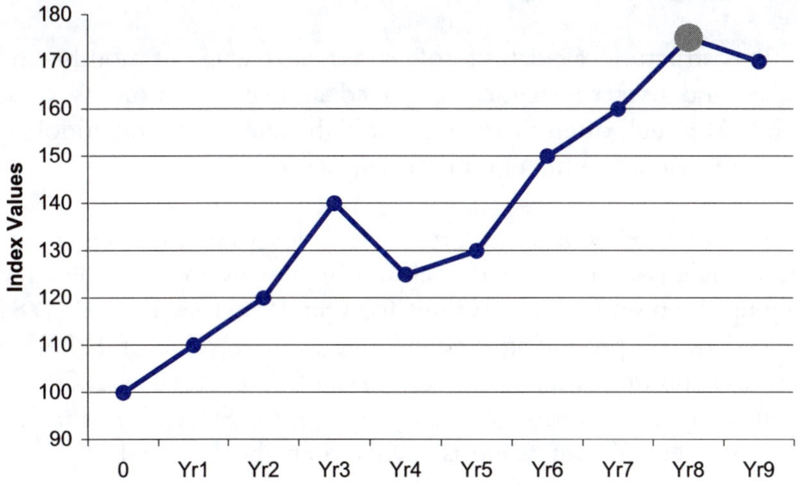

The Federal Stock Index began at a level of 100 and was at 170 nine years later. But the highest value reached on a contract anniversary was 175 on the eighth anniversary (the gray dot). The high point term method would base the gain calculation on the higher 175 value rather than the lower 170 end value, and record a total index gain of 75% [(175/100) -1 = 75%]. The index gain would then be multiplied by the participation rate to determine interest credited to the contract.

If the term high point method does a better job of protecting against late period index losses than term end point methods then why is the original version no longer offered? The reason is that it is more expensive for the insurance company to provide the protection of the high point term method because the cost of the options is higher, and so index participation would have to be much lower than it would be for term end point or rolling average structures.

Term High (Rolling) Average Anniversary

This structure calculates a rolling annual average of monthly index values and uses the highest averaged anniversary value as an end point. Although often marketed as a high water mark methodology it is not the same as a high point term structure.

This method adds up the monthly index values, divides them by the cumulative months and uses the highest averaged value. If you tally up the monthly index values for year 1 the total is 1284; 1284 is divided by 12, producing a cumulative average value of 107. If you tally the monthly values for years 1 and 2 the total is 2670; 2670 divided by 24 months (2 Years) is 111.25. Since the cumulative averaged second year value is higher than the first, it becomes the new high value.

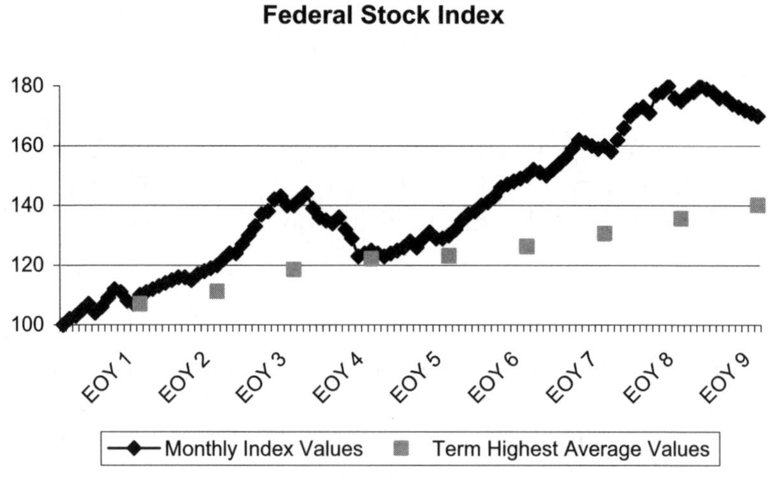

This calculation is done each year with the final averaged value compared against previous values to determine the highest. This example winds up with an end point value of 140.16 resulting in a realized index gain of 40.16% for the nine-year period (140.16/100-1). A participation rate would then be applied.

Midterms – Biennial, Triennial & Quadrennial Reset

A handful of companies calculate index movement over two year periods, and even fewer calculate index movement over three or four years, and all of the methods and variations available to the annual reset structures mentioned below apply. It is less expensive to buy one two-year, three-year or four-year option than successive one-year options, so index participation can usually be higher for these intermediate term resets. As the length of the reset increases, the likelihood of getting either a zero or a larger return increases, when compared with annual reset methods over the same years. We treat biennial methods as annual resets, because the overall differences in return distributions are very similar. On the other hand, measuring index movements over four year periods produces results that tend to look like those for five and six year periods, thus we look at quadrennial methods as term end point designs. That leaves three year period methods which may look as annual reset distribution patterns at times and follow term end point patterns at other times.

Annual Reset (Annual Ratchet, Fresh Start)

A fixed rate annuity credits interest at the end of each contract year. Index annuities crediting index-linked interest each year are known as *annual reset* or *annual ratchet* methodologies (*annual cliquet* in some academic papers). Annual reset methods begin the calculation of the next period's index movement using the closing value of the previous period.

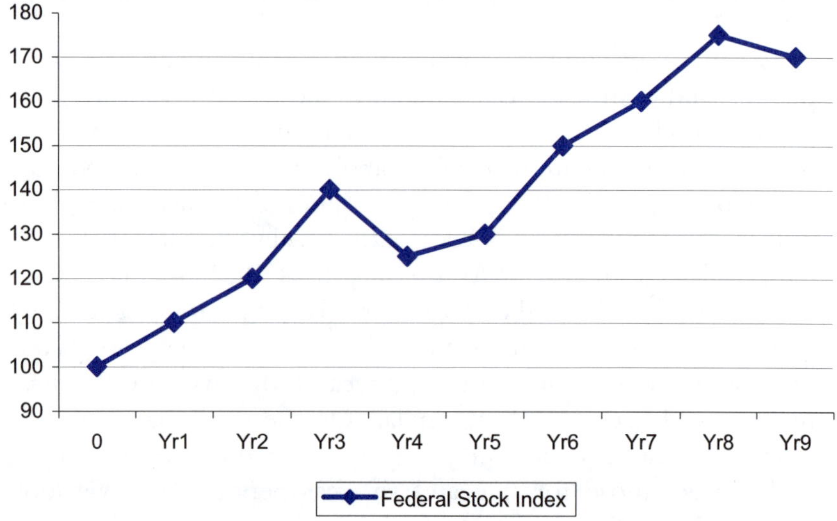

Annual Point-to-Point (APP)

Let's say that an index annuity credits 60% of any positive index movement at the end of the contract year. The Federal Stock Index level is 100 today. One year later the index has reached 110. The way this works is the beginning index value is subtracted from the ending index value (110-100 = 10) and the difference is divided by the beginning value to determine the percentage of index movement.

How Annual Reset Point-to-Point Interest Is Calculated

	110	Ending Index Value
-	100	Beginning Index Value
	10	Index Difference
/	100	Divided By Beginning Value
	.10	Index Movement
x	60%	Participation Rate
	6%	Interest Earned

We said the index annuity participates in 60% of any positive movement, so we multiply the percentage of index movement by 60% to determine the actual interest the annuity earned which is 6%.

What if the index difference had been negative? If the index difference is negative it is treated as zero positive interest.

This example shows the way an annual point-to-point crediting method works. The insurance company says in advance the extent to which the index annuity will participate in the coming year's index movement. This participation rate is applied to any positive movement produced by the index.

Annual Yield Spread (Asset Fee)

Participation in an index can be expressed as a percentage – like the 60% participation rate used above, or we could deduct an "asset fee" or "yield spread" from the index movement to determine actual interest credited to the index annuity.

How Annual Reset Yield Spread Interest Is Calculated

	110	Ending Index Value
-	100	Beginning Index Value
	10	Index Difference
/	100	Divided By Beginning Value
	.10	Index Movement
-	4%	Yield Spread
	6%	Interest Earned

Instead of saying that the annuity will credit interest equal to 60% of any positive index movement the insurer could say that 100% of the index movement will be credited minus a 4% "asset fee". If the index movement was 10% deducting a 4% fee would give us 6% interest – the same credited interest than the 60% participation rate provided.

So which is better, "times a participation rate" or "minus a yield spread"? It depends on the respective rates and the amount of gain.

In this example the two approaches resulted in the same credited rate, but what if the index increased 15% and one product had a 60%

participation rate and another deducted a 4% yield spread? Then the 60% participation rate would result in 9% interest while the 4% yield spread produced 11% interest (15% x 60% = 9%, 15% - 4% = 11%). If the index gained 5% the participation rate structure would credit 3% and the yield spread would credit 1% (5% x 60% = 3%; 5% - 4% = 1%).

Yield spread methods can credit more in big gainer periods; participation rate methods can credit more in more moderate periods.

At These Index Gains	A Participation Rate of 40%	50%	60%	70%	80%
2%	1.2%	1.0%	0.8%	0.6%	0.4%
4%	2.4%	2.0%	1.6%	1.2%	0.8%
6%	3.6%	3.0%	2.4%	1.8%	1.2%
8%	4.8%	4.0%	3.2%	2.4%	1.6%
10%	6.0%	5.0%	4.0%	3.0%	2.0%
12%	7.2%	6.0%	4.8%	3.6%	2.4%
14%	8.4%	7.0%	5.6%	4.2%	2.8%
16%	9.6%	8.0%	6.4%	4.8%	3.2%
18%	10.8%	9.0%	7.2%	5.4%	3.6%
20%	12.0%	10.0%	8.0%	6.0%	4.0%

Is Equal To The Above Yield Spreads

As mentioned before, the interest crediting "spread" can never result in a negative value because the lowest return an index annuity pays is zero. In contrast, if a variable annuity had a 4% asset fee and the index gained 3% the net to the account would be a loss of 1%; if the index lost 3% the net to the account after the 4% asset fee would be a negative 7%. However, if the same numbers were applied to an index annuity the net effect would be 0% because an index annuity cannot lose credited interest (This should not be confused with fees charged for riders that are extras the annuity owner chose to add on the annuity. Fee charges for some riders could result in a loss of account value if not enough interest is earned. This is discussed in Chapter 6).

Averaging

Many index annuities average at least some portion of index values. We will look at an index annuity with an annual reset methodology that applies a participation rate to the monthly average of the year's index values. The participation rate in any index increase is 100%.

Averaging always drives numbers to the middle. In a generally rising market averaging usually produces a lower value than an actual end point; in a falling market averaging generally produces a higher ending value than an actual end point.

In this next chart we have magnified the index values for the first contract year to show the monthly index movements. The year finished at 110, which we used for annual point-to-point calculations.

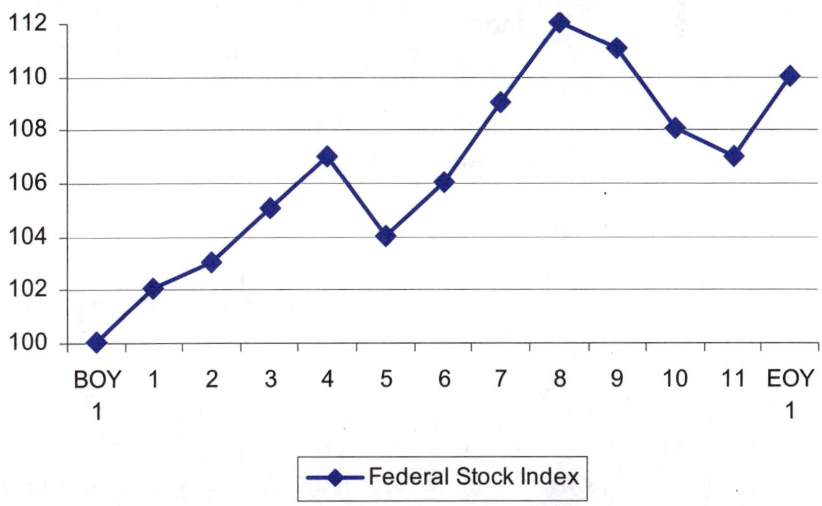

The Federal Stock Index closing monthly values for the first year are listed above. Although the year ended at 110, if you add up all the monthly values and divide by 12 you get an averaged ending value of 107.

How Annual Reset Monthly Averaging Interest Is Calculated

Beginning Value	100
Value Period 1	102
Value Period 2	103
Value Period 3	105
Value Period 4	107
Value Period 5	104
Value Period 6	106
Value Period 7	109
Value Period 8	112
Value Period 9	111
Value Period 10	108
Value Period 11	107
Value Period 12	110
Average End	107

107	Average End Value
- 100	Begin Index Value
7	Index Difference
/ 100	Divided By Begin Value
. 07	
x 100%	Participation Rate
7%	Interest Earned

If you believe that the index will rise over the next year, and you know that averaging produces a lower end value in a rising market than an actual ending point, then wouldn't you always want to go with the non-averaged crediting method? The answer is, it depends.

Crediting methods using averaging usually offer higher index participation. In this example 100% of the monthly index points produced an average end value of 107, or a 7% increase for the year. An annual point-to-point method uses the actual end point of 110, which represents a

10% increase for the year. But in our previous examples the annual point-to-point method has a participation rate of 60%, resulting in 6% interest credited to the annuity (10% x 60%). The monthly average method has a 100% participation rate, which gives 7% interest (7% x 100%). The averaging method produced higher net interest than the point-to-point method.

Caps

Another variation annual reset crediting structures may use are caps. A *cap* is a ceiling or upward limit on the interest that may be credited to the annuity and may be used in conjunction with a participation rate or yield spread structure. A cap usually reflects the maximum interest that can be credited to the annuity contract - an i*nterest cap* of 12% would mean that regardless of index movement the maximum interest credited for any one period is 12%. Another type of cap is an i*ndex cap* which limits the amount of index movement to which a crediting method is applied - an index movement cap of 12% would mean that any index movement above 12% is ignored.

It is very important to know whether the annuity you're examining uses an interest cap or an index cap. An interest cap says "this is the most interest that will be *credited*"; an index cap says "this is the most index gain that will be *recognized*". If you mistake an index (gross) cap for an interest (net) cap you could be negatively surprised.

Caps are used to boost participation rates or minimize yields spreads. Since they limit upside exposure, the cost of providing the index-linked interest is less (than if no cap were imposed), so participation in gains up to the cap are higher. Caps enable one to get "more of most" instead of "less of more."

Because caps limit the maximum interest that could be credited to an index annuity, the annuity buyer could feel that she is missing out on potential gains. However, a cap on interest may help the annuity produce higher earnings.

12% Interest Cap

30% Index Movement
x <u>60%</u> Participation Rate
18% Interest

Is 18%≤12%; No

12% Interest Credited

30% Index Movement
\- <u>3%</u> Yield Spread
27% Interest

Is 27%≤12%; No

12% Interest Credited

12% Index Cap

30% Index Movement
Is 30%≤12%; No

12%
x <u>60%</u> Participation Rate
7.2% Interest

7.2%Interest Credited

30% Index Movement
Is 30%<12%; No

12% Index Cap
\- <u>3%</u> Yield Spread
9% Interest

9% Interest Credited

Putting a cap on the potential interest paid lowers the risk. If the potential total payout is lower, the insurance company can offer a higher participation rate up to the cap.

Placing a cap on potential gains means the participation rate should be higher for the capped product than for the annuity without a cap. If index gains are modest the capped version will credit more interest. Which annuity will credit more? It depends on the relative rates and how often the interest ceiling is actually exceeded.

Suppose that one point-to-point annuity has a participation rate of 40% with no cap and another offers a 100% rate, but will credit a maximum return of 7% for the coming year. This means that in any year when the index growth exceeds 17.5% the non-cap annuity will produce a higher return. We determine this point by dividing the cap (7%) by the non-cap rate (40%). Conversely, whenever the index gains less than 17.5% the index annuity with a cap will have the higher return.

Index Gain	x 40% Rate	x 100% with 7% Cap
30%	12.0%	7%
18%	7.2%	7%
14%	5.6%	7%
10%	4.0%	7%
8%	3.2%	7%

Monthly Cap

The *monthly cap forward-not back (monthly cap on gains-not losses)* was borrowed from a Wall Street principal protection securities idea. It calculates gains and losses of the index on the monthly basis, adds up the monthly figures, and the final number is your interest for the period; the period's interest can never be less than zero. The maximum monthly gain recognized is subject to a cap, but monthly losses are not subject to a cap. This method is also called a monthly point-to-point, but this might be confusing because unlike an annual point-to-point the values are not locked each month.

With a 2% cap, a "best case" scenario would be where the index increases 2% a month for twelve months, producing 24% interest for the year. A "worst case" scenario would be if the index were to increase, say, 40% over eleven months, but then decline 22% in the twelfth month. The maximum possible gain for the eleven months would be 22% (2% x 11), which would be offset by the 22% decline in the 12th, resulting in *zero gain, even though the index would have increased by 18% for the year.*

The most common monthly cap methods do the summing of gains and loss every 12 months, but a few sum the capped gains and uncapped losses of 24 months and a few use 36 months. Since the likelihood of experiencing losing months increases as the summing period increases, the caps on the monthly gains tend to increase too, in order to recognize more positive monthly movement.

How Annual Reset Interest Is Calculated: Monthly Cap

Beginning Value	100	2% Cap
Value Period 1	102	2.00%
Value Period 2	103	0.98%
Value Period 3	105	1.94%
Value Period 4	107	1.90%
Value Period 5	104	-2.80%
Value Period 6	106	1.92%
Value Period 7	109	2.00%
Value Period 8	112	2.00%
Value Period 9	111	-0.90%
Value Period 10	108	-2.70%
Value Period 11	107	-0.92%
Value Period 12	110	2.00%

2.00%+0.98%+1.94%+1.90%-2.80%+1.92% +2.00%+2.00%-0.90%-2.70%-0.92%+2.00%= 7.42% Interest Earned

Annual Fixed Rate with Equity Component (Balanced Allocation or Equity Kicker)

Crediting a fixed rate to a portion of the premium with the remainder participating in the index was first used in the last century in an annual reset design, but sales in products with this design were small. There are a couple of variations to this theme currently in use.

In both variations, the annuity credits a fixed interest rate to a portion of the contract value, crediting to the balance interest at a rate derived from index performance. A yield spread or asset fee is then deducted from the total. Net gains are credited as interest and net losses are treated as zero interest earned.

In the *balanced allocation* method the buyer typically selects a fixed rate component (the range of rates depends on the interest rate environment) and also a term end point part that participates in positive index movements over a four, five or six-year period. The higher the fixed interest rate selected, the lower the participation rate applied to the index. At the end of the period, gains from the fixed rate and index-linked components are combined and credited. An annualized asset fee (yield spread) may be deducted from the combined return.

This "equity kicker" or "balanced" approach might look at a six year time frame and offer a couple of options. One option might allocate 50% into a fixed account paying 4% and the remaining 50% would provide a 100% participation rate on any gains in the index from start to end of the six year period. The other option might allocate 20% into a fixed account paying 4% and the remaining 80% would provide a 100% participation rate on any gains in the index from start to end of the six year period; however, a 2% yield spread would be deducted from the combined annualized gain before net interest was credited.

Let's suppose that our Federal Stock Index has increased from 100 to 150 (50%) in six years, and that the 4% fixed rate gain, compounded over those six years is 26.5%. What is the return under these two balanced method options?

Allocation	50% Index Gain	26.5% Fixed Gain	Calculated Gain
50/50	25%	13.3%	38.3%
80/20	40%	5.3%	45.3%

Allocation	Annualized Gain	Yield Spread	Actual Yield
50/50	5.5%	0%	5.5%
80/20	6.4%	-2%	4.4%

Since a yield spread was not deducted from the 50/50 allocation the total gain remains at 38.3% for the six year period and that translates into an annualized return of 5.5%, while the 80/20 allocation produced a total gain of 29.7% (after application of the yield spread) for an annualized return of 4.4%. In this example you would have better off putting half of the premium into the fixed rate "sure thing." When would the 80/20 allocation have won? If the index had gone up more than 87% the total net yield, even after the 2% yield spread, would have been higher than the yield on the 80/20 allocation.

Why is there a yield spread cost on one alternative and not the other? The potential term-end point interest the annuity owner may receive is unlimited. As the allocation to the index-linked side increases, the exposure to paying out index-linked interest increases; thus, to cover the cost of this exposure, the insurer charges an asset fee or yield spread (as mentioned, really another way of reducing the participation rate). If 90% of the premium is allocated to the index side, an asset fee of 3% might be charged, if 70% is allocated to the index side, the deduction might be only 1%, and if the split is 50/50, there might not be any reduction in the combined returns.

Biennial Variation

The other variation uses a biennial reset of the crediting period. Once again, a percentage of the index gain or loss is added to a percentage of fixed account interest, after which a charge is deducted. Losses are treated as zero gains and positive gains are compounded.

Using two year reset periods allows for a lower overall option cost than buying two annual reset options, and avoids the greater uncertainty that would result from using a longer reset period (such as four or six years). The concern is the longer one waits to lock in index gains, the greater the possibility that something might come along and cause the index to drop before you've locked in.

Assume that the Federal Stock Index increased from 100 to 114 over two years (a 14% increase), and that the 4% fixed rate compounded total gain over two years was 8.2%. One of the methods described below allocates 40% to the fixed account, 60% to the indexed account and deducts a 2.5% charge from the total. The other allocates 60% to the fixed account, 40% to the index and deducts a 0.5% charge from the total. What is the return under these two b*alanced method* options?

In this instance, it's the choice with the greatest fixed rate component that credits the highest yield, because the index component gain was not high enough to offset the increase in the yield spread from 0.5% to 2.5%.

Allocation	14% Index Gain	8.2% Fixed Gain	Calculated Gain
60/40	8.4%	3.3%	11.7%
40/60	5.6%	4.9%	10.5%

Allocation	Calculated Gain	Yield Spread	2 Year Yield
60/40	11.7%	-2.5%	9.2%
40/60	10.5%	-0.5%	10.0%

Rainbow Method

Although new to the index annuity arena the rainbow concept itself is not new. It has been used for many years in the investment world. It is an option basket whose best-performing indices are weighted more heavily than those that perform less well. It is always a "look-back" because the money is allocated based on the ranking of the performance after the period is over. Not all allocation methods are rainbows. A couple of carriers credit interest based on the blended performance of multiple indices, but the specific index allocation is fixed at the beginning of each year so they are not rainbow methods. To show how the *rainbow method* works we will compare it to the *blended indices* example used earlier.

Blended

Federal Stock Index	60%	x	35%	= 21%
Federal Bond Index	20%	x	35%	= 7%
Foreign Index	40%	x	20%	= 8%
Medium Foreign Index	-50%	x	10%	= - 5%
				31%

The *rainbow method* may also use the Federal Index, Federal Bond Index movement, Foreign Index and Medium Federal Index and allocations of 35%, 35%, 20% 10%, but the allocations are ranked by performance. After the period is over the returns will be ranked highest to lowest and then the greatest allocation is given to the best performer, then the next best, and so on.

Rainbow

Federal Stock Index	60%	x	35%	= 21%
Federal Bond Index	20%	x	20%	= 4%
Foreign Index	40%	x	35%	= 14%
Medium Foreign Index	-50%	x	10%	= - 5%
				34%

The best performer was the Federal Stock Index with a 60% gain. The *rainbow method* uses the highest allocation, 35%, and credits 21%. The next best performer is the Foreign Index at 40% and the next highest allocation is also 35% so this piece of the rainbow credits 14%. The third performer was up 20% and the third highest allocation is 20%, so 4% is credited. Finally, the lowest performer is the Medium Foreign Index with a loss of 50%. This 50% loss is multiplied by the remaining allocation factor of 10% and the resulting negative 5% is subtracted from the 21% plus 14% plus 4% gains of the other three allocations, resulting in 34% interest credited.

What if the negative returns were bigger than the gains resulting in a loss for the period? Because this is an index annuity, no loss is recorded. Instead, zero index-linked interest is credited for the period.

How does the rainbow method differ from a simple blend of indices? The blended formula's index allocations are locked in and unaffected by the ranking of the return.

The rainbow method marketing appeal has been expressed by saying that the annuity buyer gets to bet on the race after it has been run and that most of the bet will be put down on the horses that "win and place." To determine whether the different rainbow allocations may be a better horserace, we ran calculations to produce hypothetical returns for both rainbow and "S&P 500 only" crediting methods, and these are shown in the next chapter.

Other Methods

The previous methodologies represent the bulk of the index annuity sales. Most of the annuities sold use some degree of averaging, a significant number of annuities apply ceilings or caps on maximum interest credited, and whether a participation rate or yield spread is used often depends on the marketing climate. Elements are often combined. Several annual reset structures use averaging of index values, have a cap, and either use a participation rate or a yield spread. There are several other crediting methods used.

Binary, Non-Negative (Trigger) Annual Reset

The index annuity will pay a stated interest rate if the index does not go down. The insurer will declare that the "trigger" rate for the coming year is 6%. If the index does not end lower a year from now the trigger method will credit 6% interest. Whether the index goes up 1% or 90% the trigger method will credit 6%. Even if the index ends up exactly where it started, posting neither gain nor loss for the previous twelve months, the trigger method will credit 6%.

That's it. If the index is not lower at the end of the contract year the index will credit the predetermined rate.

Bond-Linked Interest With Base

Although there are a few annuities offering a bond index, or a bond index in addition to equity choices that is not what I mean. This crediting method links interest crediting to U.S. Treasury Notes. If the T-note rate is higher at policy anniversary, the annuity renewal rate is credited with a like increase. If the T-note rate is lower in subsequent years, the annuity rate goes down the same amount, but the annuity rate can never be less than the initial rate.

Hurdle

The annuity participates in index gain above a floor (the hurdle), but nothing below. As examples, say the current participation rate is 40% above a floor of 5%. If the index increased 10% next year the annuity would credit 2% (10%-5%=5% x 40%). But if the index increased 35% the annuity would credit 12% (35%-5%=30% x 40%).

Other Factors

Annuitization Requirement

Fewer than 2% of index annuities on the market require policy annuitization to receive index-linked interest earned. The minimum payout period is usually 5 years, but may be as long as 10 years and the minimum interest credited during payout can be as low as 1%.

Length Of Rate Guarantee

Almost all index annuities have the ability to reset at least one participation factor during the surrender period. An annuity may guarantee that the participation rate never changes, but the cap may be moved or the yield spread may be altered. This means that later caps, spreads or rates may be higher or lower.

A given index annuity almost always has at least one crediting part that can be changed prior to the end of the surrender period. The carrier may guarantee a 100% participation rate, but the cap or spread can change.

Free Withdrawals

The vast majority of index annuities offer some form of surrender penalty free annual withdrawals; typically 10% of the accumulated value after the first contract year. However, taking money out of an index annuity early – whether the annuity uses a term end point or annual reset design – can kill the return. If you look at multiple year index periods, the majority of the total gain for most periods are created by a few exceptional years. The index will increase 10%, then go up 3%, then, perhaps, drop 20%, and then go up 30%. If you had taken a withdrawal just before the year with the 30% increase, you would have severely limited your total return.

Taking money out of an index annuity early is like timing the market with a roulette wheel. Even if the annuity provides liquidity, it should be treated as a long-term vehicle and with the knowledge that any withdrawals could hurt overall returns.

<u>Premium Bonuses & Enhanced Rates</u>

A number of annuities offer bonuses. These are usually applied to the premium and any interest crediting is based on the premium plus the bonus. A very few policies require annuitization to receive the premium bonus, and in a few annuities the premium vests over time. There are also a few contracts that apply what amounts to a persistency bonus, by crediting a retroactive premium bonus if the policy stays in force after the surrender period ends, or taking back part of a bonus credited at time of purchase if the annuity is cashed in prematurely.

Annual reset structures may offer an enhanced first year participation rate, or reduced yield spread, that essentially represents a better rate than the index-linked pricing would permit. One point to be aware of is that unlike a fixed rate annuity in which the base rate is priced according to the insurer's current portfolio, the base fixed index participation rate also relies on the price of options down the road at time of renewal. This means even if the portfolio rate remains the same, if the option price was lower in future years the insurer could buy more options with the same portfolio interest generated, thus offering a higher participation rate..

<u>Participation Floor</u>

Many annual reset structures offer some crediting factor guarantees. These guarantees may say that the renewal participation rate can never go below X percent, or a cap may never be lower than Y, or a yield spread may never be greater than Z. These floors offer a degree of protection against uncompetitive renewal rates. However, most floors are so weak they offer little true renewal protection. Too strong a floor could cause losses for the insurer if future costs go too high.

<u>Bailouts</u>

Some annuities will waive surrender penalties if future index participation is below a specified level. For example, an annuity may offer an initial 6% interest cap, but permit the annuityowner to cash in and get the contract's accumulated value without surrender charges if a future interest cap falls below 5%.

Return of Premium

Although every state requires at least a minimum period after purchase during which the annuity buyer may cancel the purchase and get back their premium, a few annuities provide an unlimited full refund period, typically at lower participation than when return of premium is not chosen.

Compounded & Simple Interest

With very, very few exceptions the interest earned on an index annuity is compounded with new interest earned on interest already credited.

Annual Resets – How It All Works

The following is a chart of the closing monthly index values of the fictional Federal Stock Index for a nine-year period.

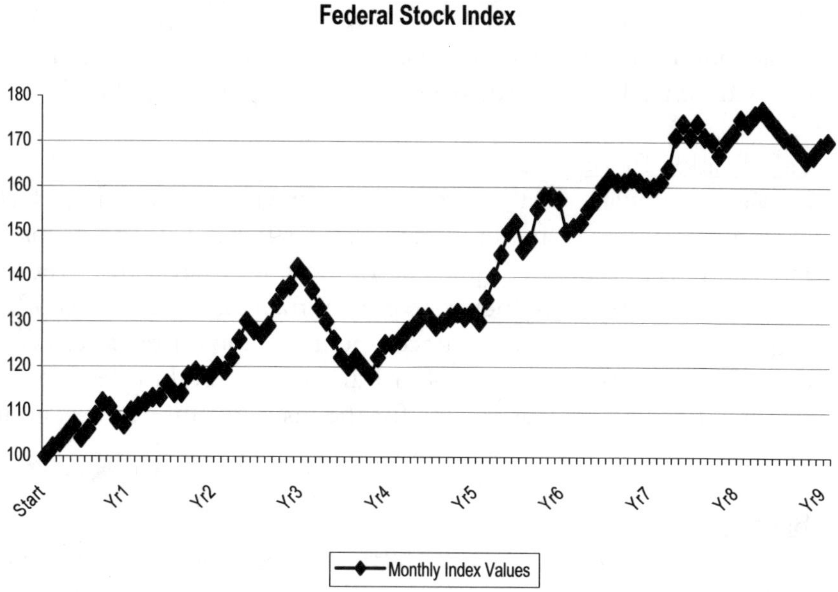

The yearly gains or losses of the index, and the annual closing index values, are these:

	Index Movement	Point-to-Point	Monthly Average	Monthly Cap
Yr 1	110	10.00%	7.00%	7.42%
Yr 2	120	9.09%	5.00%	6.68%
Yr 3	140	16.67%	9.17%	8.74%
Yr 4	125	-10.71%	-10.71%	-10.67%
Yr 5	130	4.00%	4.00%	4.00%
Yr 6	150	15.38%	15.00%	5.90%
Yr 7	160	6.67%	5.67%	6.52%
Yr 8	175	9.38%	6.25%	6.92%
Yr 9	170	-2.86%	-2.10%	-2.84%

However, because annual reset structures do not recognize negative years and begin calculating index movement using the previous year's closing value, the chart of *creditable interest* is this:

	Index Movement	Point-to-Point	Monthly Averaging	Monthly Cap
Yr 1	110	10.00%	7.00%	7.42%
Yr 2	120	9.09%	5.00%	6.68%
Yr 3	140	16.67%	9.17%	8.74%
Yr 4	125	0%	0%	0%
Yr 5	130	4.00%	4.00%	4.00%
Yr 6	150	15.38%	15.00%	5.90%
Yr 7	160	6.67%	5.67%	6.52%
Yr 8	175	9.38%	6.25%	6.92%
Yr 9	170	0%	0%	0%

And let's say we have the following methods and rates, all compounded:

65% Annual Reset Point-to-Point
88% Annual Reset Monthly Averaged Values
100% Annual Reset Monthly Averaged Values -1% Yield Spread
100% Annual Reset Point-to-Point with 7% Interest Cap
2% Annual Reset Monthly Cap Forward

We would credit these yearly returns:

	65% P-to-P	88% Month Aver	Month Aver less 1% Spread	100% P-to-P w/7% Cap	2% Monthly Cap
Yr 1	6.50%	6.16%	6.00%	7.00%	7.42%
Yr 2	5.91%	4.40%	4.00%	7.00%	6.68%
Yr 3	10.84%	8.07%	8.17%	9.10%	8.74%
Yr 4	0%	0%	0%	0%	0%
Yr 5	2.60%	3.52%	3.00%	4.00%	4.00%
Yr 6	10.00%	13.20%	14.00%	4.00	5.90%
Yr 7	4.34%	4.99%	4.67%	6.67%	6.52%
Yr 8	6.10%	5.50%	5.25%	7.00%	6.92%
Yr 9	0%	0%	0%	0%	0%

To determine the total return for the period we would compound the positive annual interest earned.

Pick The Best One

One usually selects an index annuity and knows the crediting method that will be used (at least the initial participation rate/yield spread/cap), and the only unknown variable is how the index will move. Just for fun, we want you to select the index annuity you think will produce the highest return. But unlike the real world, we will leave nothing to chance

Here are nine index annuities and the crediting methods used. There are no moving parts, every crediting component is locked in and will not change, and we will even use the same rates for the annuities from the previous section so you already know the interest credited. Which one produces the highest total return?

a. 80% Term End Point (Term Point-to-Point) period gain
b. 75% High Point Term (True High Water Mark) period gain
c. 65% Annual Reset Point-to-Point
d. 88% Annual Reset Monthly Averaged Values
e. 100% Annual Reset Monthly Averaged Values less 1% Spread
f. 100% Annual Reset Point-to-Point with 7% Interest Cap
g. 2% Annual Reset Monthly Cap
h. 6.25% Trigger, Non-Negative Annual Reset
i. 111% Term High Water Rolling Average Highest Anniversary

And The Winner Is...

It is a trick question. Each index annuity earns a total return of 56% for the period.

Even though any index annuity crediting method could produce the highest return for a given period, this example shows that you cannot pick "the best" index annuity based solely on which has the highest rate, the highest cap, or the lowest spread. Different methodologies produce different results and will react differently in different economic environments. The next chapter will help you in understanding how these crediting methods really work in different markets.

Summary

There are two main ways to credit index annuity interest. You either measure index movement over a year or two – an annual reset method, or you measure index movement over a period longer than a couple years – a term end point method.

Index movement may be calculated in dozens of different ways and any index methodology may result in the greatest return depending upon how the index moves and the degree of index participation. Because of all these variations, you cannot simply pick the index annuity with the highest rate or lowest spread and expect to get the best one.

Cheat Sheet

- There has only been one completely new methodology developed in the last six years, the *rainbow method.* Every other crediting method on the market today had its genesis in a structure used in the past.

- A typical term end point index annuity only credits interest realized from index movements at the end of the term. Interest is not calculated and credited annually. The exception is a *balanced allocation method* that may allow an interim point to be named the end point.

- An index annuity asset fee or yield spread is simply another way of saying participation rate and the interest crediting "spread" can never result in a negative value because the lowest interest an index annuity pays is zero.

- Averaging always drive numbers to the middle. In a generally rising market, averaging usually produces a lower value than an actual end point; in a falling market, averaging generally produces a higher ending value than an actual end point.

- If index movement is negative, an annual reset structures treats it as zero positive interest.

Chapter 4 – Crediting Method Truths

To compare different crediting methods you need to make certain basic assumptions. We do not declare that these assumptions are true, only that if they are false, all evaluation is a waste of time.

Our first assumption is that pricing permits index annuities to participate in a meaningful percentage of index growth. For most of their existence, the majority of index annuities have been able to offer policyowners 40% to near 100% of effective index performance and this level of participation provided the potential for competitive returns. But what if future pricing were to produce index annuities able to offer only 10% or 20% of actual index performance? At those rates, even if the index were to grow by 12% or 15% a year, the annuities would not be competitive. We have had periods where index annuity participation was not competitive, but to date these periods have been relatively brief.

Our second assumption is that the insurance company will make an effort to ensure that index annuity participation rates at renewal reflect real market pricing most of the time. In other words, if pricing forces an insurer to cut index participation in a given year, those are the breaks, but if a particular carrier were to arbitrarily drop its policy's participation rate below what market forces would require, then all of the hypothetical analysis in the world will not help in determining future returns for that annuity - because the insurer would be rigging the game.

Term End Point

The term end point design was born in the mid 1990s and it picked a lousy time to be born. The term end point concept is simple. Start with the index value today. At the end of four, five, seven, ten, or twelve years, see how much the index has gone up, and credit as interest a predetermined percentage of the increase. You get the higher of the minimum guarantee or the index-linked interest. That is how a term end point participation rate crediting method works.

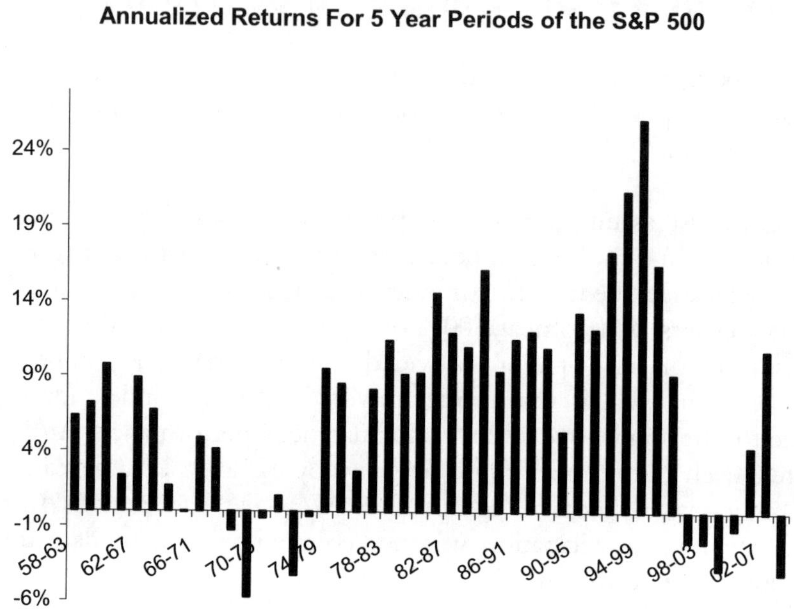

This chart shows the annualize returns for calendar year five-year periods of the S&P 500 for the last 52 years (the S&P 500 was created March 1957). Interest earned in a term end point designed index annuity would mimic the bars, except that returns would never be negative due to the minimum guarantee.

And the chart pretty much shows the good and bad of term end point designs. If index growth during the period is strong, the return can be strong. If the index is flat or declines during the period, the return stinks. Unfortunately, the index has generally been weak since term end point products were introduced, which is why the market share of term end point products has declined, from representing a third of sales in 1996 to a couple percent in more recent years.

Key Points - Term End Point

In Chapter 2, we learned that even though one 5 year option costs more than one 1 year option, it does not cost five times as much. Because their option hedging strategy costs less, term end point designs can provide significantly higher return potential than annual reset designs in rising markets. The tradeoff is that if the market period is flat or down, term end point designs are more likely to generate only the minimum guaranteed return.

The Truth Financial Writers Ignore

Financial columnists, when writing about index annuities, often use a term end point annuity as an example of how index annuities work. They then say how much better it would be – in a perfect world – if you were to put three quarters of your money into competitive zero coupons 10 year bonds and the balance in an index fund.

If you were to follow their suggestion and put 75% of your money into zero coupon bonds, you would never get back less than 100% at the end of the period – something like an annuity's minimum guarantee. However, because only 25% of your money is in the index your effective participation rate on your total investment can only be 25%. By contrast, the participation rate of a term end point index annuity often nears 100%.

But the real problem with such articles is that their authors employ a crediting method that is used by only 2% of index annuities, while suggesting (if only by implication) that its results are representative of all index annuities. That's like focusing on the performance of health care sector stocks as an example of how the S&P 500 performs.

An advantage of almost every term end point annuity is that there are no moving parts for the entire crediting period, which is often the same length as the surrender period. The risk of getting an uncompetitive renewal rate is reduced or eliminated. A possible disadvantage is that if the climate for index participation improves in the future the rate cannot be raised.

Term end point designs follow index movements. This means potential interest can be lost if the index falls back. In addition, interest is not credited until the end of the period. If a policy is surrendered, any increases in the index from the beginning of the period are ignored and a charge may also be assessed. However, most index annuities treat death as the end of the cycle, credit any interest earned, and waive surrender charges.

What Is The Reality?

Given the same option budget, you get more bang for your buck with a term end point design than with an annual reset method, and if the index cooperates, you also get a higher potential return. However, the historical reality is that -

Most buyers of an index annuity with a term end point design have earned only the minimum guaranteed return

The reason is simple: There have been very few five year periods from 1996 on that were truly bullish. The S&P 500 hit 950 in the summer of 1997 and kept rising for 3 more years leaving high starting points for future index performance calculations. The next decade was then "bookended" by the millennium bear market and the 2008-2009 bear market. From 1997 to 2007, the index rose 51.3% percent – an annualized return of 4.2% - and the return from a 10-year term end point purchased in 1997 was even less. As a result, most buyers of index annuities that used a term end point design have earned only the minimum guaranteed return. A relatively few lucky buyers managed to eke out money market returns. That said, a lot of stock market investors would have been delighted to wind up with money market returns over those same periods.

Key Points On Term End Points

- Term End Point designs can significantly beat annual reset returns in rising markets, but in a lousy market you're more likely to only get the minimum return
- No Moving Parts during crediting period and no "trust me" at renewal times
- Potential gains are usually not locked in until the end (except with the balanced method)

Term High Point (High Water Mark)

On 15 February 1995, the first index annuity was purchased. When the surrender period ended five years later the buyer of that contract had realized an annualized return of 19.78%.

A true high water mark has not been offered since 2004

The first index annuity ever purchased used the high water mark method, and the high water mark method overcomes the biggest objection of regular term end point designs, which is that nothing is locked in until the end of the period.

An annuity with this method typically vests any index gains, a bit each year, so you could get some or most of any gains if you surrender early. And this method locks in the highest anniversary level of the index, so you avoid late period index losses.

If you look back at, say, ten-year periods over the last 50 years the high point term method would have produced a higher total gain than a term end point method 44% of the time.

So, Why Doesn't Anyone Use Term High Point Anymore?

As it is much more expensive for the insurance company to provide the protection of the high point term method, index participation is lower than it would be for term end point structures. Because many buyers focus chiefly on the participation rate when choosing an index annuity, no insurer currently offers a true high water mark.

Key Points On Term High Point

- The term high point (high water mark) method provides the return potential of term end point designs in a rising market while still protecting any gains
- Because of the cost of protection is so high, no one currently offers this method.

Annual Reset

We showed this chart in Chapter 2. It shows the annual returns you would have realized had you been able to purchase the S&P 500 at the end of every month beginning December 1957. The first bar represents the annual return for calendar year 1958. The last bar represents the 12 month period ending in August 2010. The returns do not include reinvested dividends.

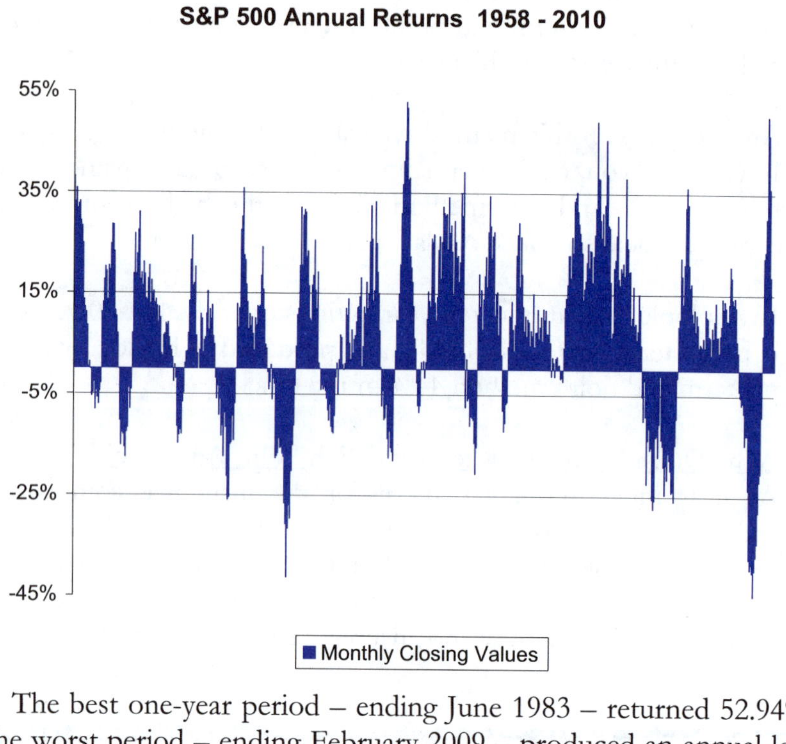

The best one-year period – ending June 1983 – returned 52.94%. The worst period – ending February 2009 – produced an annual loss of 44.76%. Had you been able to invest in the S&P500 in every one of the periods, your average annualized return would have been 8.19%.

Index annuities using annual reset crediting methods link interest earnings to movement of the index - with three very significant differences from term end point designs:

- Annual Credited interest cannot be lost if the index declines
- Years of negative index movement are treated as years of zero growth
- Index values are reset at the beginning of each year

Take a look at the same chart if the index had employed an annual reset approach.

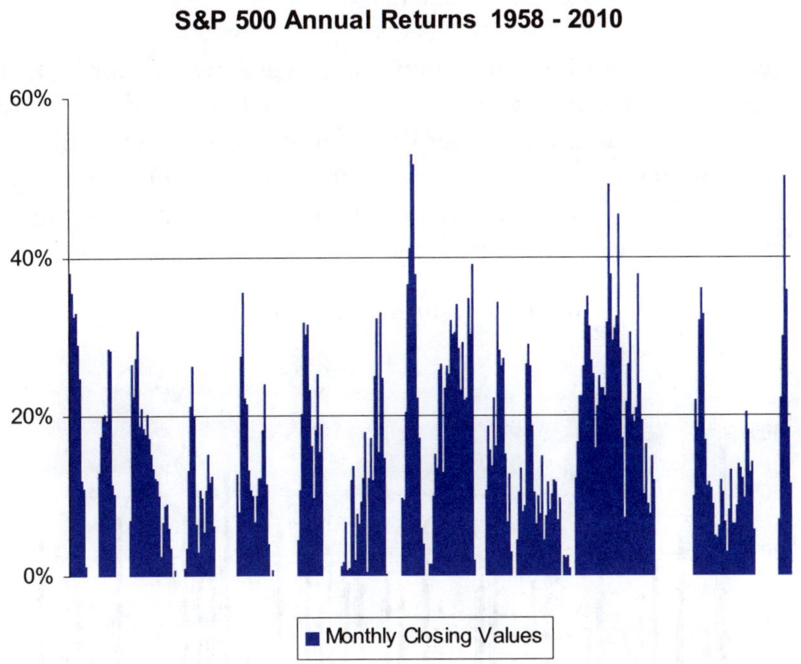

The best one-year period would have returned 52.94%. The worst period produced no loss, so no previous gains were lost. Had you been able to invest in the S&P500 in every one of the periods, and had that index employed the "annual reset" approach, your average annualized return would have been 11.23%.

Averaging

The majority of index annuities sold are contracts that employ annual reset designs that average index values to determine index movement. There are two basic facts underlying the averaging of index values, and they're well worth remembering:

First, averaging always drives numbers to the middle. In a steadily rising period, averaging produces roughly half of the gain of an unaveraged line. In a steadily falling period, averaging produces roughly half of the loss of an unaveraged line.

Second, the return of an annuity using averaging will not look like the index return that appears in the newspaper. The index does not average index values; the insurer does that calculation. The following chart compares the annual calendar year point-to-point return of the S&P 500 with calendar year returns that use a monthly average of index values to determine the year's index gain or loss.

Annual Returns 1958-2009

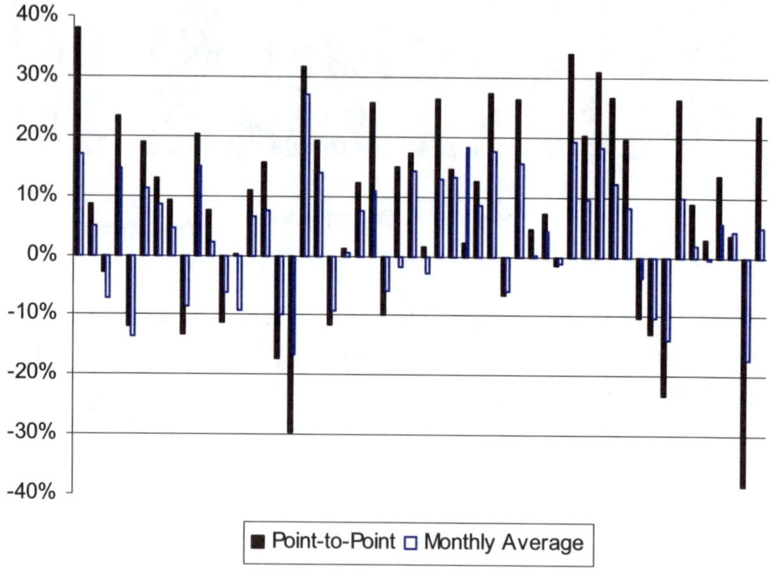

As we've noted, averaging drives numbers to the middle. "Smoothing" index values means you will never finish a year locked in at the lowest index point of the year, but it also guarantees you will never hit the highest point. In fact, if you look at an entire half-century of returns, the overall monthly average index return is 50% of the point-to-point annual return; the overall daily average return is 48% of the point-to-point annual return. This does not mean, however, that index annuities using monthly averaged crediting methods will necessarily perform only half as well as unaveraged ones, or that an averaged design needs double the index participation of an annual point-to-point structure to produce the same return.

If an index annuity does not use averaging in a formula, it will either have to offer a lower participation rate (than it would if it used averaging) or impose a cap to limit gains – or both.

Annual reset designs treat years of negative index performance as zero returns. If you substitute all of the negative index years with zeros, the effective monthly average return rises from 50% to 57% of the point-to-point return, so the averaging return is likely to be not 50%, but nearer to 60%, of the point-to-point return. And the relationship between the two can vary depending on how the market moves. For example, in the '80s the monthly averaged index return was 60% of the unaveraged return; in the '90s the averaged returned was almost two-thirds of the unaveraged returns.

The truth is that, over time, if a point-to-point index annuity and an averaging index annuity have identical crediting criteria – the same rates, caps or spreads – then the returns of the index annuity using averaging would be 55% to 65% of the point-to-point annuity. However, index annuities using averaging offer higher rates or higher caps or lower spreads than point-to-point methods, so the highest return is dependent on the relative index crediting factors.

Using the last half century, the return of a monthly averaged structure has been 57% of the return of a point-to-point structure. Another way to say this is a monthly averaged structure needed 168% of a point-to-point's index participation to achieve the same return. If a contract using the annual point-to-point method offers a participation rate of 45%, a contract using the monthly average method would need to offer a 76% rate to produce the same return. This just happens to be the rate we used to produce the same return in the examples shown in Different Methods & Different Markets later in the chapter.

The 168% factor mentioned above might be a rough rule of thumb to judge whether participation rates of unaveraged and averaged index methods are comparable, but it is not a universal law. In the '90s the factor would have been 150%, meaning a 45% APP (Annual Point to Point) rate would have produced the same returns as a 68% monthly averaged rate. That said, the factor would likely be different for other market periods. In addition, only a relative handful of index annuities use only an unadorned participation rate. Both averaged and point-to-point structures employ caps or interest rate spreads, either alone or in combination. We know of no quick and dirty comparison rules of thumb to compare different methodology that will produce reliable results.

There is nothing inherently wrong with an index annuity that uses averaging of index values. That method can, under certain market conditions, provide significantly better results than unaveraged methods. The most interest ever credited in one year to a fixed annuity policy utilized averaging of index values.

Key Points On Averaging

- Averaging always drive values to the middle, but that does not mean index annuities using averaging will have half the return of an index annuity with a point-to-point design, because averaging structures typically have higher rates or higher caps or lower spreads than unaveraged ones.

- The use of averaging does mean that you cannot figure out what your index annuity interest is earning by looking at the finance page in the newspaper.

Caps

A cap is a ceiling on interest earned – that is the negative. The cap allows you to get higher participation on index gains than you would get in the absence of that cap – that is the positive. An index annuity using a methodology with a reasonable cap can be very competitive with non-cap index annuities in most markets and provide the best returns in modest markets. However, too a low a cap can hurt overall returns because market returns have a wide range.

There is an altitude cap on where we can walk. Once we get over 18,000 feet or so, the air gets too thin to breathe and this limits our travels. But since we do not normally climb Mount McKinley or hike in the Himalayas, this cap usually will not affect us. It is at least arguable that if the cap is high enough, it will probably not limit gains unduly, because the index will probably not increase enough to trigger that cap.

<u>And When A Cap Can Limit A Return</u>

Say that you had a choice between getting 100% of any index gains up to an 8% interest ceiling or 50% of any index gain. When the index gains 16% or less, the cap version comes out better (8% cap divided by 50% rate). Applying actual historical returns to our hypothetical comparison, we find that in only seventeen years out of the last fifty two years would that non-cap version have credited more interest than the capped version.

Continuing with our comparison of the hypothetical capped and uncapped annuities, if the index in any year declines, but advances 32% in the following year, the non-cap version would credit 16% interest in that second year. But in that same scenario, the capped version would earn only 8% in that year. A "problem scenario" for an annuity with a low cap is a string of flat index years followed by a year with a humongous gain. The non-cap version would still come out okay because it offsets the zero years with one great year, but the cap version gets too little of the upside of that one great year.

S&P 500 Postive Annual Returns 1958 - 2009
White is annual return portion above 16%

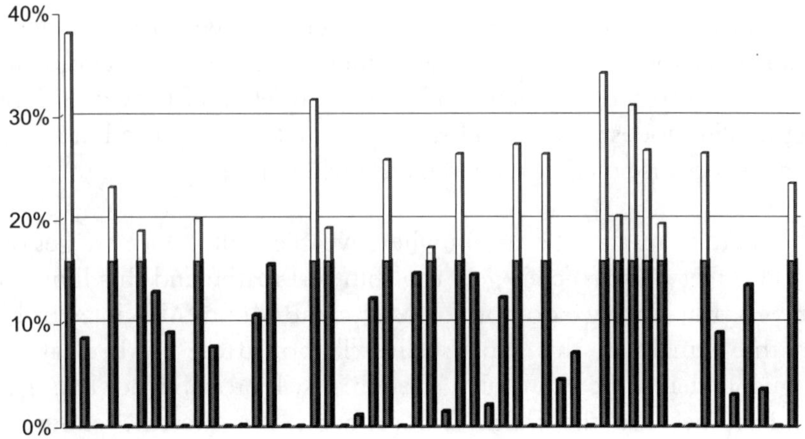

<u>Index Versus Interest Caps</u>

There are two types of caps and agents need to understand the difference. An interest cap means this is the most interest that will be credited. An index cap means this is the most index gain that will be recognized.

Say that you are looking at two index annuities. Both deduct a 2% yield spread, and both have a 12% cap. But one annuity has an interest cap and the other has an index cap. How will these caps affect returns?

▶ Index goes up 12%. Each annuity would subtract 2% from the 12% index gain and credit 10%.

▶ Index goes up 20%. The interest cap would subtract 2% from 20% resulting in 18%, and then ask is 18% higher then 12%? Since the answer is yes, this annuity would credit 12%.

▶ Index goes up 20%. The index cap asks is 20% higher than 12%? Since the answer is yes, this annuity uses the index cap of 12%, subtracts 2%, and credits 10% interest.

Another example: Two annuities each have a 12% cap and each have a 70% participation rate. But one annuity has an interest cap and the other has an index cap. How are returns affected?

▶ Index goes up 12%. Each annuity would multiply 12% times 70% and credit 8.4%.

▶ Index goes up 20%. The interest cap would multiply 20% times 70% resulting in 14%, and then ask is 14% higher then 12%? Since the answer is yes, this annuity would credit 12%.

▶ Index goes up 20%. The index cap asks is 20% higher than 12%? Since the answer is yes, this annuity uses the index cap of 12%, multiples it by 70%, and credits 8.4% interest.

Key Points On Caps

- Whether a cap is a real limit depends on what it is. A high cap may never come into play because most stock market years aren't blockbusters. However, too low a cap means you may never participate in enough good index gains to offset the bad years.
- If you do not know whether your annuity uses an interest or index cap, you could be unpleasantly surprised. Use the book's examples and ask the carrier what interest would be credited under their cap method.
- A low cap combined with averaging – a cap of less than 20% based on our analysis – often depresses returns because averaging means the calculated index gain in rising markets would tend to be around half of the unaveraged return, even before applying the cap. However, averaging methods with 20%+ caps or no caps can perform very competitively.

Because an index cap is a lower effective ceiling than an interest cap, an annuity using an index cap usually has a higher cap than one with an interest cap (all other factors being the same). However, you won't read much (if anything) about "interest rate caps" and "index rate caps" in annuity marketing materials, because most contracts employ "interest rate caps". "Index rate" have been seldom used. However, some contracts do use them. If the annuity you are considering imposes a cap, you need to know for certain which sort of cap it uses. Sadly, you often cannot tell from the marketing pieces.

Monthly Cap On Gains (Monthly Cap or Monthly Point-to-Point)

The monthly cap method (where the cap applies to gains but not to losses) hit the index annuity scene at the start of 2003 and became the top selling index method for a couple of reasons. One reason is it is a legitimate method that can produce, and has produced, returns that meet or exceed the returns of other methods. The other reason is that it can produce a mistakenly (or misleadingly) high expectation of the contract's return potential.

<u>You Won't Earn The Cap</u>

Based on historical index performance, it is extremely unlikely that a 3% monthly cap will ever produce a year with a 36% return, or even a 20% return for that matter. Indexes do not tend to go straight up, and returns depend on when you begin and end the years.

If we look back day by day, over the last 50 years, and apply the 3% monthly cap method, we find that the purchaser of an annuity using this method would have earned a 20% plus return in only three of those fifty years (in contract years ending during calendar years 1996, 2004 and 2010), and then, only if the contract year ended during the school year. If we analyze this method using contract years that began during the summer months, we find that there was only one year, of the last 50, that would have produced 20% plus returns using this method.

What about a two-year design with a 5% cap on monthly index gains? Well, you never hit a return of 120%, but unless you bought in the spring of the year you had at least one two year period in the last half century that delivered a 50% gain.

The correct way to describe a 3% monthly cap or a 5% biennial monthly cap is to say, "this method limits monthly index gains to 3% (or 5%) but any upward movement is not locked in and the cap does not apply to index losses." The wrong way to describe this method is to say, "your annual cap is 36%" or "you could make 120% in two years." It is inaccurate to multiply the cap percentage by the number of months in the holding period because it creates an unrealistic picture of potential returns.

Monthly Cap Designs Are Legitimate

Monthly cap designs are not going to produce great returns when the market becomes more volatile; although we have had several annuity producers tell us this. The monthly cap structure has a greater potential than some other methods for producing at least some index-linked return in highly volatile times where other methods will not.

Higher volatility means index-link sellers demand more money because the risk of big market swings – both up and down – has increased. Because the risk of catching the index-link seller on a big upswing is greater in periods of high volatility, the cost of the index-link goes up in such periods. Higher costs mean insurers cannot buy as much index-linkage so traditional caps and/or participation rates go down.

Monthly cap methods share in this volatility, and with caps on monthly gains but not losses, the index-link seller can be more generous on up cap limits, hoping that the down months will offset. This does not mean monthly cap designs will post great returns in bad markets – 2008 was a year of high market volatility and monthly cap designs credited the same zero returns as other methods – what it does mean is during periods when high volatility may effectively shut down returns from some crediting methods the monthly cap design will still have caps that offer the potential for index-linked returns.

This chart shows calendar year annual returns (the negative years are replaced by zeros) assuming monthly caps of 1.5%, 2.0%, 2.5%,

3.0%. Although the highest theoretical annual returns are 18%, 24%, 30% and 36% respectively, the actual highest returns that would ever have been reached are 14%, 19%, 23% and 26%. The respective average returns over the 50 years are less exciting, being 2.0%, 3.3%, 4.5% and 5.7%.

Monthly Cap Annual Returns

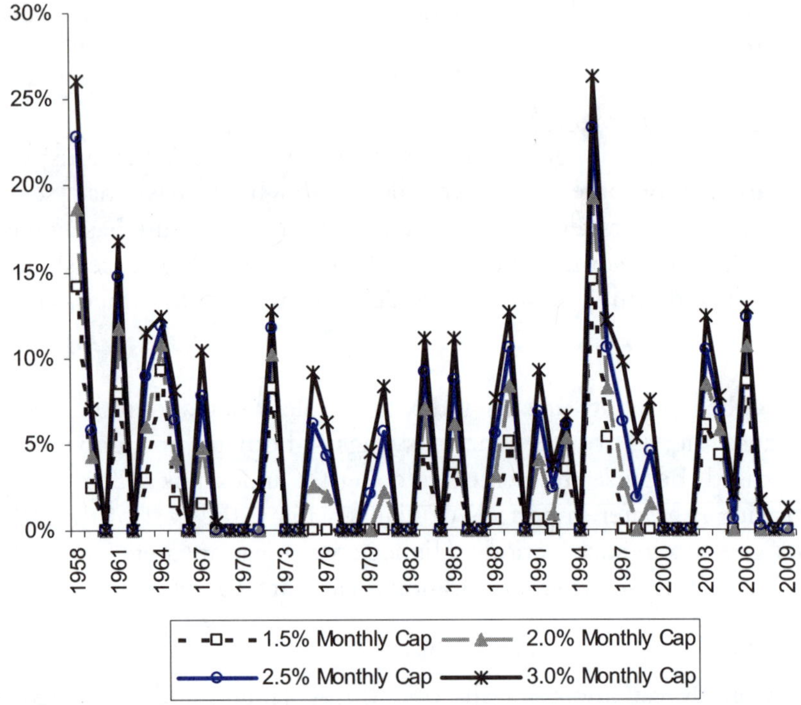

Key Points On Monthly Cap

- You won't earn the cap. For a 3% cap the highest annual return was 26%, but the long-term average was 5.7%.
- It is legitimate. In both actual index annuity returns and hypothetical modeling the monthly cap is very competitive with annual point-to-to-point methods and usually beats averaging with cap methods

Different Methods & Different Markets

Index annuities have been around for only 15 years and several individual crediting methods have an even shorter history, so we do not know how the different crediting methods would have performed over the long term. However, the purpose of this section is not to "guestimate" what index annuity returns might have occurred, but to conceptually get an idea of how different annual reset structures might perform in different markets, if priced correctly.

While we do not know what crediting rates might have been over the last 50 years, we do know that annual reset point-to-point structures have often had actual participation rates of 45% for quite awhile. And we can plug a 45% participation rate into every up year of the last 50 years of S&P 500 returns (because annual reset index annuities treat down years as zeros), and determine the annualized return for all of the rolling ten-year calendar year periods is 5.2%. We can then use the Mean (average) return for this Annual Point to Point design and see what index participation rates other designs would have to offer to equal the return produced by the 45% APP method. There is not a particular reason for using ten year periods; we simply picked ten years.

If you could have purchased an index annuity for every ten-year period since 1960, with this 45% APP annual reset structure your annualized interest rate would have been 5.2%. By contrast, if you had purchased an annuity with a 100% APP and an 8.45% interest cap (where you would never have earned more than 8.45% interest in a given year) your overall annualized return would have been 5.2%.

If you had purchased an index annuity using monthly averaging with a 76% participation rate, you would also have averaged a 5.2% annual return. And we can do the same analysis for other crediting methods. What we are trying to build is a level playing field using interest crediting factors that have actually been used, but we are adjusting them so that they all would have produced identical long term results. It does not matter which structure you picked, they all earned 5.2% on average.

Here are the rates needed by all of these different crediting methodologies to match the same 5.2% annualized returns.

What Is Required To Produce The Same Annualized Return		
Crediting Method		Effective Rate
Annual Pt-to-Pt	45%	74%
Monthly Averaging	76%	74%
Daily Averaging	80%	74%
Annual Pt-to-Pt	100% with 8.45% cap	74%
Monthly Cap	3.05% cap on monthly gain	74%
Monthly Averaging	100% less 2.75% spread	74%

If we could have deposited the same amount of money into annuities using each of these different index annuity crediting methods over the last 50 years, our overall returns would be the same for each crediting method. We are not saying this is what index participation would have been; we are simply saying if you apply these crediting factors for the half century you get the same returns.

The main conclusion here is that simply choosing the annuity with the lowest spread, or the highest rate, or the best cap will not ensure you of getting the highest return.

What Is The Effective Rate?

The annualized actual return of the S&P 500, without dividends, was 7.0% for all calendar 10-year periods since 1960. The different crediting methods shown generated an annualized return of 5.2%, which means the owners of our hypothetical index annuities were effectively getting 74% of what the index actually returned (without dividends) -(5.2%/7.0% = 74%). The effective rate could also be called the "real rate of index participation".

You could express participation in a particular crediting method as 45% of the annual point-to-point movement, 80% of the daily averaged movement, or 100% of the monthly averaged movement less a 2.75% yield spread, but these numbers rarely represent the actual degree of index participation. Whether the stated or nominal rate is expressed as 45% or 80% or 100%, what the hypothetical contract owner would actually have received was 74% of the index return (without dividends) for all those 10 year periods.

How can we get an effective real participation rate of 74% if our stated or nominal annual point-to-point participation rate is 45%? It's because index annuities with annual reset structures treat negative years as zeros instead of losses, whereas returns for the index include years with losses. If you eliminate years with negative returns, and only include years with positive or zero returns, your average return must, necessarily, be higher than if those negative years were included in the calculation. This is why a lower participation rate can still provide competitive returns.

We adjusted crediting factors so that each method would have identical returns over a 50 year period. We are now going to plug in the same crediting factors in decidedly different stock market environments and see what happens to returns.

The '80s

This was a transition decade. It began with a hard and long bear market, and ended with a short and mild bear market. In between, were six-years of double digit gains. The 1980s brought a new phrase into the investor lexicon- "Black October." If you look at ten-year periods of S&P 500 performance ending in the 1980s the average annual return is 7.34%. What were the returns of our different crediting methods?

This is about as "normal" a period as you can find. With the exception of the monthly cap method, the different crediting structures all produced about the same return. The reason for the low monthly cap performance is that the period had high volatility, and it only takes the subtraction of one really bad month to louse up a string of capped gains. The effective index participation rate of these annuities is around 73%.

Hypothetical Annualized Return For 10-Year Periods Ending In The '80s		
Crediting Method		Annual Return
Annual Pt-to-Pt	45%	5.24%
Monthly Averaging	76%	5.36%
Daily Averaging	80%	5.39%
Annual Pt-to-Pt	100% with 8.45% cap	5.23%
Monthly Cap	3.05% cap on monthly gain	3.97%
Monthly Averaging	100% less 2.75% spread	5.52%

The '90s

The 1990s represent the conclusion of the strongest bull market in American history. If you look at ten year periods of S&P 500 performance ending in the 1990s the average annual return is 12.50%. How did the index annuity structures do?

Hypothetical Annualized Return For 10-Year Periods Ending In The '90s		
Crediting Method		Annual Return
Annual Pt-to-Pt	45%	6.20%
Monthly Averaging	76%	6.91%
Daily Averaging	80%	6.82%
Annual Pt-to-Pt	100% with 8.45% cap	5.81%
Monthly Cap	3.05% cap on monthly gain,	6.46%
Monthly Averaging	100% less 2.75% spread	7.20%

The best performing method deducted a yield spread. The lowest returns resulted from cap structures. The effective index participation rate of these annuities for the decade, when compared with actual index returns, is from 46% to 58%.

The '00s

The 2000s were a nasty decade for the stock market beginning with a three year bear market and ending with a two year decline. If you look at ten-year periods of S&P 500 performance ending in the 2000s the average annual return is 6.46%. What were the returns of our different crediting methods?

The highest returns were from the monthly cap and straight participation rate method designs, averaging methods fared worst. The effective index participation rates of these annuities for the decade are 66% to 95%.

Hypothetical Annualized Return For 10-Year Periods Ending In The '00s

Crediting Method		Annual Return
Annual Pt-to-Pt	45%	5.70%
Monthly Averaging	76%	4.47%
Daily Averaging	80%	4.50%
Annual Pt-to-Pt	100% with 8.45% net cap	5.05%
Monthly Cap	3.05% cap on monthly gain	6.16%
Monthly Averaging	100% less 2.75% spread	4.29%

Annual Reset Return Analysis

We chose an actual annual reset point-to-point participation rate available from the past, calculated the annualized return for the half century using this rate, and then worked backwards to find the crediting criteria for other methods that matched my selected return. We rigged the results so that overall returns would be the same over the long haul. The reason we did this was to highlight how different crediting structures can react in different markets. You can see that any method could produce the best return, depending upon actual index movement and the degree of index participation.

Option sellers use the same pricing models as insurers and they do their best to keep the playing field level for all crediting methods. But this does not mean that index annuity crediting is an efficient market whereby the return produced by one crediting method will equal the return produced by another. The index annuity rate market is not efficient either by accident or design. One needs to be aware of how crediting method variations affect returns.

Truth #1 Annual Reset Crediting Methods Are Priced To Perform The Same

After doing hundreds of thousands of historic "what if" modeling exercises and examining the actual participation credited by the carriers over the previous fifteen years, we found that annual reset product crediting methods were priced to perform the same over time. This means that if the same money is spent on options, and the patterns of the historic stock market repeat, the returns will come out pretty much the same over the long haul, whether you use an annual point-to-point or a yield spread or averaging or a monthly cap. The choice of the crediting method is the least important factor affecting the returns of annual reset annuities over time. Since we have been often misquoted on this topic here is what we are saying and not saying.

The crediting method used is the least important factor

We are not saying that a method crediting 100% of the annual point-to-point index participation will deliver the same returns as another method crediting 100% of the monthly averaged values of the index. Over the past half century earning 100% of the monthly averaged annual return worked out the same as earning approximately 57% of the annual point-to-point index calculation. What we are saying is this: If you had, say, 6 cents available to buy an option to earn index-linked interest on a dollar of premium, and you were able to use the 6 cents to get 100% participation in the monthly average value, and if you spent a different 6 cents on an option that measured the annual point-to-point gains in the index, the participation on the annual-point-to-point option would be around 57%.

This doesn't mean index annuities will produce the same return

This does not mean that if you spent 6 cents each to buy the monthly averaging method at 100% participation and another 6 cents to buy the annual point-to-point without cap method, at 57% participation, these two methods will produce the same return next year. Different methods produce different results depending on how the actual market moved, which is why averaging methods produced the highest returns in 1998 and annual point-to-point with cap methods were the winners in 1999. However, over time the returns are priced to average out about the same.

How is this possible?

Insurance companies typically go to index-link sellers (option sellers) to buy the options providing the potential for index-linked interest. These index-link sellers look at the crediting method used, look at past performance of the index, look at current economic realities, and then calculate the probable potential returns for the different methods. The seller's goal is to make sure that all the different methods have the same upside potential for the money received. The seller's goal is to keep the playing field level so that no one crediting method has a greater probability of a bigger payoff than another method if the seller received the same amount of option money for both.

If policies using an annual point-to-point, monthly average, or cap forward crediting methods each paid 6 cents out of a dollar of premium to buy index-linked gain potential on that dollar of premium, the person guaranteeing to pay any index-linked gain would want to make sure that the probability of a payout was equal for all methods, or else everyone would flock to the crediting method with the best odds and the option seller would lose over time. To use a gambling analogy, regardless of which number you place a bet on at the roulette wheel the odds are always 35 to 1. The reason why is that the casino has enough historical experience to show that over time the probability of each number coming up is the same and the odds are priced to reflect this probability.

The seller of the options covering the hedge uses past index performance history and a guesstimation of how other factors like yields on alternative investments, volatility and such will affect the index movement, and then says what potential upside will be offered on the 6 cents received. The gain payer's task is to try to ensure that everyone gets the same 'spin of the wheel' for their 6 cents.

Just as a casino would not give better odds on one number at the roulette wheel the index annuity gain payer (option seller) tries to ensure that the odds on the different crediting methods are also the same

This means that one annuity might offer, say, 100% of the point-to-point gain up to a 7% cap, while another gave 80% of the monthly average gain and still another used a 2.5% monthly cap structure to measure performance, but the gain payer (usually, the index option seller) believes that these crediting methods, at these rates, have the same return probabilities. Of course, that does not mean that all those methods will produce the same returns.

Efficient Markets Or Crystal Balls

We have presented the previous information and then been asked if this "theory" results from a belief in the efficient market hypothesis or are we followers of the reversion to the mean school of stock market movement. Our answer is that we're not dealing with theory, but with what we see happening in the real world. We will leave the question of why it happens to other authors.

Truth #2 Annual Reset Crediting Methods Are Priced To Perform The Same*

***except when they are not**

The index annuity gain payer, usually the seller of the options covering the index annuity, considers many factors to try to ensure that everyone gets the same spin of the wheel for their 6 cents. Does this mean that different methods perform the same each year?

No, it doesn't. As we saw, different methods react differently in different market environments. What the gain payer is betting on is that if its analysis showed that a 76% monthly averaging rate and a 45% annual point-to-point have produced the same returns over the long haul in the past, this same pattern will occur in the future. The roulette wheel might come up showing 16 four times in a row, but over time, the other numbers will come up, and it will all even out. The option sellers give every method the same spin of the wheel...until they choose not to.

The following table shows the average hypothetical return, for three actual products from three different insurance companies that offer multiple crediting methods within the same product. It applies each method's participation rates that were in effect on a random day in 2007 to calendar year S&P 500 Index movements for the previous 50 years. The percentages shown are the overall hypothetical average return for the 50 year period, where zeros were substituted for negative years (to reflect an annual reset methodology).

Crediting Method	Product 1	Product 2	Product 3
Annual Point-to-Point – no cap	5.83%	5.83%	
Annual Point-to-Point – cap	4.11%	3.67%	4.17%
Monthly Averaging – no cap	5.04%	5.83%	4.90%
Monthly Averaging – cap		4.61%	

These are different crediting methods within the same product. In all three examples, policy expenses are the same for each product and the same percentage of annuity premium was used to purchase index options. Given the option seller's desire for a "level playing field", this should have resulted in roughly equal 50-year average returns.

But that is not what happened. In all cases, the uncapped methods with effective participation rates of around 45% had average hypothetical returns that were significantly higher than the methods paying 100% of index gain up to a specified cap. Why? It's because of the option seller's expectations.

If you are the seller of options, and you believe that the broad patterns of past financial markets tend to repeat, you would try to keep the payoffs the same for the same sized bet. This means you might limit your average exposure to, say, paying around 4.11% on every crediting method. But in our example, that didn't happen, because on this day in 2007, option sellers were predicting low index gains for the coming year and their pricing of options reflected that expectation.

Picking the best crediting method over the short term usually means being able to predict the future, but in this case some crediting methods were given better odds than others. On this day in 2007, these three insurers offered index annuities with an index participation choice that was somewhat akin to a roulette wheel paying 35 to 1 on some numbers, 45 to 1 on others and 25 to 1 on the rest. On that particular day, the option sellers were saying, in essence, "I do not care what my pricing model says, I want to play a hunch." Since index returns were negative the following year their hunch did not hurt them. However, there have been times when a form of "index annuity arbitrage" is possible. Or, viewed another way, there are times when you can see how the carriers are predicting the future.

Truth #3 Annual Reset Crediting Methods Are Priced To Perform The Same*

***except when the carrier changes the equation**

Normally, products with similar surrender terms, commissions, minimum guarantees, and bonuses offer similar rates and caps when the underlying methods are the same. But it should be remembered that unlike the casino, the index annuity carrier can change the odds while the wheel is spinning – during the surrender period – so regardless of any temporary advantage today's pricing may produce, the "end game" result is still determined by the carrier on subsequent spins.

Ultimately, it is the carrier that decides how much money is available to fund the index-link. This is why we continue to believe that the most important factor in index annuity returns is not the crediting method, but how the carriers will treat the annuity owner when they reset that cap or rate in the future. The only way we know of to get even a hint of possible future treatment is to see how they have treated customers in the past, and that means asking for annuity renewal histories.

The real question is not whether renewal rates have gone up or down – external financial conditions affect renewal rates – but whether the carrier will furnish them at all. What if the index annuity is new and the carrier says there is no history? Fine, show the renewal histories of your other index annuities. What if the carrier will not furnish a renewal history? Well, if you were going to have an operation and the doctor refused to tell you how many patients survived, would you use that doctor?

Truth #4 Annual Reset Crediting Methods Are Priced To Perform The Same*

***except when the available money is different**

As we've said, the option seller is trying to keep the probable payoffs the same for the different methods if the options are all the same price. Over the long term (fifty years, let's say), each of these different methods can be expected to produce the same long term return even though the rates for the various "moving parts" may be different, and if the cost for the point-to-point one-year option is 6 cents the probable cost for the same one-year options associated with the other methods would be six cents too. However, even if the cost of each one is six cents that does not mean each index annuity has six cents available to pay the option.

Crediting Method (option money)	Effective Rate
Annual Pt-to-Pt (6¢) at 45% participation	74%
Monthly Averaging (8¢) at 100% participation	96%
Daily Averaging (4¢) at 53% participation	49%
Annual Pt-to-Pt (6¢) with 8.45% cap	74%
Monthly Cap (4¢) 2% cap on monthly gain	38%
Monthly Averaging (6¢) less 2.75% yield spread	74%

In the second chapter, we said the insurance company invests the premiums, earns a return, and then after paying the expenses and covering the cost of the minimum guarantee buys the option. What if the sales commission on Index Annuity A is 7% but Index Annuity B pays a 4% commission? As the expenses for Annuity B are less, that annuity issuer has more of the premium available with which to buy options. If the lower expenses gives Annuity B 8 cents left over (after buying enough bonds to secure contract guarantees) instead of the 6 cents left over in Annuity A, Annuity B can buy one-third more options, which means that the owner of Annuity B can participate in more of the index gain than can the owner of Annuity A. Costs matter!

What if Annuity B has a higher minimum guarantee, but all other factors are equal (to those in Annuity A)? If Annuity B guarantees 3% when Annuity A guarantees only 1%, Annuity A might have 4 cents with which to buy options, when Annuity B has only 2 cents. In this scenario, Annuity A can offer a higher participation rate.

Suppose the expenses for both annuities are identical, but Company A can invest its money at a higher rate (by buying bonds with longer maturities or rated less highly than the bonds bought by Company B)? Once again, Company A will have more money with which to buy options. (Of course, it will bear more risk with regard to the contract's guarantees if its bond portfolio is more at risk).

Truth #5 Annual Reset Crediting Methods Are Priced To Perform The Same*

***with the possible exception of the rainbow method**

Several carriers offer rainbow allocation crediting methods, but as said in the previous chapter not all allocation methods are rainbows. There are index annuities out there that also credit interest based on the blended performance of multiple indices, but in those other annuities, the specific index allocation is fixed at the beginning of each year- which is why they are not rainbow methods.

Do rainbow methods run a better horse race?

The rainbow method has been explained by saying that the annuity buyer gets to bet on the race after it has been run and that most of the bet will be put down on the horses that "win or place." To determine whether the different rainbow allocations may be a better horse race we ran calculations going back to 1991 to produce hypothetical returns for both rainbow and S&P 500 only crediting methods. We attempted to compare rainbow methods with "S&P 500 only" methods within the same or similar carrier products. Because index annuities are used, any negative returns were replaced with zeros.

A problem with most rainbow indices is their short history. With the exception of the Dow Jones Industrial Average and S&P 500, the indices used in current rainbow methods have been around less than 25 years; we are unsure whether this provides enough of a track record to be meaningful. For example, three of the four carriers offering index annuities using the rainbow method include the EuroStoxx 50 in their mix; that index has been around less than a decade, with almost all of its history occurring in a bull market. In considering this problem, we discovered that a composite index made up of half German DAX and half French CAC 40 values had a 0.99 correlation with the EuroStroxx 50 since its inception, and the DAX and CAC 40 have longer histories. Therefore, because a 50/50 mix of the DAX and CAC has essentially mimicked the EuroStoxx 50, we have used this composite DAX/CAC index as a proxy for the EuroStoxx 50 prior to July 2003.

We examined rainbow method products from most of the carriers, and tried to compare apples with apples; we picked products without bonuses and with surrender periods of 10 years or less. These examples apply current rates to 195 past rolling 12 month periods. We want to emphasize that the past does not predict the future and, due to the short history of our indices, we're not sure that the past even predicts the past. Moreover, the participation rates could change wildly in years to come, so the hypothetical returns should not be viewed as real numbers. That said, we believe that the following comparisons provide some insight into how well the rainbow method performs, vis a vis single indices.

Rainbow A

Rainbow A uses the S&P 500, Nasdaq-100 and Dow Jones Industrial Average that are allocated 50%/30%/20% at look-back. At the time the method used 100% monthly averaging (MAVG) less a 5% yield spread. It is compared to the product's S&P 500 only methods – one that credited 100% of the annual gain up to a 7.25% cap, and one that used 100% MAVG less a 5.5% yields spread.

	Average Return	Rainbow Correlation
Rainbow Method MAVG -5.0%	6.60%	1.00
S&P 500 MAVG -5.5%	3.10%	0.79
S&P 500 100%APP w/7.25%	5.35%	0.47

Rainbow B

The S&P 500, Dow Jones Eurostoxx 50, and Nikkei 225 are allocated 50%/30%/20% at look-back. The method used 100% of annual gain up to a 7.5% cap (APP). It is compared to an S&P 500 only method crediting 40% of the annual gain.

	Average Return	Rainbow Correlation
Rainbow Method 100% APP	5.22%	1.00
S&P 500 APP 40%	5.02%	0.61

Rainbow C

The S&P 500, Dow Jones Eurostoxx 50, Hang Seng and Nikkei 225 are allocated 40%/30%/20%/10% at look-back. The method used 80% monthly averaging less a 1.5% yield spread. It is compared to an S&P 500 only method crediting 90% monthly averaging less a 1.5% yield spread.

	Average Return	Rainbow Correlation
Rainbow Method MAVG -1.5%	6.64%	1.00
S&P 500 MAVG 90%-1.5%	4.90%	0.59

Rainbow D

The S&P 500, Dow Jones Eurostoxx 50, and Russell2000 are allocated 50%/30%/20% at look-back. The method used 85% of annual gain up to a 5.75% cap. It is compared to S&P 500 only methods crediting 85% of the annual gain up to a 5.75% cap and one using 55% of daily averaged gains.

	Average Return	Rainbow Correlation
Rainbow Method w/5.75% cap	4.45%	1.00
S&P 500 DAVG -55%	3.51%	0.54
S&P 500 APP w/5.75% cap	4.29%	0.91

<u>Correlation</u>

Correlation shows the extent to which the returns of one index track another. Example: In this scale if the Dow moved exactly like the S&P 500 they would have a correlation value of 1.00; if the Dow moves were completely unlike the S&P 500 the correlation would be 0. For the periods measured the current rainbow methods produced correlation values of .53 to .92 when compared with the S&P 500.

S&P 500	1.00
DJIA	0.93
Nasdaq-100	0.81
EuroStoxx 50	0.77
Russell 2000	0.70
Nikkei 225	0.37

Correlation Of The Different Rainbow Methods

S&P 500/DJIA/Russell	0.92
S&P 500/DJIA/Nasdaq	0.84
S&P500/Russell/EuroStoxx	0.83
S&P500/EuroStoxx/Nikkei	0.71
S&P/EuroStoxx/Nikkei/Hang*	0.53

All allocate 50/30/20 except the last at *40/30/20/10

Rainbow Model Hypothetical Annual Returns

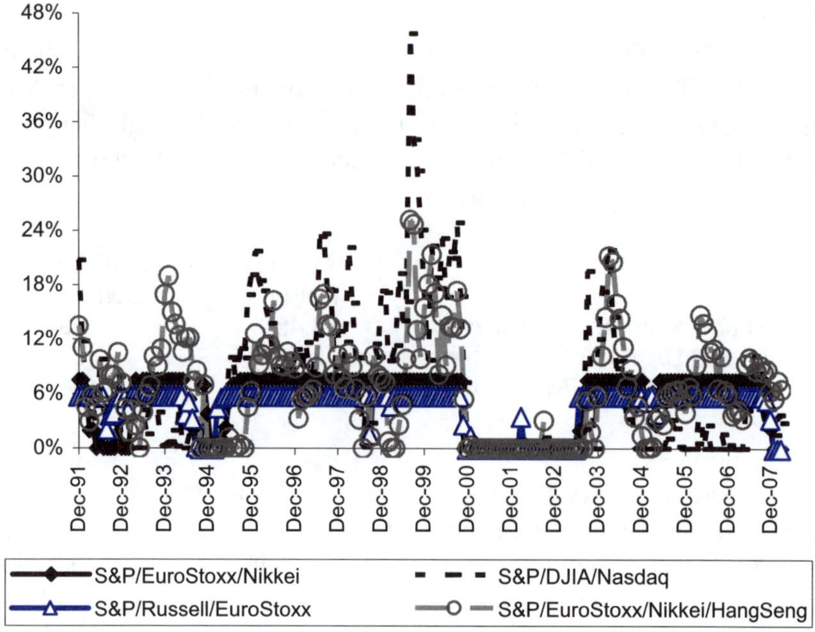

<u>What We Found</u>

If the S&P 500 is having a rotten year, a rainbow method probably will not produce a great return either; all stock markets tend to respond to news and changing economic conditions similarly. However, the rainbow method could offer higher returns than the S&P 500 alone in good times if pricing of the options is similar.

The advantage of the rainbow method in having greatest participation in the top performing index is reduced by application of a cap. Actually, capping the rainbow method defeats, somewhat, the main attraction of that method. However, if the option cost of the rainbow method permits higher caps than the S&P 500 alone might receive, then the rainbow method could offer an advantage.

In all cases the Rainbow produced higher average returns

Our goal, in the above exercises, was to see which method would have performed better (hypothetically, of course) – the rainbow method or the S&P 500 only methods. We discovered that in all cases the rainbow method produced higher average returns. However, the data are insufficient for us to conclude whether this is the result of an inherent superiority of the rainbow method or is simply due to an aberration in current option pricing.

The rainbow method is a legitimate addition to index annuity methodology. We believe it provides the greatest potential interest when offered without a cap, even when offered at lower participation rates or higher spreads. However, if the rainbow method uses a cap, and the rainbow cap is higher than the cap for the S&P 500 alone, we would pick the rainbow method at a higher cap every time.

Comparison Between Annual and Term End Points

One can graph the hypothetical returns of index annuities by looking at their distribution patterns. There are several ways to do this, but for this example, let's simply see how often returns occur within certain ranges.

I've used 7 year periods going back over the last 50 years and computed the annualized returns for each 7 year period using three different crediting methods. The first is the term end point method that applies a 75% participation rate to the total gain over each 7 year timeframe. The second uses the annual reset point-to-point method applying a 75% participation rate to annual gains, but also applying a

12% interest cap to any yearly gains. The third method uses an annual reset monthly average method with an uncapped 90% participation rate calculated on annual averaged index gains. I assume a minimum annualized return of 1%.

I am not saying these are necessarily realistic rates. As I did in the previous chapter I've purposely set this up so each method would have produced identical returns over the entire 50 year period to provide a level playing field. I then separated the returns for each method into five categories and added up how often each method produced hypothetical annual returns of under 4%, 4%, 5-6%, 7% or 8%-11%. When we calculate the percentage of time the return numbers from the three methods fell into the categories we get this chart.

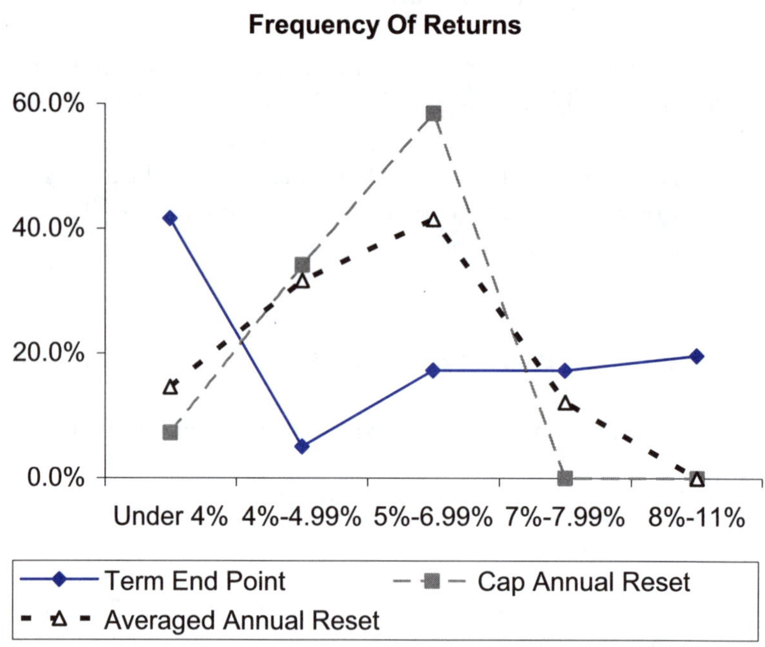

The frequency of the annual reset returns shows a small percentage of very low returns, a small percentage of very high returns, and a lot of returns in the middle. The term end point method shows more very low returns, more very high returns, and fewer returns in the middle. The distribution patterns are dissimilar even though the overall returns over the entire period are identical.

Why is there a difference in annual return distributions? Term end point designs, and other methods that measure index movement over long periods of time, tend to follow the actual performance of the index. A stock index often has a large number of years of very high returns and very low returns with relatively few returns in the middle.

Annual reset returns look more like a bell curve. Annual reset annuities ignore years with negative returns. This limits the periods with very low index returns, but annual reset structures tend to have higher total pricing costs than term end point structures, which mean the annual reset methods usually have a lower effective participation rate than term end point designs. This means annual reset structures do not tend to produce extended periods of very high returns.

The shape of the graph lines depends upon the methodology and the rate applied. If the term end point and annual reset rates slipped lower the lines would shift to the left. If rates had increased, the lines would shift to the right meaning higher returns.

Reading Annual Statements

The annual statements for annual-reset structured annuities tend to look like fixed rate annuity statements – with one big difference. Almost every index annuity will, if the index movement is flat or negative, reflect zero interest in the accumulated value column and not the minimum guaranteed rate. The minimum guarantee comes into effect only if the overall actual credited interest is lower than that minimum, in which event, minimum interest is retroactively calculated and credited, to bring the account value up to the level guaranteed. An annual reset structured annuity might show 7% interest in year 1, 0% interest in year 2, and then 9% in year 3.

Statements from term end point styled annuities are a different matter because interest is usually not credited until the end of the term. So, even if the index gained 40% in the first year, the statement would only reflect the minimum guaranteed interest. Most insurers also provide a kind of running summary of hypothetical performance in their annual statements, as if the interest crediting period were to terminate on the statement date. It is a good idea to review a sample annual statement before purchasing such an annuity, if only to avoid future surprises.

Selecting An Index Annuity Carrier

Financial Strength

Pick a carrier with finances you feel comfortable with. If you like to use third party ratings, pick a carrier evaluated by a rating service you like and define the minimum ratings you will accept. Better yet, look at that carrier's ratings from multiple ratings services. These services use different methodologies in arriving at their ratings, and a carrier might be rated more highly (even much more highly) by one service than by another. We look at a lot of factors when we are evaluating insurance companies and, in some situations, we may feel that a "B+" carrier offers the same relative safety as one rated "A+" because rating services "scores" are merely one measure of an insurer's stability.

Renewal Rates

We strongly believe that a carrier's treatment of renewal rates is far more important than the crediting method – or even the actual movement of the index – in estimating how much interest an annuity is likely to give us.

By renewal history, we do not mean interest credited to the policy; we mean the history of how the level of index participation in that particular annuity changes over time.

The problem is this: Some annuity issuers maintain a contract's participation in the underlying index at a fair level after the initial period. Others don't. This isn't an issue only with index annuities; it's been happening with non-indexed fixed annuities for years. Some insurers attract purchasers to their fixed annuity with high initial interest crediting rates. But once the guarantee period for the initial rate expires, they'll drop the renewal rate sharply. This may be especially likely when the initial rate seems uncompetitively high.

The same thing can happen with index annuities. An insurer can offer initial participation in the index that is unusually high, because it expects to drop that participation as soon as it can change the level of the "moving parts" (e.g.: decrease participation rate and/or the cap or increase the yield spread.

One possible solution to this renewal rate risk is to avoid annuities that can change any aspect of their index crediting during the surrender period. This works with annuities with term end point crediting methods because the product pricing can to a large part be worked out at policy issue. But locking in all moving parts of an annual reset structure can be so expensive that it makes the product uncompetitive.

The insurance company needs the flexibility to change index participation factors because financial markets change.

Almost every index annuity using annual or biennial reset methods has at least one moving part that can move during the surrender period. The annuity may guarantee the participation rate for the life of the contract, but the cap can change. Or the cap and participation rate are locked, but the yield spread can change. Even if products have limits on minimum caps or maximum spreads, forced crediting at these limitation levels would produce terrible returns.

The reality is this: the insurance company needs the flexibility to change annual reset index participation because financial markets change. You do not want to lock the insurance company into a situation where it might be placed in financial jeopardy – forcing a carrier to go belly up is a lot worse than getting a 20% participation rate for one year. Moreover, if the product pricing environment improves, this flexibility gives the carrier the ability to raise index participation at renewal. And before anyone goes "yeah right, an insurance company actually raising renewal rates", actual collected renewal data shows that every carrier furnishing renewal data has raised renewal rates at some point in the past.

How do you determine how carriers will treat you at future renewals? You can't know for certain, but you can look at how they have treated their customers in the past. We look at three things:

Will the carrier provide renewal information? If there is a renewal history and the carrier will not furnish it, why would you do business with that carrier? You do not need the rate of every policy ever issued; a representative sample will be sufficient.

Does the renewal rate reflect market changes? The carrier does not need to raise and lower index participation every time market volatility changes, but if a carrier cut p articipation when pricing costs went up then that carrier should also raise participation if conditions improve. Did that happen?

Did the carrier keep its promises? A promise might be an insurer's spokesperson assuring you that his company will not change rates for five years, even though the annuity contract permits annual changes. If that insurer drops the rate in year three, that's a broken promise. Similarly, an insurer might advertise a second year "base rate" that it expects to credit after expiry of the higher initial rate. Unless pricing conditions worsen during that first year, that insurer should renew at the base rate. If it doesn't, it has broken its promise. Insurance companies need to keep their promises – not only those contained in the contracts they offer, but also the assurances they make to prospective buyers and annuity representatives in their marketing materials.

What if the annuity does not have a renewal history? If there is insufficient index annuity history, look at their fixed rate annuity renewals. If a carrier has treated customers fairly in the past, that's a promising sign.

We firmly believe in the index annuity concept, and are optimistic about the ability of index annuities to competitively participate. The only thing that could really screw this up is if carriers are not fair at renewal time.

More Questions To Ask

- What moving parts to the interest crediting formulae can change in value before the end of the surrender period and how often can they change?
- How is cash surrender value calculated. Can you give me an example?
- What is your renewal history?
- What happens to the policy after the surrender period is over (any new charges)?

What Can Go Wrong?

- The stock market can be flat or decline for a prolonged period – for any number of reasons
- Overall interest rates in the economy can drop so low that index annuity participation stinks
- Option Prices can get so high that index annuity participation stinks
- Insurance company management could decide to increase company profits by cutting renewal rates
- If the insurer's pricing people didn't hedge their risks in offering an index annuity properly, renewal rates could drop to, and stay at, the guaranteed minimum, possibly for years
- The annuity buyer, failing to understand why his index annuity return is less than expected, might sue his agent
- The insurer could go out of business. It's happened.
- This List doesn't cover everything. Remember Murphy's Law.

Cheat Sheet

- The jump up and down extraordinary points about annual reset crediting are credited interest cannot be lost if the index declines, years of negative index movement are treated as years of zero growth, and index values are reset at the beginning of each period.

- Simply choosing the annuity with the lowest spread, or the highest rate, or the best cap won't ensure you of getting the highest return.

- Any crediting method can produce the best return for a given period.

- It is not the nominal or stated rate, but the effective rate that is important. The nominal rate only tells you how much of the crediting method calculation you are participating in; the effective rate says how much of actual index performance you are getting.

- Because index annuities with annual reset structures treat negative years as zeros, instead of losses and only include years with positive or zero returns your effective return goes up. This is why a lower participation rate can still provide competitive returns.

- Averaging always drives values to the middle, but that does not mean index annuities using averaging will have half the return of an index annuity with a point-to-point design, because averaging structures typically have higher rates than unaveraged ones.

- Averaging needs to be explained because you can not figure out what your index annuity interest is by looking at the finance page in the newspaper.

- Caps generally mean you get more of most instead of less of a lot, because an annuity with a cap has higher index participation than a similar annuity without a cap. A high cap may have minimal effect of returns because relatively few stock market years are stratospheric, but too low a cap can kill returns because you cannot use higher years to offset zero years.

- Although locking in all the crediting factors eliminates renewal rate risk it is very expensive to do so with an annual or biennial design.

- The integrity of the carrier is far more important than selection of a crediting style.

- A premium bonus is never free.

P.S. – Effective Participation During Bullish Times

This study shows how different index crediting structures and rates would have hypothetically performed for ten year periods ending during the 1980s (71-81, 72-82...80-90) and 1990s (81-91...90-00) calculated as a percentage of S&P 500 Index returns. For measurement the study uses the end of the year value for the S&P 500 index in calculating the returns. The results obtained should not be taken as a representation of actual returns for any product or period.

Example: The annualized S&P 500 Index return for ten year periods ending in the 1980s averaged 7.88%; the average for ten year periods ending in the 1990s was 13.06%. If you apply the term end point method with a 75% rate averaging the last 52 weeks of the period to ten year periods in the 1980s the average return of the method equaled 78.2% of the S&P 500 Index. Or, applying an annual reset offering 60% of annual point-to-point gain approach to ten year periods would have produced an average return that was equal to 88.2% of the average S&P 500 index return for the same ten year periods.

	% of Annualized S&P 500 Return	
	'80s	'90s
Term End Point		
75% of term gain, last 52 weeks averaged	78.2%	78.4%
100% of gain, 12% caps, 5 yr high pt look-back	64.0%	59.0%
annualized gain less 1.9%, last year averaged	74.5%	80.1%
Annual Reset		
60% of annual point-to-point gain	88.2%	65.3%
50% of annual point-to-point gain	73.7%	54.6%
100% of annual point-to-point gain, 9% cap	70.7%	47.5%
100% of annual point-to-point gain, 8% cap	63.3%	43.2%
100% of annual point-to-point gain, 7% cap	56.0%	38.9%
100% of monthly averaged gain	90.2%	69.5%
80% of monthly averaged gain	72.6%	55.9%
60% of monthly averaged gain	54.8%	42.1%
100% of monthly averaged gain, 10% cap	65.4%	48.1%
100% of monthly averaged gain, 9% cap	60.2%	44.3%
100% of monthly averaged gain, 8% cap	54.7%	40.1%
4% monthly cap	76.1%	70.4%
3% monthly cap	49.2%	51.3%
2% monthly cap	21.5%	28.9%
Biennial Reset		
5% monthly cap	68.3%	67.4%
4% monthly cap	48.7%	54.1%
3% monthly cap	25.6%	37.7%
100% of two year point-to-point gain, 17% cap	72.3%	56.4%
100% of two year point-to-point gain, 15% cap	67.3%	51.1%
100% of two year point-to-point gain, 13% cap	61.1%	45.3%

Chapter 5 – Hypothetical & Real Returns

Whether we are looking at an historical comparison of mutual fund returns or last week's winning numbers in the state lottery, we must always be aware that past performance – however calculated or represented – cannot be used to predict the future returns of any financial vehicle. We all know this; yet we try to use past data to predict future events or look for a modern Cassandra to tell them to us (though if we could actually hear the truth about the future we would, like the hearers of her prophesies, probably ignore it).

Hypotheticals based on the past will not tell you what future results will be or even, with any real reliability, the probability of certain results. Even results based on the finest computer models can only tell you the probability of certain outcomes *if the model's assumptions are correct.* Unfortunately, some people *do* use the results of hypothetical index annuity models to tell consumers the returns they can *expect* to earn in the future.

Hypotheticals don't predict the future (and often not even the past)

Hypotheticals Do Not Even Predict The Past

Most index annuity models cannot even predict the past because today's cap rate or participation rate or yield spread can be changed. In the last year alone, caps on most products have swung from 25% higher to 25% lower than where they started. Two hypothetical studies looking at the same historical period could post results 50% apart, depending upon the day you ran the illustration. Because of this variation in "moving parts" (including, but not limited to, caps), you cannot use hypotheticals to say how a method might perform even if the past were to repeat perfectly.

<u>Real Returns Were Happening</u>

Much of the early hypothetical modeling of index annuity returns was done because there was no actual history available. Today, we have several index annuity issuers with ten year track records and many with at least five year track records of actual returns. For many carriers and crediting methods one can get actual interest rates credited on policies and make actual real-life comparisons with other annuities and other financial instruments. We've done that, and we will examine those returns later in this chapter.

Curiously, some carriers persist in showing hypothetical returns for a crediting period even when they have actual returns for their crediting method available for that same period. We can understand the use of hypotheticals when the crediting method used is new, or when the actual returns history is short, but we believe that a carrier should make available both actual and hypothetical returns.

Hypotheticals Can Help Detect "Too Good" Rates

In the fixed rate world, things are easier. If ten products have similar surrender periods, similar guarantees and similar commissions, but one of those products credits an initial interest rate 2% higher than all the others, we ought to ask why that one company's rate is so much higher and what that mean about that company's future renewal rates. But index annuities are more difficult to compare, due to the wide variety of crediting methods used, which is why hypothetical models are useful in detecting returns that are so far outside the norms that questions ought to be raised.

A while back, we plugged into 50 years of index movement the then-current annual reset participation rates, caps and spreads of over 40 actual index annuities, and determined their hypothetical annualized returns, broken down by surrender period. We found -

The 5-year surrender period products had an average annualized return of 4.53% (ranging from 3.08% to 5.03%) for those 50 years.

The 10-year surrender period products had an average annualized return of 5.12% and all but one had average returns between 3.98% and 6.15%. That one annuity paid an average of 7.12%

The hypothetical returns produced by almost all of these products were within 1% of the average return for their surrender period (which reflected similar pricing), with two exceptions. One 5-year annuity had a 3.08% average return, which was well below the others; one 10-year annuity had a 7.12% return; well above the others. Why?

By digging a little deeper, we found that the carrier that issued the 5-year annuity with the 3.08% return was discouraging sales of this product by offering a less competitive rate because they were promoting another product; the low rate was a temporary situation. The carrier with the high 10-year index annuity return represented a bigger red flag. How could it offer a rate which resulted in a hypothetical return that was almost 40% higher than the average for the group? The answer may very well be that it could not, and that future renewal rates for that contract will have to be less competitive to make up for that over-crediting.

Backing Your Claim

Hypothetical models may also be used to verify marketing claims. None of these annuities at then-current participation rates, ever produced, in those fifty years, a 10% or greater return for the entire surrender charge period, so, if someone claims their annuity will give consumers "double-digit" returns you have reason to doubt the veracity of their message.

These hypothetical returns *should not* be interpreted to mean that, if you had purchased any of those index annuities, that you would have earned an average return of 4.53% over the next five years or 5.12% over 10 years. For that to happen the future would have to unfold exactly as the past did, , and the participation rates or caps would have to be as they were then, and stay that way. The hypothetical results we presented are just that – hypothetical illustrations of *past* events; they are *not* predictions of future returns.

Beware Hypotheticals That Cherry Pick The Past

Depending on the actual movements of the index, the crediting structure utilized, and the participation rate applied, any methodology could result in the highest return for any given period.

The following analysis examines three index annuity crediting methods, using the return data for the same 50 year period used earlier. We looked at seven-year periods and made the following assumptions: (1) interest crediting is based on calendar year movements of the S&P 500, (2) a minimum interest guarantee of 1%, compounded on 87.5% of premium, and (3) a participation rate for each method such that each method produces the same average (mean) return for the entire fifty year period. This requires the term end point structure to use a 75% rate, the annual reset point-to-point to have a 75% rate with a 12% interest cap, and the annual reset monthly average to have a 90% rate.

We are not saying these are necessarily realistic rates. As we did in the previous chapter, we have set up this demonstration so that each method would have produced identical returns over the entire 50 year period, so as to provide a level playing field. Let's look, first, at hypothetical distributions based on *seven-year periods* for the last 50 years.

50 Years	Over 10%	8.00%-9.99%	7.00%-7.99%	5.00%-6.99%	Under 5.00%
Term End Point	13.3%	26.7%	13.3%	8.9%	37.8%
Pt-to-Pt w/Cap	-0-	17.8%	8.9%	60.0%	13.3%
Monthly Average	4.4%	17.8%	17.8%	37.8%	22.2%

50 Years	Over 10%	8.00%-9.99%	7.00%-7.99%	5.00%-6.99%	Under 5.00%
Term End Point	6	12	6	4	17
Pt-to-Pt w/Cap	-0-	8	4	27	6
Monthly Average	2	8	8	17	10

There are 45 seven-year periods within 50 calendar years. When we apply the 75% participation rate for the Term End Point method to the actual returns for the 50 years, we find that that method produced a 10% or higher annual return for 6 of the periods (13.3% of the 45 periods). For 12 of the periods (26.7% of the 45 periods), that method produced an average return between 8.00 and 9.99%. In

13.3% of the periods, it produced a return between 7.00 and 7.99%, and so forth.

"Customized" periods with shorter time frames may not reflect realistic hypothetical performance. These are the distributions if you plug in the rates and your seven-year periods end during this recent fifteen-year time frame.

1986 – 2002	Over 10%	8.00%-9.99%	7.00%-7.99%	5.00%-6.99%	Under 5.00%
Term End Point	50.0%	20.0%	30.0%	-0-	-0-
Pt-to-Pt w/Cap	-0-	30.0%	20.0%	50.0%	-0-
Monthly Average	-0-	60.0%	10.0%	30.0%	-0-

Based on only this example, you would probably conclude the term end point structure is the best one. However, let us look at a different fifteen-year time frame.

1965 – 1980	Over 10%	8.00%-9.99%	7.00%-7.99%	5.00%-6.99%	Under 5.00%
Term End Point	-0-	-0-	-0-	-0-	100.0%
Pt-to-Pt w/Cap	-0-	-0-	-0-	60.0%	40.0%
Monthly Average	-0-	-0-	10.0%	50.0%	40.0%

If you assume this timeframe will be representative of the future, you would probably select the annual reset methods. However, the data derived by "cherry picking" your periods may give a distorted view of the actual return parameters and probabilities. When you look at hypothetical returns, it is important to use a timeframe that is long enough to include a variety of market conditions.

3 Card Monte Hypothetical

You are shown three index annuity returns representing the hypothetical results obtained from plugging in current rates to historic index movement. The hypotheticals produced show you a best return of 12%, a median or middle return of 5%, and a worst return of 0%. This seems fair. The problem with this is that if we do not get any other data we will mentally give each outcome the same odds of occurring. Since 3 returns are listed we subconsciously conclude there is a 1 in 3 chance of earning 12% and a 2 in 3 chance of earning at least 5%, and conclude that those are pretty good odds.

Worst	Median	Best
0%	5%	12%

The problem is that the above statistics do not tell us *how often* those results occurred in that hypothetical analysis. What percentage of the total results does that 12% return represent? In this example, based on actual annuity marketing materials and looking at the time frame used by the insurer, the distribution of outcomes was like this: in 1% of outcomes, the return was 12%, in 30% of the outcomes, the return was 0%; and in 69% of the outcomes, the return was between 4% and 6%. If that's the case, the probability of achieving a return of less than 12% (if the past repeats exactly) is 99%.

Worst	Median	Best
0%	5%	12%
30%	***69%***	***1%***

If you are going to look at hypothetical results, be sure you look at the whole range of outcomes to get a better feeling of not only *how good* a result might be but also *how likely* it is.

Key Points On Evaluation

- Although we do not know how the stock market will perform tomorrow, for any evaluation method to have validity we need to believe that long term trends hold true.

- Be wary of index annuity hypothetical illustrations that "cherry pick" certain periods. Any index annuity can be made to look good if you carefully select the right time frame.

- If an illustration shows three possible outcomes it does not mean there is a 33% chance that each will occur.

Real Returns

The middle of this chapter is about real index annuity returns and how they compare against other real returns. The index annuity data is for real. It was usually obtained by getting copies of actual annuity owner annual statements with the personal information blacked out, or sometimes by examining the published renewal histories that a few carriers make available. However, one should view the data with this in mind:

The data is limited. The data collected are very few for some periods. Nonetheless, the contracts for which we have data are real contracts and reflect actual crediting rates that were provided to annuity owners over time under twelve different crediting rate structures.

The data is "cherry-picked" due to necessity. Index annuities have only been around since 1995, which is a short timeframe. We do not have actual performance over broad market periods because it simply isn't available.

The data is what it is. We make no claims that the data is representative of what will happen or even what did happen. The data is what it is.

Best Index Returns By Crediting Method

The chart below assumes you had purchased the best performing annuity for each crediting method on the last day of each month beginning in January 2003 through December 2006. So the first yearly return ranking for the methods is for the period beginning January 2004 and ending January 2005, and the final period begins December 2006 and end December 2007.

The chart ranks from highest to lowest actual first year interest credited by Annual Point-to-Point, Monthly Cap, Averaging or Trigger (Binary, Non-Negative) crediting methods over the previous 12 months based on the best rates, caps and spreads in effect at time of purchase for all index annuities. These are not hypothetical results. We examined the roughly 300 index annuity products on the market during each of the 36 periods, calculated the first year returns, and then ranked the best performing annuity in each method.

Best Returns By Crediting Method

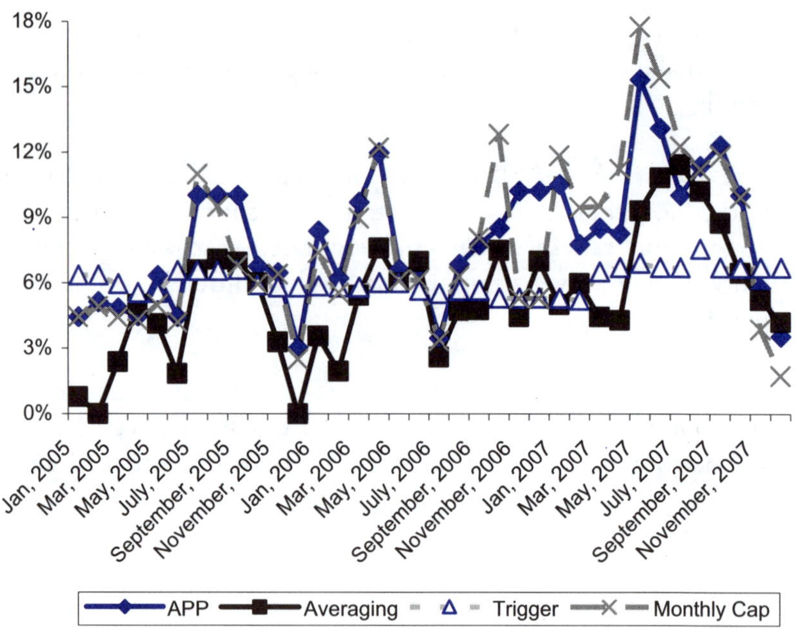

For the period ending January 2005, for example, the trigger method annuity with the highest return beat the best performing annual point-to-point annuity, which in turn bested the winning annuity using a monthly cap method, and the top performing annuities in these three methods won over the annuity with the top averaging returns.

The chart breaks down the crediting method universe into four broad categories and then picks the best performing index annuity in each category. What does it indicate? That there is not one best method for a particular market period.

The period in question witnessed the S&P 500 rise from around 1100 to 1500 in a fairly steady manner, and yet no one method consistently had the highest returns. Annual point-to-point won in fifteen months, but a monthly cap design was on top for eleven, and even the trigger method led the field for nine months. Averaging methods only led the field once.

The Key Point.

There is not a "best crediting method" for a particular market environment.

Real Returns – All Index Returns By Crediting Method

The previous chart shows the best first-year returns you could have earned, but not everyone purchased *the best* products for each method. Let us look, now, at periods ending in 2010 and say that in 2009 you purchased *every* available index annuity on the last day of each month. The following chart shows the range of interest that "woulda" been credited based on participation rates, caps and spreads in effect at time of purchase based on different index annuity products.

Range of 1st Year Actual 12 Month Returns - All Index Annuities

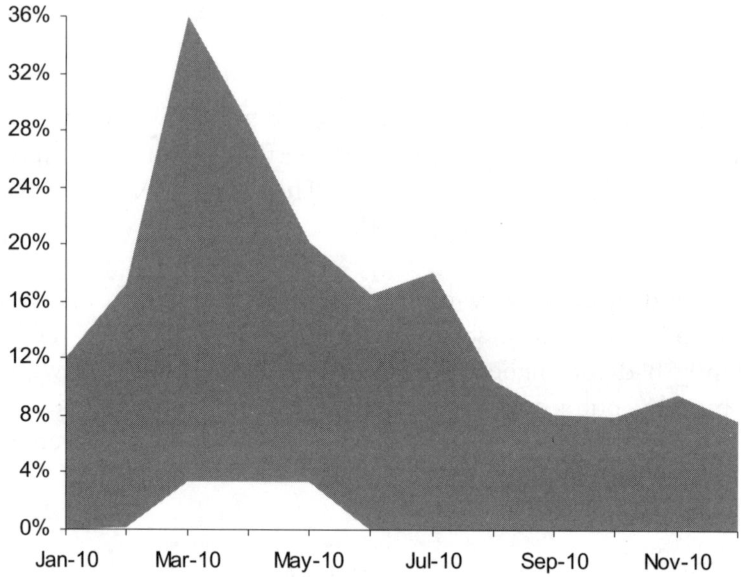

If you had purchased the best performing annual reset index annuity on 31 January 2009 you would have earned 17.21% interest on 31 January 2010. However, if you had purchased the lousiest index annuity on that date you would have earned a miserly 0.18% for the same annual period.

This shows how even a month's difference in annual periods can greatly affect returns, and what a difference the crediting method and participation in that crediting method can make over the short term. Depending on the annuity purchased your average return for all 12 annual periods ranged from less than 1% to over 16% in 2010.

The Key Point.

Over the short term the day the annuity is purchased and the crediting method used have a tremendous effect on the return, but to be able to take advantage of this you would need the ability to forecast the future.

Index Annuity Returns Are Competitive

We compared fixed rate annuity, fixed index annuity and taxable bond fund returns for five year periods beginning in 1992 and ending in 2009. Our conclusions are that both fixed rate and fixed index annuities have been competitive with U.S. taxable bond mutual funds for these periods.

From 1997 thru 2009 the taxable bond fund averaged 4.79% a year while the index annuity averaged 5.63%

If you look at the period from 1997 through 2009, the 5-year annualized returns for the index annuities averaged 5.63%. The average taxable bond fund return was 4.79%; the average one year certificate of deposit return was 3.43%, and the average fixed rate annualized return was 4.42%. For the periods from 1992 through 2009 the average taxable bond fund return was 5.34%; the average one year CD was 4.18%, and the average fixed rate annuity return was 4.92%.

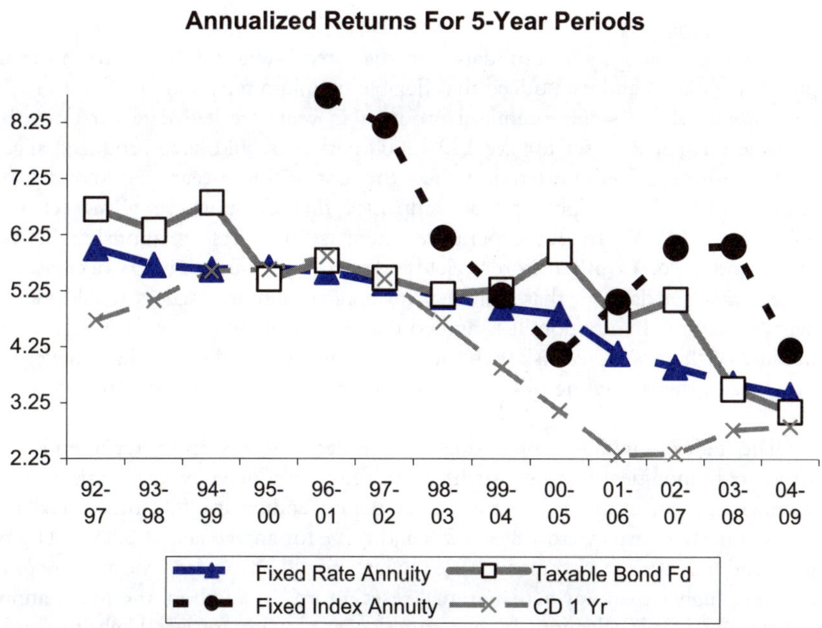

Stats – Annualized 5 Year Periods

1992-2009 The average fixed rate annuity return is 4.92% with a standard deviation of 0.882. The taxable bond fund average is 5.34% with a standard deviation of 1.099.

1997-2009 The average fixed rate annuity return is 4.42% with a standard deviation of 0.757. The taxable bond fund average is 4.79% with a standard deviation of 0..988. The average fixed index annuity return is 5.63% with a standard deviation of 1.317.

The Data

Best's Review was the source of the earlier annuity data representing the initial and renewal rates for 56 carriers for the first four 5-year periods. Fixed rate annuity returns for later years reflect rates for annuities offered by "AA" or higher rated carriers not using MVA. The index annuity returns reflect reported annual reset returns ranging from 3 carriers for the period ending in 2001 to 18 carriers for the most recent figures. We have 5 year data for the period ending in 2000, but for only one index carrier and we decided not to show it. The taxable bond fund data reflects the average annualized returns for taxable bond funds for the five year periods as reported by *The Wall Street Journal.* The index annuity data reflects 1 October to 1 October periods, all other data reflects 1 July to 1 July years.

Data Concerns

Fixed rate annuity return data for the first 5-year period is from flexible premium policies and we noticed that flexible premium rates were tracking 11 to 18 basis points above single premium products in years we had data for both. It is possible a larger data set for the 1998-2000 periods would have produced slightly higher returns. Fixed rate returns for the last seven 5-year periods are from annuities issued by highly rated companies that do not use a market value adjustment (MVA). In our experience, there is an inverse relationship between rating and yield. In other words, yields tend to increase as ratings decrease. We believe a larger data set that included lower rated annuity carriers would increase average returns. In addition, it is argued that MVAs allow carriers to increase rates because of the sharing of risk with the annuityowner. Although we have never seen evidence of this, including MVA products might increase overall reported yields.

The index annuity sample does not reflect returns from term end point structured annuities because such inclusion would have severely skewed the numbers. As an example, for the 5-year period ending in 2002 the annual reset index annuity returns were 7.8%, 8.2% and 8.7% for an average of 8.23%. The two term end point returns averaged 10.7%, which would have raised the average return to 9.3%, higher than any actual annual reset return. In addition, the index annuity return data is self-selecting. In our experience, carriers are less likely to send in return data when they perceive their own returns as low. We believe, therefore, that the average index annuity returns shown are higher than a larger, more random sample would have produced for the periods.

Finally, the fixed rate and bond fund data uses July to July years whilst the index annuity years start and end three months later. We do not believe moving the fixed rate and bond fund returns by three months would substantially impact the data relationships or conclusions reached.

* *The Wall Street Journal*, Average Annualized 5-Yr Taxable Bond Fund Returns; 7/3/96, 7/3/97, 7/6/98, 7/5/99, 7/10/00, 7/5/01, 7/5/02, 7/7/03, 7/5/04, 7/5/05, 7/5/06, 7/3/07. 7/3/08, 7/6/09 CD: Federal Reserve, bankrate.com

** *Best's Review*, 3/96 p.51-57; 4/97 p.38-42

*** Companies rated AA or better by S&P or Moody's. Based on policies with equal annual premiums; consequently, renewal rates are influenced by premiums arriving in years 2-5. Extrapolation 08, 09 No MVA or two-tier products.

**** *Best's Policy Reports* notes from 10/00

What Does It Mean?

Although past performance does not predict future results, the data support a conclusion that index annuities are a viable alternative to taxable bond funds. And although overall fixed rate annuity returns averaged roughly a half percent less than bond funds in the study, we believe if less than top financially rated carriers had been included in the data, the results would have been much closer. Index annuities may well be a better choice than bond funds if the consumer is apt to fall into the trap of selling when rates are falling and buying when fund yields are peaking (moves that many investors have made in the past). This logic would also make *fixed rate* annuities a better choice than bond funds for many consumers.

An index annuity should never be viewed as a place for "safe high returns" – an oxymoron – but as an alternative to the risk of stock investments for those consumers who want the potential to earn more than they will likely get from fixed investments such as fixed-rate annuities and bonds and who are so risk averse that they cannot tolerate the market risk associated with equity investments. This is *not* to say that an index annuity is a reasonable alternative to buying stocks (or a stock mutual fund); the risk and return characteristics of those two investment types are so hugely different that they are not, properly speaking, "alternatives". That said, index annuities do offer the *potential* for greater return than fixed-rate annuities or CDs, from interest *linked to* the *upside* performance of an equity index. Based on their performance vis a vis other safe money benchmarks, index annuities should be recognized and respected index for doing what they were designed to do.

More Real Returns

We have collected actual return data since 1997 and calculated the effective five-year annualized returns of this data. Therefore, the first five-year period data collection ends in 2002 and includes yearly returns for the annuity contracts purchased in 1997 for policy years ending in 1998, 1999, 2000, 2001 and 2002. The next data group uses annuities purchased in 1998 and returns for the next five years ending in 2003 were collected, and so on. These individual returns are then compounded and the annual return for the five-year period calculated.

These are *real* numbers about *actual* index participation. This data and the following chart reflect both annual reset and term end point returns. With the exception of the 1997 – 2002 returns, which use calendar year returns, all of the other five year periods use annual periods that begin and end on or about 30 September each year. How has index annuity participation compared with the actual index?

Index Annuity Participation Rates

As mentioned in the previous chapter_the effective rate could also be called the real rate of index participation. It is the percentage of actual index gain the index annuity credited as interest. The effective participation rate can never be negative because index annuities do not participate in index losses.

9/05 – 9/10

The S&P 500 closed down 7.1% for the 5 year period; therefore an effective participation rate cannot be determined. However, the average annual reset index annuity returned 21.0% for the period

9/04 – 9/09

The S&P 500 closed down 5.2% for the 5 year period; therefore an effective participation rate cannot be determined. However, the average annual reset index annuity returned 22.8% for the period

9/03 – 9/08

The S&P 500 was up 17.0% for the 5 year period. The effective participation rate for annual reset annuities, when compared with the actual index gain, ranged from 110% to 269% for the entire period (the reason for the high effective rate is in the fifth year the index declined 24% wiping out a large part of the previous gains, but index annuities cannot lose credited interest).

9/02 – 9/07

The S&P 500 was up 87.3% for the 5 year period. The effective participation rate for annual reset annuities, when compared with the actual index gain, ranged from 18% to 57% for the entire period.

9/01 – 9/06

The S&P 500 was up 28.3% for the 5 year period. The effective participation rate for annual reset annuities, when compared with the actual index gain, ranged from 63% to 122% for the entire period.

9/00 – 9/05

The S&P 500 closed down 14.5% for the 5 year period; therefore an effective participation rate cannot be determined. However, the average annual reset index annuity returned 23.6% for the period

9/99 – 9/04

The S&P 500 closed down 13.1% for the 5 year period; therefore an effective participation rate cannot be determined. However, the average annual reset index annuity returned 25.8% for the period

9/98 – 9/03

The S&P 500 closed down 2.1% for the 5 year period; therefore an effective participation rate cannot be determined. However, the average annual reset index annuity returned 30.5%

1/97 – 1/02

The S&P 500 was up 56.67% for the 5 year period. The effective participation rate for annual reset annuities, when compared with the actual index gain, ranged from 80% to 91%.

A common criticism of index annuities is that they do not allow the annuity owner to get full participation in the index because they do not take account of dividends. While technically true, that suggests an incorrect conclusion. Even if you add an additional 11% to the index returns (to reflect the equivalent of average reinvested dividends on the S&P 500 index for these years), the "full" index representing reinvested dividends would have beaten all index annuity returns in only two of the seven 5-year periods and beaten only some index annuity returns in a third. The "full" index with reinvested dividends would have lost to index annuities in 63% of the periods.

The larger problem with comparing index annuity participation to the index is one mentioned previously: namely, that index annuities are targeted as savings vehicles and their goal is to be competitive with other savings vehicles, not with a direct investment in equities. A reasonable – and fair comparison would be between the return a consumer got from his index annuity with the interest he was paid on his CD, rather than the return produced by an investment that he would never have considered in the first place. We feel an appropriate benchmark for fixed annuity returns is the average rate of return on short term certificates of deposit. Using this metric, index annuities have participated very well.

Actual Annualized Returns

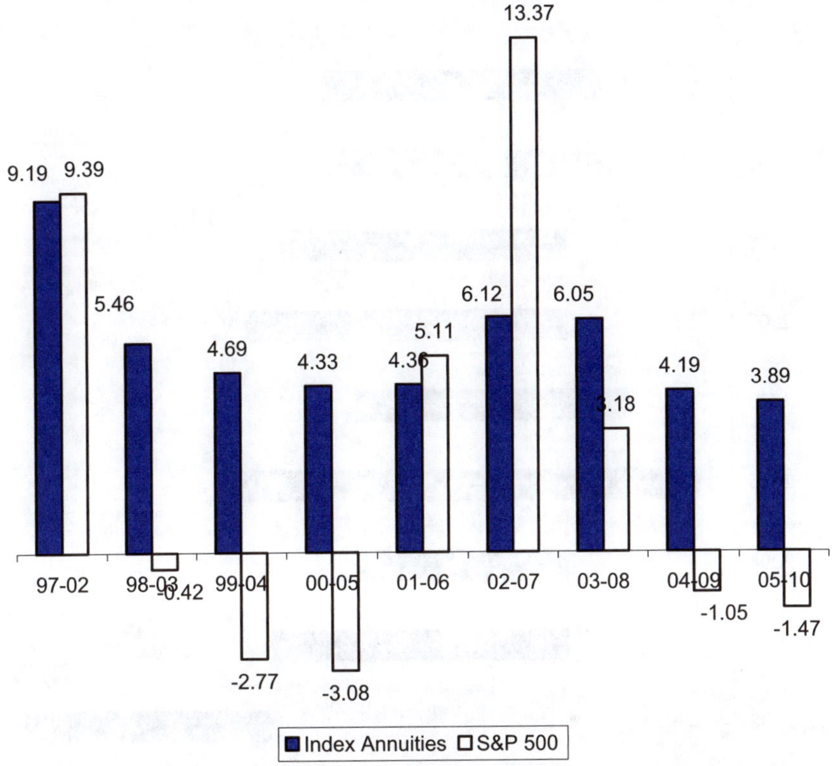

Real Ranges Of Returns

The previous chart compare the average reported index annuity five-year annualized return with the corresponding return for the index, the following chart shows the range of annualized returns credited to the index annuities. The variance in returns over the same period reflects the crediting method used – different methods perform differently in different markets – but it also reflects the renewal rates of the reset methods.

Range Of Annualized Index Annuity Interest Earned During 5 Year Periods Ending Years 2002 through 2010

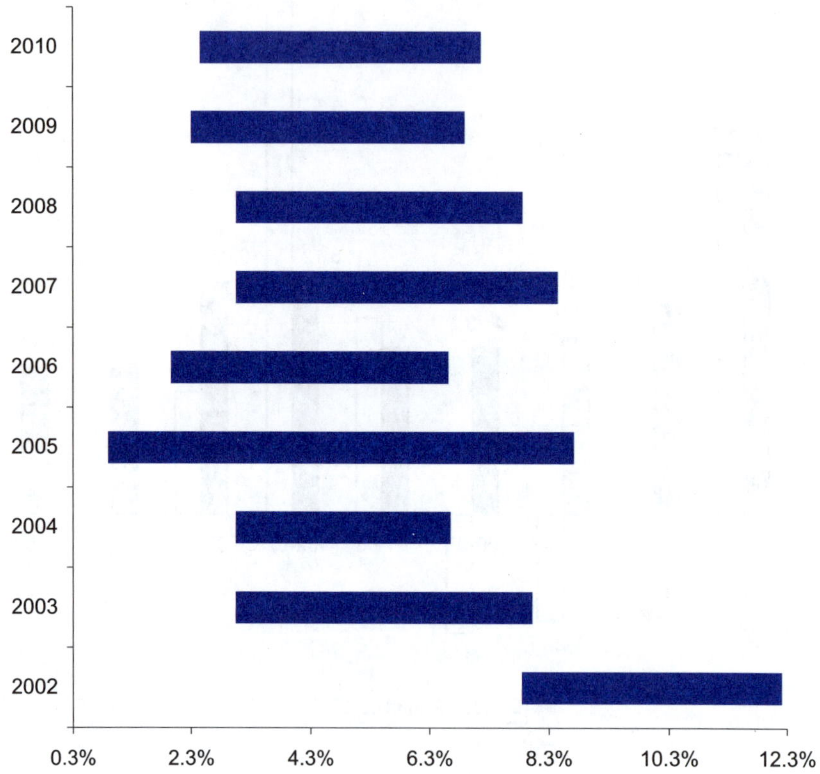

Although the index return data gathered represents several hundred "years" of actual returns it is still a very skinny picture of the real returns. Depending on the period start and stop dates, there were several periods in the 1990s, and even in 2010, where index annuities earned over 20% interest in a single year, and some products using averaging earned over 30%. Offsetting these very good times are bear market periods in which term end point designs credited only the minimum return. The problem with building a comprehensive picture of index annuity return reality is the same one that exists on the fixed rate side – it is difficult to obtain adequate documentation on renewal histories.

Never Use The Fixed Bucket...Unless

Based on our modeling, and on the actual results we examined, we believe that index annuity buyers should allocate 100% of their index annuity accounts to the indexed accounts offered, rather than to the "fixed accounts" available in those contracts. And we believe this should be the case 100% of the time - with three exceptions. We'll get the exceptions out of the way first.

The carrier offers a five year or longer fixed rate of 6% or higher.

We realize that the average index annuity yield was 8.2% from 1997 to 2002, but the reality is that 6% is likely to be better than many 5-year index annuity returns.

You use a balanced allocation method and you leave it alone.

In our current-rate modeling the balanced method combining a 2 or 4 year index-linked term end point return with a fixed account model, was competitive with annual reset methods. Our modeling also shows a higher index/fixed account allocation, even with that allocation's higher charge, is usually better than going for a more fixed rate balance.

You can predict the future.

Everyone laughs at the foolishness of trying to predict the future, and then tries to do it.

<u>Fixed Rate – You'll be right at least once</u>

In almost every 5-year period, at least one year is down, and a fair share of the time, you will see two down years. This means the index bucket will be showing goose eggs part of the time, but it doesn't take much for the index account to win. Here are a few Rules of Thumb: If the annual point-to-point cap is 175% or more of the fixed rate, or the averaging method cap is at least double the fixed rate, or if the uncapped participation rate is at least 35% for an annual point-to-point, or 55% for an averaged method, it makes sense to go for the indexed option. A 4% fixed rate over 3 years is equaled by 2 years of 6% index performance and 2 years of 8% indexed interest will equal 4 years of 4% fixed returns.

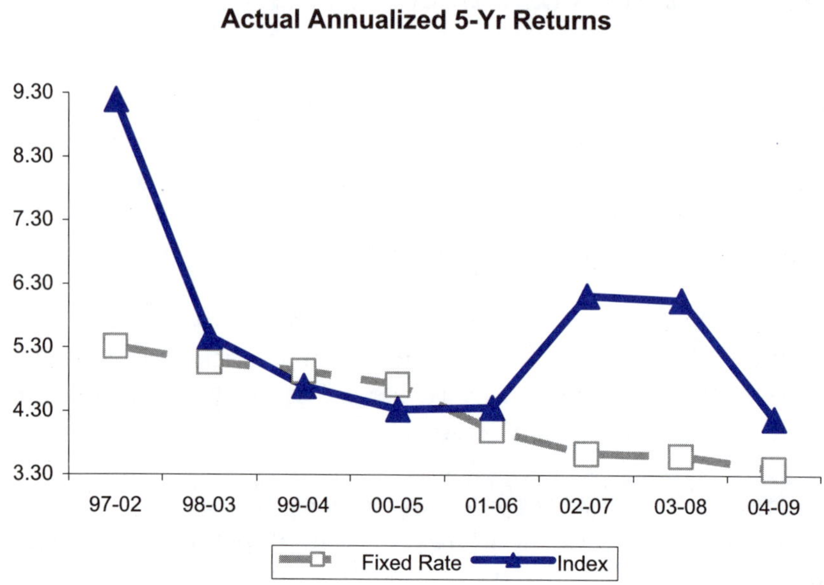

It's Not A Stock, Don't Act Like It Is

A fundamental reason for using asset allocation with investments is that if you put all of your eggs in one basket, someone might squash that basket and you could lose *all* your eggs. But the worst case scenario with an index annuity is you won't earn new interest. Therefore the "prevent loss" reason for asset allocation doesn't apply. Putting your money in the fixed account to avoid the variability of future returns means you are trying to preserve a 3%-5% gain and avoid the possibility of a 6%-20% gain. Huh?

Don't Listen To The Voices In Your Head

We've talked to enough people to have concluded that the primary reason why so many of them choose the "fixed bucket" option is not a poorly conceived asset allocation strategy or a dislike of low caps, but is, rather, due to their belief that they know how the market will perform over the next12 months. We are only batting .500 predicting what the weather will be the day after tomorrow; yet many people tell us that they *know* that the market will be down in a year, so they're picking the fixed account, or they're putting half of their money on the fixed side and half in the averaging strategy "because it will be a choppy year". Well, either of those *might* prove to be the most successful strategy. But, for our part, we acknowledge that we don't know where the index will be in a year, so it makes sense, to us, to go with what produces the best returns in *most* years.

Let The Index Annuity Work

Index annuities were designed to give fixed annuity buyers a real shot at earning higher than fixed annuity yields. When you put the premium in the fixed bucket, it defeats the purpose of the index annuity. Unless "this time is different", or unless one of the exceptions mentioned earlier applies to you, you'll be better off allocating your premium among different indices or crediting methods and not touching it again until you cash in the annuity.

Cheat Sheet

- Hypotheticals based on the past will not tell you either what future results will be or the probability of certain results.

- Hypotheticals based on the past cannot even predict the past because today's participation rates can be changed.

- Data derived by "cherry picking" your past periods may give a distorted view of the actual return parameters and probabilities.

- Based on only the limited return data collected, index annuity returns have been competitive with taxable bond funds, fixed rate annuities, certificates of deposit and index funds.

- An index annuity should never be viewed as a place for "safe high returns" – an oxymoron – but as an alternative to the risk of stock investments for those consumers who want more upside potential than is likely to be produced by CDs or fixed-rate annuities, *and* who are unwilling to accept the *principal loss* possible if they invest in stocks (or bonds, for that matter)..

P.S. – Flawed Studies Of Index Annuity Naysayers

We have noticed two basic flaws that often appear in studies and articles that attempt to describe potential index annuity performance. The first of these consists of choosing crediting methods and crediting rates that are rarely used, using those methods to create results, and declaring the results to be representative of index annuities in general. The second flaw consists of making assumptions that are not well supported and which appear to have been created to make data fit the authors' prior conclusions ignoring, in the process, how index annuities have *actually* performed.

Unrepresentativeness

Often, a financial writer will dismiss the index annuity concept by proposing that a consumer would be better off by purchasing a long-term zero-coupon bond and an index fund, instead of the annuity. Writers making thise suggestion often use the term end point crediting method as representative of all index annuities. However, term end point designs represent, historically, less than 5% of index annuity sales. Indeed, one study based its conclusions on a term end point that uses a cap - yet fewer than 1% of the products have ever placed a cap on a term end point crediting method.

Calling a term end point with a cap structure representative of index annuity crediting methods is akin to saying utility stocks may be used as a proxy for the Wilshire 5000. The writer's basic assumption is flawed because the sample is not representative of the population.

The sample is not representative of the population because the method was not used in over 95% of sales.

The assumed participation rates may also not be representative. Looking at annual reset methods, one study assumed 55% index participation, subject to a 7% annual cap or 60% averaged index participation, subject to a 7.5% cap. Another study compared returns from 1990 through 2007 of the S&P 500 with a hypothetical annual reset point-to-point design with a constant 6.5% cap. Were the assumed values *reasonable?* Not even close! Our review of *actual* new money rates for annual reset designs from 1996 on reveals that one would have been subject to participation rates this low at only a few points in the last few years. Indeed, many averaging products were offering 100% first year participation without a cap in the late '90s, and many annual point-to-point products offered, during these periods, 100% participation up to double digit caps.

Some studies will use term end point methods. There is nothing wrong with showing how a term end point method might have performed. There is something very definitely wrong in implying that the hypothetical performance of a method not used in over 95% of sales is representative of how all index annuities perform. There is also something wrong with plucking crediting methods rates out of the air and claiming they illustrate potential performance.

Flawed Assumptions

<u>#1 Participation Rates Never Change</u>

Almost every anti-index annuity study we've examined assumes that index annuity participation rates, caps, and yield spreads will remain constant over long periods of time. This is a fatal flaw. It does not take into account those changes in interest rates that occur in the real world or the effect of market volatility on the cost of providing the index participation. One cannot assume that today's rate would have existed in the past because the financial conditions of the past are often quite different. One cannot simply make-up an index rate, hold it constant, and then attempt to say it is both reasonable and representative, merely because it supports your predetermined conclusion. By no means does *every* study treat index annuity participation as a viewing of the movie *Groundhog Day* (where the world never changes), but too many fail to understand that index participation is driven by bond yields and option costs and that factors these change over time.

<u>#2 Stock Market Returns of 17.6% Are Normal</u>

One study said that many attempts to show index annuity comparisons are exercises in "data mining" and we agree. *Many*, but not all, employ gross "selection bias". There are different ways to enforce such a bias. One way is to make long-term predictions based on using low participation rates that do not represent the reality of long-term markets. Another is to select, intentionally, time periods that favor the outcome one wants to show. Both methods produce results that are neither accurate nor respectable.

Many performance comparisons pit index annuities against stock market investments over the '80s and '90s when the stock market returned averaged 17.6% – and ignore the preceding eight decades with their average return of 8.5%. If you get to pick the period of time, you can "find" almost any result you want.

#3 No People Are Involved

Over 95% of index annuity sales are of products that may change at least one element of their interest crediting methodology after the reset period. Two primary factors affecting subsequent index participation are bond yields and the price of call options. But it's important to note that the ultimate determining factor in setting index participation in future years is not either the interest rate environment or the cost of options. It is what the management of the issuing insurer decides to do. This human element introduces a random and unpredictable variable that cannot be quantified – which makes any attempt to project returns with confidence difficult, if not impossible.

Conclusion

Much of the analysis published on index annuities is based on hypothetical returns that are generated by using selected time periods and crediting criteria to produce a desired conclusion. If the analysis is produced for the annuity industry, the conclusion is generally positive; if it is directed towards the securities industry, the conclusion is usually negative. The reality is this: At least some index annuities have produced returns that have been truly competitive with certificates of deposit, fixed rate annuities, taxable bond funds, and, at times, even equities. How will index annuities perform in the future? We do not know, but the concept has proven to work in the past and any articles should reflect this.

Chapter 6 – Rider Revolution

Let's suppose you're fifty years old and plan to retire at 65. You're considering putting $100,000 into a mutual fund this year. What amount will you be able to withdraw each year from that fund, starting at retirement, and be *guaranteed* that the income will last as long as you live? Is that too tough a question? Here is another. What will that mutual fund be worth fifteen years from now?

When we priced this example, there were deferred annuities available that would provide a 50 year old buyer with the assurance of a lifetime income of at least $12000, starting at age 65, based on minimum contractual guarantees. This requires *annuitization* (election of an "annuity payout option"), which amounts to a *conversion* of the annuity cash value to an *income stream.* When you annuitize an annuity contract, the decision is generally irrevocable (meaning that you cannot "undo" the conversion); you trade control of (and access to) the annuity's cash value for the right to those income payments.

GLWB Comparison

Start With $100,000 @ age 50
Lifetime Guaranteed Income @ Age 65

	Income	**Principal**
Stock Market	**?**	**?**
Fixed Annuity Annuitized	**$12,000**	**$0**
Index Annuity GLWB	**$15,000**	**$100,000+**

There is another option. As we write this there are several index annuities where, if we paid our $100,000 premium at age 50, we could receive $15,000 a year or more for life at age 65 based on the annuity's *guaranteed lifetime withdrawal benefit (GLWB).* The GLWB removes uncertainty over the amount and length of the payments; it offers the same protection against living too long that annuitization does, but we also have access to the annuity's cash value. The GLWB is transforming the retirement income landscape.

Retirement Income Planning

The reason why purely investment thinking (and investment mathematics) won't supply answers to these retirement income questions is simple. ***Retirement income planning isn't really an investment problem; it's a risk management problem.*** The risk is that you won't have enough income in retirement (or that you will, for a while, but that you'll run out of money if you live long enough). If the annual income that you need in retirement exceeds the *income* from your investments (e.g.: bond coupon income, stock dividends), you'll have to tap *principal* for the difference. If your investments grow, each year, by at least that amount, you'll be fine. But if they don't, you could run out of money.

The GLWB Concept

The GLWB concept is simple. The annuity owner may choose to withdraw, each year, no more than a specified percentage of the value of the annuity and is guaranteed by the insurer to receive this payout for as long as he or she lives, even if the cash value of the annuity drops to zero. This is *not* "annuitization". When a deferred annuity is annuitized, its cash value is converted into an income stream. By contrast, an annuity with a GLWB remains a deferred annuity, even when its owner is taking withdrawals under the GLWB rider. That owner retains control of the contract value. He or she may stop the withdrawals at any time, and, whether taking GMWB withdrawals or not, has access to the contract values. (However, withdrawals of more than the specified maximum GLWB percentage will reduce the amount of the withdrawals guaranteed under the GLWB rider).

- *The later the start date, the higher the income.* Most GLWB's guarantee that the value upon which the withdrawals are based will increase by at least a minimum amount for each year the annuity owner delays the start of receiving guaranteed withdrawals.

• *The later the start date, the higher the income.* Most index annuity GLWB's increase the guaranteed percentage of annuity value that may be initially withdrawn as the annuity owner age increases.

• *Joint payouts usually reduce income.* The GLWB may often be set up to cover two lives providing an income up to the second death, but the percentage payout is usually reduced.

An example

At age 65, George invests $100,000 in an index annuity offering a GLWB. George may begin withdrawing, say, 5% beginning the following year (most index annuities require a one-year waiting period before withdrawals may begin), and this income is guaranteed to last as long as George lives - even if the account value goes to zero. But there's more. Almost every index annuity guarantees the income will increase by a minimum percentage for each year the onset of withdrawals is delayed. Suppose that this GLWB guarantees that the amount of the annual income will grow at a minimum of 7% a year, compounded. If George waits one year before commencing GLWB withdrawals, his guaranteed withdrawal will not be $5,000 – $100,000 times 5% – but $5,350 ($5,000, compounded at 7% for one year).

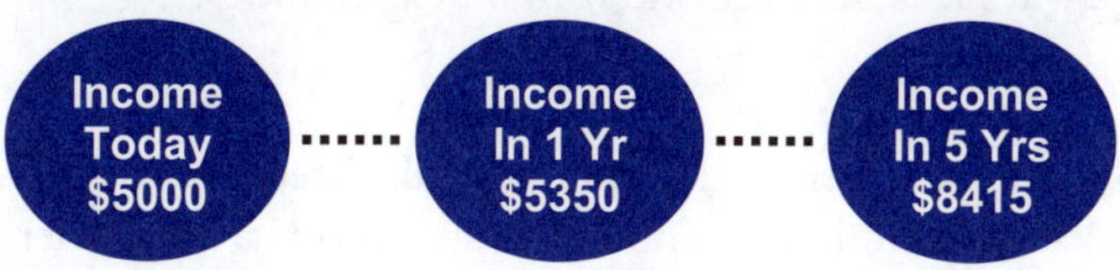

Suppose he waits 5 years to begin withdrawals? We might suppose that his income should be $7,013 ($5,000 x 1.07 x 1.07 x 1.07 x 1.07 x 1.07), but it could be even higher - because George is now is older.

In this hypothetical example, the annuity GLWB guarantees a 5% withdrawal rate if the contract owner is between age 65 and 69, and a 6% withdrawal rate if the contract owner is age 70 or older *at the time that GLWB withdrawals commence.* George is age 70 when he takes his first GLWB withdrawal and is therefore guaranteed a 6% withdrawal rate, (reflecting the fact that he's older and will probably get fewer annual withdrawals over his remaining lifetime). However, George's guaranteed withdrawal amount is not $6,000 ($100,000 times 6%), but $8,415! The minimum payout growth rate of 7% is calculated on this higher withdrawal rate ($6,000 x 1.07 x 1.07 x 1.07 x 1.07 x 1.07).

George put $100,000 in the annuity at age 65. He was guaranteed a lifetime income of at least $5,350 a year if he began withdrawals at age 66 (because this annuity required a waiting period of one year before GLWB withdrawals). By waiting to age 70 before commencing withdrawals, his annual guaranteed minimum income increased to $8,415. The choices were his. And he never had to annuitize.

As we write this, almost every index annuity GLWB increases the withdrawal percentage as certain age levels are reached, and every index annuity guarantees some type of minimum payout growth of the GLWB. Since all of this is done in a variety of ways we'll talk about the differences shortly.

What if the annuity owner wants to guarantee withdrawals for two people? Most index annuities will guarantee the payout for as long as either lives, but the payout percentage for two lives is almost always less than for one with index annuities.

Will the payout increase after the withdrawals begin? Possibly. Almost every index annuity will "step up" or increase the guaranteed payout if the annuity cash account value increases by more than the guaranteed payout growth percentage. There are also a few index annuities that promise to increase the payout each year, but they start you at a lower income payout.

What if the index annuity accumulated account value grows more than the 7% guaranteed payout growth each year? The guaranteed lifetime withdrawals would be higher.

What if the index annuity accumulated account value grows less than 7% a year? The annuity owner still receives at least the guaranteed withdrawal payout for life even if the annuity runs out of money.

What does the annuity owner get upon cashing in the annuity? The annuity *surrender* value (The cash value, less any applicable surrender charges).

Let's say the annuity owner put $100,000 into the annuity at age 65, took out $5,350 at age 66, and then cashed in the annuity at age 67. Assume that the contract earned zero percent interest. The cash received would be calculated as $100,000, plus zero interest, minus $5,350 - $94,650, less any surrender charges. What about the 7% guaranteed growth rate? It's not a factor. That guaranteed growth rate is a feature of the GLWB and applies *only* to GLWB withdrawal benefits. It has nothing to do with the cash or surrender value of the annuity contract itself.

Could the annuity owner (or the annuity owner's beneficiary) get back less than the original premium – or even zero – if he or she cashes in the annuity <u>after receiving guaranteed lifetime withdrawals</u>? Of course! That's why you buy the GLWB in the first place – to protect the income even if the principal declines to zero.

The GLWB guarantees an income for life – the same guarantee provided by a life-contingent immediate annuity or by annuitization (using a life-contingent payout option). The difference is that with an immediate annuity or annuitization of a deferred one, you typically lose control of the principal, because you have converted a capital asset into an income stream. However, even when you receive guaranteed withdrawals from a GLWB on a deferred annuity contract, that contract remains a deferred annuity. As the annuity is not "converted", the withdrawals can stopped or decreased, or the annuity cashed in at any time and the net cash value received. Could you get back less than you put in? Absolutely! If you're earning, say, 5% and withdrawing 6% the account balance is going down and can fall to zero – that's basic math. But with the GLWB you have complete control all of the time and you know what your annuity is worth at all times.

Is there a cost to a GLWB? Yes, there is either an implicit or specific cost for the benefit

Is the GLWB mandatory? Unless it is built-in to the annuity and offered without an explicit charge to the annuity owner the GLWB is usually offered as a *rider* to the contract. A rider is an optional feature the annuity buyer may choose to add or not. As an optional rider a fee is charged that is expressed as a percent of annuity value.

GLWB Parts

A decade ago a regulator remarked that index annuities are like snowflakes, in that no two are exactly alike; the same can be said about index annuity GLWBs. This section talks about the parts of GLWBs, the variations, and what they mean.

Controlled Asset Allocation

Every *variable* annuity we researched offering GLWBs placed limitations on how subaccount assets may be invested, either by requiring a certain percentage of the assets to be placed in bond funds or by limiting selection to specified bond-equity balanced subaccounts. *Index* annuities generally do not have limits.

Payout Step-Ups (Resets)

Almost every variable annuity or index annuity that offers a GLWB includes a "step-up" feature that allows an annuity owner to lock-in increases in principal value at predetermined intervals, which in turn increases the payout. The annuity owner may turn down the step-up if an increase in the rider fee would result.

Withdrawal Benefit Guaranteed Growth

As stated earlier almost every index annuity guarantees the payout will increase. Here's the way the GLWB growth is usually presented.

The age 65 annuity buyer puts in $100,000. The benefit base/income account/income base grows at 7% a year. These are the values and the payout you would receive:

Contract Year	GLWB Base	GLWB %	Guaranteed Withdrawal
0	$100,000	NA	
1	$107,000	5%	$5,350
2	$114,490	5%	$5,725
3	$122,504	5%	$6,125
4	$131,080	5%	$6,554
5	$140,255	6%	$8,415

Most annuity marketing materials apply the guaranteed growth rate to the original premium to determine the GLWB "benefit base" and then multiply that result by the GLWB percentage to determine the amount of the guaranteed withdrawal ($100,000 x 1.07). It is also possible to multiply the appropriate GLWB percentage (for the year in which withdrawals begin) to the original premium and compound that result by the number of years that elapsed before withdrawals ($5,000 x 1.07). Regardless of whether we compound the base or compound the actual payout, we wind up in the same spot. The problem we've run into – many times – is that many annuity owners believe that the benefit base (also known as "income base" or "income account") is the annuity's ***cash value*** (that they are able to take as a lump sum). ***It's not!*** And no matter how clearly, or often, the marketing material explains that the "benefit base" *cannot be taken in a lump sum*, at least some buyers don't get it. They see the increasing benefit base and confuse it with the annuity's *cash value.* Worse, they look at the guaranteed growth rate of that benefit base (in this example, 7%) and see it as a guaranteed return on their "principal. ***It's not!***

We suggest that this confusion could be avoided by focusing directly on the guaranteed increases in the *withdrawal amount* and not on the guaranteed increases in the *"benefit base"* (which is, after all, only a "shadow account", from which the guaranteed minimum withdrawal amount is calculated), and that the guaranteed growth could be shown as illustrated on the next page:

Contract Year	Guranteed Withdrawal
0	
1	$5,350
2	$5,725
3	$6,125
4	$6,554
5	$8,415

This would place the buyers' focus on the benefit that they will actually get.

The benefit growth is usually expressed as a compounded rate that will continue until withdrawals commence or until the end of a specified period (e.g.: 10 years). The lowest annual guaranteed growth we've seen is 4% a year, but several carriers offer 7% to 8% guaranteed benefit growth.

The guaranteed benefit growth aspect of GLWBs has been the subject of a lot of marketing creativity and can be very confusing. Many of the GLWBs with high percentage annual growth will limit the initial guarantee to 10 years; others may use simple (instead of compound) interest. Still others offer a high initial benefit bonus, and a few will increase the payout based on how many years the annuity has been owned. No one method is better or worse than another. The value of any method to the buyer depends upon what that buyer intends to do with the annuity and we'll discuss this a little later.

Fees

A few index annuities have embedded fees because the GLWB is an integral part of the annuity. This does not mean the benefit is free. Guarantees cost money and an annuity with a GLWB should have a lower renewal rate than one without the benefit. In other words, if two products are identical, except that one offers an embedded GLWB and the other doesn't, the one with the GLWB will have lower caps or a lower participation rate at renewal time.

Most index annuities charge explicit fees, which have ranged from 0.10% to 1.5%. Though GLWB fees in variable annuities are normally higher for joint payouts (for two lifetimes) than for single life payouts, this is not the case with GLWB fees in index annuities, because index annuity GLWBs typically reduce the guaranteed payout percentage for joint payouts.

Current fees are in the 0.40% to 0.75% range, but may be increased if the annuity owner exercises a "step up" option or renews a benefit growth guarantee. For example, an annuity offers a GLWB for a fee of 0.60%, which is guaranteed for the life of the contract, and guarantees that the GLWB payout will increase at 7% per year for 10 years (or that the "benefit base" will do so, which produces the same result). At the end of 10 years, the annuity owner will have the option to renew the growth rate guarantee for an additional 10 years, but at whatever rider fee is then in effect (not to exceed the maximum rider fee specified in the contract). The owner can elect not to renew the growth rate guarantee and continue to pay the 0.60% rider fee, but there will be no further guaranteed growth of the GLWB amount.

Impact Of The GLWB Rider Fee On Annuity Cash Value

Generally speaking, the "principal" (premium contributions and already-credited interest) in a fixed annuity (either fixed-rate or indexed) is guaranteed; it cannot be lost or reduced, except by surrender charges. But with many indexed annuities, there's an exception to that rule.

You could lose principal if you earn zero index-linked interest in a year. Zero interest occurs whenever the index growth calculation is negative and this happens with regularity. *A very few* index annuity contracts guarantee that the GLWB rider charge will never be more than interest credited; most index annuities do not offer this assurance. this means that, with *most* carriers, annuity owners, after being hit by account statements showing that they failed to earn *any* interest in the previous year, will also get hit by seeing their account balance *decline* by the GLWB rider fee (which might be hundreds, or even thousands, of dollars).

Payout Percentage

Generally, the percentage payout guaranteed under a GLWB is 4%, if withdrawals are begun when you're in your fifties; 5%, in your sixties; 6%, in your seventies; and 7%, in your eighties, However, some carriers increase the percentage payout by 0.1% each year; others bump up 0.5% all at once at age 55, 65 or 75. A few increase the percentage based on how long you've owned the contract as well as age. Almost all offer a joint payout at 0.5% to 1.0% less than a single payout. A few carriers offer an annually increasing payout option, where the payout increases by 2% to 3% a year, but the initial payout is generally 1% less than the initial payout in the flat (not increasing) payout option.

<u>Enhanced Living Benefits</u>

A few carriers will significantly increase the payout if the annuity owner is confined to a nursing home or is unable to perform two of the Activities of Daily Living – a 6% payout might increase to 8% or 9%. We expect to see more of this type of enhancement in other annuities.

<u>Step-Ups</u>

Many GLWBs provide that if the annuity cash value rises above the "benefit base" (in other words, the credited interest has exceeded the guaranteed GLWB growth rate), the "benefit base" can be "stepped up" to equal the cash value (or, seen another way, the GLWB income amount will be increased to the level that would be produced by multiplying the GLWB payout percentage by the cash value). How likely is it that this "step up" option will ever become available? Well, it *can* happen. If the GLWB growth rate is 7.2% for 10 years, the annuity would need to earn at least 7.2% per year, *after deductions for all annual fees (GLWB fee, and any other fees)*. Some index annuities have, in the past, earned that much in certain years. But few have produced an *average* return that high over more than a few years, so the "step up" option, while *potentially* valuable, may be less likely than many brochures advertising it would suggest.

Other Elements

Minimum/Maximum Age

Guaranteed withdrawals may typically commence as early as age 50 and as late as age 90 (but, as discussed in Chapter 8, there may come a point where one may be too old to benefit from a lifetime guarantee).

Starting and Stopping Payouts

Annuity owners may start and stop the withdrawals as needed, but the only economic incentive to forego withdrawals would be to preserve the annuity's *cash value* (for example, where the annuity owner is considering cashing in the annuity).

When must you buy the GLWB?

Most index annuity carriers require you to purchase the GLWB when you buy the annuity; some let you add it on later.

Can I stop the GLWB?

Unless the GLWB is built into the index annuity (no separate fee), most index annuities will let you drop the benefit (and stop paying the rider fee) at any time, but a few will require you to stick with the GLWB for five years before you can drop it.

What if I take out too much?

All carriers reduce the protected account value on a proportional basis for excess withdrawals. For example if the value is $100,000 and your maximum guaranteed withdrawal is $5,000 but you take out $10,000. The next year you would be guaranteed $4,750 (5% of $100,000 minus the extra $5,000 withdrawn or $95,000 x 5%).

> A calculating actuary from Glider
> tried to create a new life income rider
> Of "joint life" he'd heard
> But he added a third
> Which made the rider a little bit wider

The Behavioral Attraction Of GLWBs

Since the days of the Roman Empire, annuities have offered a way to provide a certain income that cannot be outlived. Unless the retiree has a need to provide a bequest, it has been argued by many classical economists that a retiree should annuitize all of his or her investment assets upon retirement. But this does not happen. One comprehensive study done on annuitization of existing annuities found that less than 1% of deferred annuities are ever annuitized (according to Linda Koco, Retirement income studies point up opportunities for insurers, brokers, *National Underwriter*, 2002, 106; 27:12). Sales of *life contingent* immediate (income) annuities have been essentially flat for the last 15 years. Indeed, our review of life contingent immediate annuities revealed that sales have been flat over the last fifteen years – even though the over age 65 population increased 11% during that period. Why don't more people annuitize?

<u>Annuicide</u>

You might swap a million dollars for a very respectable lifelong annual income of, say, $80,000, but in doing so, you are transformed from a millionaire into a *pensionaire* - from being an independent financial player into a person on an allowance.

annuitization has the smell of death

This is not to say that life income annuities are bad; far from it. Annuitization is often the most rational choice for all or a substantial portion of the retiree's assets. Annuitization provides the solution to the problem of running out of money – an outcome feared by many retirees. However, the annuitization solution offered by currently available contracts creates *annuicide* concerns – loss of control of the asset and the loss of the asset itself – which is why annuitization is so seldom elected.

Another problem with the "annuitization solution" is that there is a "smell of death" about it. When you annuitize, you get a guaranteed income for life, but that guarantee places a spotlight on your own mortality. You are no longer hoping to build assets to use in the future, but instead, have admitted that you will die in the future.

Essentially, annuitization of a deferred annuity – or the purchase of an immediate annuity – means a loss of hope of building for the future. By contrast, Guaranteed Lifetime Withdrawal Benefits provide guarantees of income for life, but can also preserve hope. With GLWBs, your account balance may fall to zero when (or before) your blood pressure does, but it may not. Indeed, it may even grow, permitting you to both "eat your retirement cake and have it, too" - to pass on to your heirs.

GLWB History

In 2002 Hartford Life introduced the first variable annuity with a *guaranteed minimum withdrawal benefit (GMWB).* The GMWB allowed investors to withdraw 7% or 10% a year from their variable annuity with the assurance that they would receive at least their original principal through these withdrawals, even if the account value declined to zero. The GMWB guarantees only a return of the original premium (or, in some cases, the original premium plus a "bonus" or specified minimum interest earnings). *It does not guarantee an income for life.* As fixed annuities (including indexed annuities) guarantee both a return of principal and a minimum interest rate, a GMWB rider offers no benefits to buyers of these contracts (which, sensibly, do not offer it).

In 2003 the first variable annuity with a *guaranteed lifetime withdrawal benefit* (GLWB) was introduced. This rider became very popular, and our research indicates that most VA sales in recent years have been in products offering some type of guaranteed living benefit. The value proposition of a G**L**WB (also called a *lifetime benefit rider* and other names) is that the annuity owner will receive a steady stream of equal withdrawals for as long as he or she lives, regardless of the account value. This arrangement has greater attraction for the consumer than a simple G**M**WB because with a lifetime payout there is a higher perceived potential that the ultimate return will be greater than zero. Because the potential payout period of a GLWB may be much longer, the payout percentage on a GLWB is typically less than that of a GMWB. Unlike a GMWB, a GLWB could be appropriate on a fixed annuity, providing the guaranteed payout percentage exceeds the minimum interest rate guarantee

The first index annuity carrier to offer a guaranteed living withdrawal benefit was American National Insurance Company in June 2006, quickly followed by the AmerUs Group/American Investors (now Aviva). By the end of 2008, almost all of the major index annuity carriers were offering GLWBs, with many more carriers preparing to launch. The financial crash that began in 2008 caused concern among insurers that the lifetime nature of these guaranteed benefits would lead to unanticipated future costs and some insurers ceased offering the benefit. However, by late 2009 most of those that had withdrawn returned to the GLWB arena.

Guaranteed withdrawal benefits have changed the focus of the annuity marketplace. No longer is the emphasis solely upon growth (as has been the case for decades); now, the focus is upon *safety of income,* with the *possibility* that *principal* will be preserved.

Variable and Fixed Index Annuity GLWBs

The impact of guaranteed withdrawal benefits is greater in the variable world than it is in the world of fixed annuities. Although both preserve the hope of growth, the variable annuity's value proposition has changed. No longer is a variable annuity simply a "mutual fund in a tax-deferred wrapper"; it's now an investment alternative with income guarantees the mutual funds cannot match (although a few mutual fund companies have figured out a way to add to lifetime income guarantees to their funds).

The availability of variable annuities with guaranteed lifetime withdrawal benefits has also altered the fixed annuity market. If Joe Consumer wants an accumulation vehicle with no market risk, then the availability of income guarantees in a variable annuity should have little impact on his decision as to what kind of annuity to buy. However, if what Joe is looking for is greater certainty of current or future income, then a VA with a GLWB may offer the same certainty with the possibility of greater potential growth.

Whether a VA with a GLWB or a fixed annuity (with or without a GLWB) is "better" depends upon which is more important:
(a) Greater growth of future income or
(b) "No market risk" cash availability

Does A VA With A GLWB Make Fixed Annuities Obsolete?

No, because they're different tools, designed to do different jobs; comparing them is like comparing apples with oranges.

We have heard people say that a variable annuity with a GLWB makes index annuities and fixed rate annuities obsolete because of the GLWB guarantees. They argue that because a GLWB provides guaranteed payouts (and often guarantees some growth of this payout), a VA with a GLWB is necessarily better than an index annuity (because of that potential for higher returns). This argument reflects confusion over how the GLWB actually works.

With a fixed annuity, your principal is protected from loss, and if you decide to take your money and leave, you know pretty much what leaving early will cost. A variable annuity, even with a GLWB, protects only the income and not the principal; the principal is still fully exposed to market risk.

A GLWB does not protect principal

If you put $100,000 into a fixed rate or index annuity and cash it in a year from now, you will get back your original principal, plus minimum guaranteed interest and any additional interest credited to the policy, less any surrender charges. Even if the annuity has a *market value adjustment* (MVA), annuity owners still know in the worst case scenario they can get back (say, $88,000).

FIA GLWB
Principal + Interest – Surrender Charge = Cash Value

VA GLWB
Principal ± Market Gain(Loss) – Surrender Charge = Cash Value

If you put $100,000 into a variable annuity with a GLWB and cash it in, you will get back the market value of the annuity less surrender charges. In the worst case scenario, you'll get back nothing.

There is no GLWB cash value. The cash value of the variable annuity will be higher or lower than the fixed annuity, reflecting the market risk and potential gain inherent in investments. What this means is this: If a consumer's primary goal is to protect her principal from market risk, a variable annuity - with or without a GLWB – is the wrong choice, because it will not give that protection.

Guaranteed living benefits reduce the risk of owning a variable annuity, but they do not turn it into a fixed annuity because principal – and income growth – is still subject to market risk.

Rational Economic Behavior

From a purely rational economic view, the utility of using a GLWB with a fixed annuity, whether stated rate or indexed rate, is not always apparent. Using the maximum GLWB withdrawal percentages currently offered on any fixed annuity at any age, the annuity remains in force past age 90, even if only a 3% average return is earned, making the cash last at least a third longer than expected life expectancy at any issue age (based on the 2002 U.S. Life Tables). If a 4% return is earned, the maximum withdrawal payouts last into the second hundred years of living *for every annuity owner*, regardless of when the payouts start.

Essentially a GLWB on a fixed stated rate or indexed rate annuity is an insurance policy that probably will not be used. However...

Unless bond rates continue to fall and index-link option prices increase forever, the buyer of an index annuity should be able to maintain comparable lifetime withdrawal levels without needing a GLWB rider. In essence, a GLWB on an index annuity is an insurance policy that probably will not be used. However, the reason we buy insurance is to provide protection to cover unlikely losses.

How long an individual will live is unknowable, and average life expectancy continues to increase. According to a July 2006 study by the Society of Actuaries, a man turning age 65 in 2005 had a 23%

chance of making it to age 90 while a woman had a 37% chance, and the odds of at least one of them hitting age 90 was 52%. Advances in medicine and healthier life choices continue to extend longevity. A 55 year old in 1971 might have had a 10% chance of living to age 95, but today a 55 year old might have a 22% probability of making it. Indeed, average life expectancy has been improving for males between ages 55 and 80 at a rate of 1% a year.

All of this means that using an retirement planning end point of age 95 or even 100 may be too short for a significant portion of those close to retirement today, and self-insuring retirement income may mean either depriving oneself of income today (by taking overly cautious payouts), or taking more aggressive payouts and increasing the chance of running out of money. Transferring longevity risk to a carrier via a GLWB guards against the nuisance of actually benefiting from a jogging, low-fat, chocolate-denying lifestyle and making it pass the century mark.

GLWBs Have Strong Emotional Appeal

The financial problem associated with an immediate annuity is that the annuity buyer gives up an asset in exchange for an income. The emotional problem is that he or she also gives up all hope of future gains. Annuitants (those who made that exchange, by buying an immediate annuity) may regret their decision. They know their income is protected but they may regret the fact they will never again be a millionaire on paper. Moreover, those who are considering purchase of an immediate annuity *anticipate* that scenario and will often elect not to purchase the annuity because they're not willing to make that trade-off.

The financial problem associated with spending down assets to create retirement income is that doing so might result in spending those assets down to zero. The assets may leave this world before the retiree does. The thought of that prospect can leave one with a fear of future poverty, and most people have an aversion to dipping into capital that can make them income poor, but asset rich. GLWBs may overcome both sides of the problem because they banish the fear of future poverty while offering the hope of future growth.

Eliminate Regret

The buyer of an immediate annuity transfers the uncertainty of maintaining an income stream to an insurance company by buying an annuity; the cost of that transfer is that the buyer "loses" control of the money used to buy it. Some consumers may feel regret and a loss of hope. An annuity with a GLWB preserves control of the asset while guaranteeing an income stream, thus avoiding regret aversion.

Not Understanding The Risk of Living

The main consumer risk that has generated so much interest in GLWBs is *longevity risk*. We know we will die but we cannot control when (although suicide is arguably a way to do that). At retirement, we are expected to change our lifetime habit of *saving for tomorrow* into *spending for today*, which puts us in unfamiliar territory. And we may experience doubt as to the reality of this risk by recalling that Aunt Sal lived to be 103 while Uncle Bob died at 66, which makes believing in rules of thumb (like "average life expectancy") difficult. There are other money risks in retirement: loss of purchasing power due to inflation, unexpected illness, unforeseen liquidity needs, allocating assets efficiently, but these risks are often less feared because we have at least the illusion that we can exercise some control to lower their impact on us.

Annuitization is one sure way to eliminate longevity risk, but it requires that we cede control of the annuitized asset (which means that we cannot use that asset to deal with the other money risks). From a behavioral point of view, there are a few ways to increase the use of life income annuities. One way would be to give the owner of an immediate annuity (or annuitized deferred annuity) the right to "commute" (to exchange the remaining income payments for a lump sum) or to make withdrawals in excess of the regular annuity payments, in exchange for a reduction in the amount of such payments (or, perhaps, a reduction in the annuity payout period). A few – a *very* few – annuities offer such options. Another might be to emphasize that the decision to annuitize is not an "all or nothing" proposition. One need not annuitize *all* of his or her assets. One option that is getting a lot of press lately is to make an immediate annuity a *mandatory* and nonconvertible part of all employer-sponsored retirement plans.

To be very clear on this, we are not against annuitizing deferred annuities or buying income (immediate) annuities. Our studies show, time and again, that an immediate annuity is, in many planning scenarios, the most rational solution to the problem of providing *adequate* retirement income on a *fully guaranteed* basis, but we accept the reality that consumers do not make completely rational decisions.

GLWBs' Emotional Appeals

- Greed – owners of annuities with GLWBs may feel that they can still make a killing someday, because they still have control of their capital.
- Loss Aversion – The GLWB income is a certain income that cannot be lost, so long as one lives.
- A Reward for Self-Sacrifice – the annuity owner does not get penalized by running out of money for living longer due to the personal sacrifices made to maintain a healthier lifestyle

GLWB's Relieve

- Anxiety – remove uncertainty of future income
- Mistrust – annuity owner, and not the insurance company, retains control of asset

GLWBs May Help Women Plan For Retirement

Our analysis of 150 studies finds that men are generally comfortable taking greater financial risks than women. In addition, as a man's belief in his financial capability grows the more risk, he takes. However, even when women increased their financial capability and understanding, studies show that they do not take on more risk.

What this says is this: Guys are more inclined than gals to pick investments with higher potential returns, even when the risk goes up, and when you educate men about investments and the realities of risk and return, they choose investments with even greater risk/return possibilities. However, even when women are educated about risk and return, they still do not become more risk oriented.

Educating women about risk/returns does not make women strive for higher yields riskier yields, but insuring against the risk does.

A problem often mentioned in retirement planning articles is that because women are more conservative when investing for retirement, they do not earn the returns that men do; thus, they have less money to draw on during retirement. A solution proffered by many, including the SEC, is that educating women about investments will encourage them to select the higher risk/return portfolio needed. However, the studies we examined say otherwise:, that educating women about risk/return does not cause them to take on more risk.

A Case For GLWBs

A recent study* asked both men and women respondents if they would be more likely to put $20,000 into a stock mutual fund if, for an annual fee of $200, the mutual fund guaranteed no losses and a minimum return. The study then educated the respondents on the possible risks and returns of the mutual fund.

After this education about how the mutual fund worked, men were significantly more likely to buy the mutual fund without the insurance. However, after the same education, the women were no more likely to buy the mutual fund without the insurance than they were before, but *were much more likely to buy the fund and pay the $200 "insurance fee."*

The implication is that educating women about the investment world will not turn them into risk oriented investors, but educating women on how they can "buy insurance" against losses may make them a lot more likely to look beyond conventional insured

*Xin He, Inman, Mittal. 2008. Gender jeopardy in financial risk taking. *Journal of Marketing Research. 45:* 414–424

instruments (such as CDs) to satisfy retirement needs. If this is true, women should be more attracted to the index annuity message than men, and more attracted than men to the guarantees of GLWBs and less influenced by cost of the "risk insurance."

This suggests a need for different stories in the product explanation process. The index annuity or GLWB story, given to a man, should focus on the potential return, while the story, given to a woman, should tell how the protection allows her to try for higher potential returns without greater risk of loss.

GLWB Risks To Insurers

We probably wouldn't be writing about insurer risk if it weren't for the severe problems with guaranteed benefit riders experienced by issuers of variable annuities in recent years. Most VA issuers were forced to reduce the guarantees of these benefit riders, raise the fees they charged for them, or both. Some actually stopped issuing these riders (although many of those companies have resumed offering them).

An insurance company's exposure to loss is much less when offering GLWBs on *index* annuities, chiefly because index annuities present less downside volatility. For example:

Both a variable and index annuity might provide a $5,000 annual lifetime withdrawal for a $100,000 premium for an age 65 annuity buyer, but what happens if the stock market falls 50% over the next year? The index annuity account still has $100,000 and a withdrawal of $5,000 represents 5% of that contract value. The variable annuity account is now worth $50,000 and that same $5,000 withdrawal represents 10% of that contract's value. Ten annual withdrawals of $5,000 each would, thus, put the insurance company that issued the variable annuity in the position of having to use *its own* money for the next withdrawal (assuming no change in the underlying index). If the index were to decline further, that result could occur earlier.

However, even if the index continues to decline forever, the owner of the *index* annuity will spend 20 years burning through his or her own money. Indeed, because minimum interest is guaranteed, he or she might be age 90 or older before the insurance company needs to dig into its own pocket for that $5,000 withdrawal.

And there's another element at play here. If the variable annuity owner is collecting, essentially, a 10% guaranteed payout, it is unlikely that another insurer will offer a similar incentive to that annuity owner to switch contracts (via a "Section 1035 exchange), so that annuity will stay on the books of the variable annuity carrier and remain a long-term obligation. Bottom Line: The worse the exposure for the insurer, the more likely it is that guaranteed payments will remain a liability.

Guaranteed living benefits also represent an "*adverse selection*" *problem* for the issuing insurer. "Adverse selection" (or "anti-selection") refers to the tendency of those who are more likely to make claims under insurance coverage to elect such coverage, compared to those who are less likely (lower risk). If an insurer is guaranteeing a $5,000 annual payout to the owner of a deferred annuity, it makes more sense for that person to begin receiving payments when the contract value is as low as possible (rather than when the contract is performing well) because he or she won't find a better rate of return anywhere else. And if annuity owners know that the insurer is on the hook for at least $5,000 per year, it makes sense for them to invest in those investment alternatives (in the annuity contract) with the highest risk/reward potential – because their payout can only go up. This is precisely why all variable annuity issuers restrict the investment selections available to policy owner who have purchased a guaranteed living benefit rider.

An index annuity avoids almost all of the market related anti-selection problems because the account cannot lose value due to market forces. However, issuers of both variable and index annuities that offer GLWBs face another adverse selection problem. What if the people who buy their annuities live significantly longer than actuarial expectations (so that the insurers will pay out more income to those individuals than they had anticipated)? Insurance actuaries manage that risk in various ways, including imposing restrictions and limitations on the income guarantees.

Hedging

All living benefit guarantees need to cope with the same concern – that, in delivering income payments under a guaranteed living benefit option, the insurer will spend more of *its own money* than expected.

Withdrawals under a GLWB reduce the account balance, so that in delivering a payment to the owner of an annuity with a positive account balance, the insurer is really using the policy owner's money. It's only when that account balance has fallen to zero that the insurer, in making annual GLWB payments, is using its own funds.

In the GLWB world, variable annuities guard against anti-selection by using investment diversification restrictions and sometimes limiting additional premium deposits; both index and variable annuities may prohibit the annuity owner from canceling the benefit soon after issue (or, in some contracts, at all), and may make benefit selection mandatory.

How does the insurer handle these risks? One way is reinsurance, but when it is available (and sometimes it is not), it's often expensive; another is buying *put options* to hedge against downturns – which may be expensive. A third way is to "grunt it out and hope" – essentially retaining the risk. Finally, there's *dynamic hedging* – a sophisticated bundle of techniques that insurers may use to offset the risk represented by guaranteed living benefit income guarantees.

GLWB Comparison

We compared the performance of some index annuity GLWB designs and used certain assumptions. We placed $100,000 in each annuity using issue ages 50 and 65. We then calculated the income benefit account value (the "benefit base") based on the product guarantees, and multiplied the values by the respective payout factors at ages 65, 70, 75 and 80 to produce the initial annual lifetime payout at those ages. We did the same thing assuming the annuities grew 6% per year, less the cost of a GLWB rider costing 0.4%, so the net effective annual growth was 5.6%. The result is a list of the initial lifetime payouts that would be received by different GLWB growth income factors if the cash value grew at only the guaranteed rate (Table 1) or at 5.6% per year (Table 2).

There is a little fudging. Although many annuities require a one year waiting period, we assumed the 65 year old purchasers could begin taking an annual income immediately. We also assumed the following payout percentages: Age 65 – 5.5%, Age 70 – 6.0%, Age 75 – 6.5%, Age 80 – 7.0%, 75. The 25% bonus rider calculation assumes the payout percentage remains 5% regardless of the age at first withdrawal. A final assumption is that all growth is compounded, with the exception of the second example that specifically says "simple" interest income acct growth.

Buy At Age 65

If you put $100,000 in at age 65, what initial lifetime payout would you receive at age 65, 70, 75 or 80? The first two charts show single life payouts based on buying the annuity at age 65 at both guaranteed growth (Table 1) and 6% (Table 2) account value growth rates. Although some of the riders stop guaranteed income growth after ten years, we assumed that growth continues until the first withdrawal.

Table 1 Initial Payout Assuming Annuity Purchase Age 65

Guaranteed Results: 100,000 Deposit @ Age 65	**65**	**70**	**75**	**80**
25% income acct bonus, then 5%/yr	6,250	7,977	10,181	12,993
10%/yr ***simple interest*** income acct growth	5,500	9,000	13,000	17,500
8%/yr income acct growth	5,500	8,816	14,033	22,205
7%/yr income acct growth	5,500	8,415	12,786	19,313
1% payout growth each 5 yr deferral	6,000	7,000	8,000	8,000

Which GLWB is "best" depends upon how it is used. In Table 1 the rider with the large up front income factor (the rider crediting an initial 25% bonus) has the highest payout if withdrawals begin quickly, but the 5% payout factor makes it less attractive at older ages.

A $100,000 deposit at age 65 to an index annuity that earned only the minimum return of 2% for 5 years – a possibility in a bad economic patch – would have an accumulated value of $110,408. Yet a GLWB rider *on that same annuity* could guarantee a lifetime income of $8,000 to $9,000 a year! This represents a payout percentage of over 8% of the *account balance* and *that's a "worst case" scenario.*

Table 2 assumes the annuity accumulated value growing at 6% a year, but deducts an annual GLWB rider fee of 0.4% meaning the account is growing at 5.6%.

Table 2 Initial Payout Assuming Annuity Purchase Age 65

6% (5.6% after rider fee) Growth Results: $100,000 Deposit @ Age 65	**65**	**70**	**75**	**80**
25% income acct bonus, then 5%/yr	6,250	7,977	10,181	12,993
10%/yr simple interest income acct growth	5,500	9,000	13,000	17,500
8%/yr income acct growth	5,500	8,816	14,033	22,205
7%/yr income acct growth	5,500	8,415	12,786	19,313
1% payout growth each 5 yr deferral	6,000	9,192	13,795	18,115

In Table 2 (which assumes a 5.6% net growth rate), the only payout method providing a higher value than it would have produced at the GLWB guaranteed growth rate (Table 1) is the payout based method (1% payout growth each 5 yr deferral), which uses the annuity accumulated account value. In all the other methods, the payout under the GLWB growth guarantee rate is higher (which is why the numbers in Table 2, for all other methods, are those from Table 1). Unless one assumes index annuities will produce significantly higher returns than they have produced historically, the payouts generated solely by the income factor growth guarantees may be what a 65 year old can expect from a GLWB.

Buy At Age 50

If you put $100,000 in at age 50 what initial lifetime payout would you receive at age 65, 70, 75 or 80? Table 3 shows the single life payouts based on buying the annuity at age 50 at guaranteed growth. Since the accumulation timeframe before initial withdrawal has increased to 15 though 30 years I have shown the effects of the income account factor growth stopping after 10 years and 20 years for the 7%, 8%, and 10% factors.

Table 3 Initial Payout Assuming Annuity Purchase Age 50

Guaranteed Results: $100,000 @ Age 50	**65**	**70**	**75**	**80**
25% income acct bonus, then 5%/yr (20yr)	12,993	16,583	16,583	16,583
10%/yr simple interest income acct (20yr)	13,750	18,000	19,500	21,000
10%/yr simple interest income (10yr)	11,000	12,000	13,000	14,000
8%/yr income acct growth (20yr)	17,447	27,966	30,296	32,627
8%/yr income acct growth (10yr)	11,874	12,953	14,033	15,112
7%/yr income acct growth (20yr)	15,175	23,218	25,153	27,088
7%/yr income acct growth (10yr)	10,819	11,803	12,786	13,770
1% payout growth each 5 yr deferral	10,767	13,374	14,765	16,302

Consider two 50 year olds that buy income riders that each guarantee 8% growth, but one stops growth in ten years and the other in twenty. At age 70, one rider pays $27,966 while the other pays $12,953 a year!. What this means is the annuity owner needs to make some assumptions on when the payout will be used to pick the rider best suited for them.

Table 4 again assumes the annuity accumulated value grows at 6% a year, and deducts an annual GLWB rider fee of 0.4% meaning the account is growing at 5.6%.

Table 4 Initial Payout Assuming Annuity Purchase Age 50

6% (5.6% after fee) Growth Results: $100,000 @ Age 50	**65**	**70**	**75**	**80**
25% income acct bonus, then 5%/yr (20yr)	12,993	16,583	16,583	16,583
10%/yr simple interest income acct (20yr)	13,750	18,000	19,500	21,000
10%/yr simple interest income (10yr)	12,000	12,000	13,000	14,000
8%/yr income acct growth (20yr)	17,447	27,966	30,296	32,627
8%/yr income acct growth (10yr)	11,874	12,953	14,033	15,112
7%/yr income acct growth (20yr)	15,175	23,218	25,153	27,088
7%/yr income acct growth (10yr)	10,819	11,803	12,786	13,770
1% payout growth each 5 yr deferral	18,115	26,762	35,143	46,149

The big winners here are riders that increase the payout based both on the age when the first withdrawal happens and the amount of time the policy remains in force. By age 75 – with the exceptions of the rider that guarantees 8% account growth for twenty years and the payout growth rider – you would have been better off not buying the rider at all, earning the full 6% on your accumulated value, and then buying an annuity with a GLWB rider when, and if, you needed it because the accumulated value by age 75 would have grown to $429,187 at 6%, but a lower $390,479 assuming 5.6% . This highlights the point of GLWB riders in general. If the annuity performs well you did not need the rider.

Other Comparisons

Payout Percentage

Although starting withdrawals at age 60 often means a payout of 5%, your percentage payout at age 67 might be 5%, 5.5% or 5.7%. This means you cannot simply go with the highest growth factor or highest percentage payout: you need to compare the dollar amount of the payout for each alternative.

Some carriers increase the payout based on both age and time spent in contract. This rewards persistency, and has been used as an alternative to an income growth account factor. Our analysis shows that these persistency payouts do quite well if the annuity earns 5% or better, and often beat the growth account methods; however, if returns are close to the annuity's minimum guarantee, the persistency payouts suffer, because they are based on the accumulated value.

Increasing Income Factors

A drawback with typical GLWBs is that the first payout income check the annuity owner receives will probably be for the same amount as the final one. Although most index annuity GLWBs allow for the payout value to be raised if the account value increases after payouts begin, our research indicates it is unlikely (or at least unlikely with any kind of consistency). While it is true that some annuities will guarantee to increase payout amounts by 2% or 3% a year, the initial payout for such contracts begins at 1% less than their level payout choice.

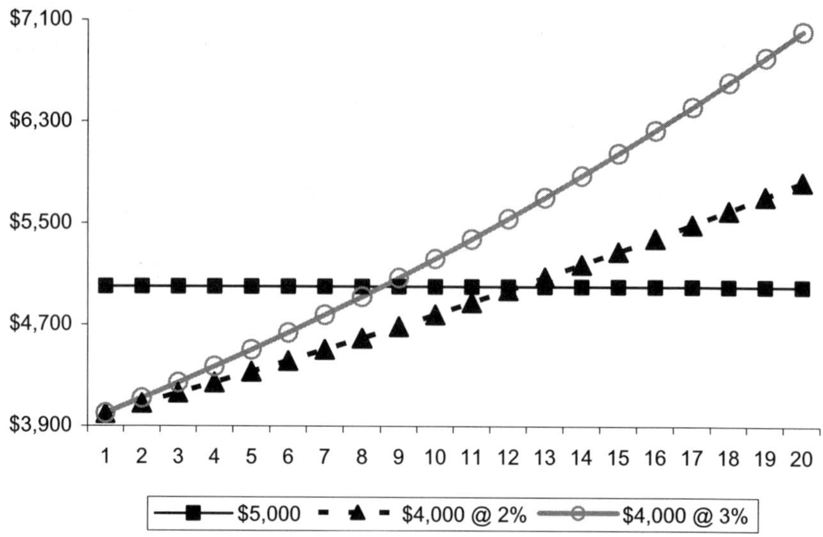

What this chart shows is the difference in income between choosing an annual payout of $5,000 – that remains at $5,000, versus accepting $4,000 initially and that the $4,000 increases at a guaranteed rate of 2% a year or 3% a year. The crossover point hits after 9 years at 3% growth and 13 years at 2% growth. After this point the growth payouts have surpassed the $5,000 flat payout. After 20 years the 3% growth option has resulted in a payout of $7,014 and the 2% option is paying $5,827. This may mean unless the annuity owner needs the full payout today, or can find a more profitable use for the extra 1% gleaned from the level payout, the increasing payout annuities may prove to be a better choice if the guaranteed growth rate is attractive and the annity owner lives long enough to enjoy the higher income.

Long Term Care Payouts

A couple of index carriers increase payouts if the annuity owner is confined to a nursing home or needs nursing home style care. We anticipate more developments in this area in the future.

GLWB Perception & Reality

"I am 69 years old. I recently lost $150,000 in the stock market, and I have about $150,000 dollars left to invest in something safe. I have been talking to a representative about XYZ annuities. They guarantee that the account value will always grow at 7% every year. This sounds too good to be true. Is it?"

This was the text of a real email and the response was "Yes, it is too good to be true" and tried to explain what she had really been presented.

GLWBs solve one of the main retirement concerns – outliving your money – and unlike annuitization, does not require the annuity owner to surrender control of the asset. This does not mean that the annuity value will not decrease over time – it probably will and may even go to zero, which is why you buy the benefit in the first place. But the annuity owner retains control at all times and may increase, decrease, or even stop the income and take whatever is remaining in the annuity account. The problem for agents selling annuities with GLWBs is to ensure that the annuity buyer has a clear understanding of how the GLWB really works.

The Income Growth Factor Is Not A Yield

Alice buys an annuity for $100,000 at age 60. Let's say that her actual cash value account value ten years later, at age 70, is $153,817. Most index annuity GLWBs would promise a lifetime payout of 6% at age 70, which would guarantee Alice $9,229 every year for as long as she lives, protecting her from outliving her *money and* giving her the flexibility to access the cash value if she chooses.

In the last few years, index annuity carriers have enhanced the potential payout of GLWB provisions by guaranteeing a minimum growth rate of the income factor (sometimes called the "benefit base") on which the payout is based. Although the actual cash value of Alice's annuity ten years after issue, was $153,817, the GLWB payout would be based on the original principal's growing at, say, 7.2% a year (which rate might be guaranteed until the later of the first withdrawal or ten years or even longer). Thus, after 10 years, Alice's 6% payout would be based on a $200,000 income factor and her *minimum* lifetime payout would be $12,000.

Alice's payout has increased by almost $3,000 from what it would have been without the guaranteed growth rate for the income factor ("benefit base"). She'll get $12,000 per year instead of $9,229 This is a wonderful benefit! But has that GLWB given Alice a guarantee that she'd have $200,000 ten years after buying the annuity? No! Her *cash value* at that point was $153,817. And did she receive a 7.2% *guaranteed yield?* No! The *yield* on her *cash value* was 4.4%. The 7.2% was a growth rate on a factor that could be used only to produce an income stream. It was *not* a *yield,* or a *return on her principal.*

How GLWB Growth Really Works

The first money received back is the annuity owner's actual cash, which is based on actual net interest credited. Any income account specific "bonus" or "guarantee" only produces a real hard dollar return after the annuity owner's money is used up, which will take years.

If the annuity continues to earn a net return after rider fees of 4.4% – the yield used to produce the $153,817 – and pays out $12,000 a year the cash value will remain above zero for 20 years. If

Alice dies before age 91, the 7.2% income guarantee would have had no value, because her own money (the cash value of the annuity), growing at 4.4% would have supported withdrawals of $12,000 per year through age 90 anyway. How long would you have to live to realize the 7.2% income guarantee as a true return? Assuming a return of 4.4%/year for the years during which withdrawals are taken, you would have to reach age 101 to have earned 7.2% in those first ten years! What this means is if a producer tells a consumer they are "getting a 7.2% return on their income account" they might want to end with "if you live to be a hundred."

The Payout Is Not A Return

You receive a 5% income for life, what is your return? To figure out the return, you need to know what you will receive and what (if anything) your heirs will receive. If you start with $100,000, receive $5,000 a year for 10 years, and your heirs receive $100,000, your real return is 5%.

But what if you receive $5,000 for 10 years and your heirs get $80,000? The real return is 3.3%.

And what if you receive $5,000 for 10 years and your heirs get $50,000? The real return is 0%.

You Need To Win The Longevity Lottery

If you look at a group of one hundred 65 year olds, fifty of them will be dead by age 84, seventy-five dead by age 91, and ninety-seven will be dead by age 100 (according to the United States Life Tables 2002). If you put $100,000 into an annuity at age 65 and begin withdrawing $8,500 at age 70, your income will continue past age 100 so long as you earn a little over 5% interest. Even if you manage to average only a 3% return, your money will not be used up until you're age 88.

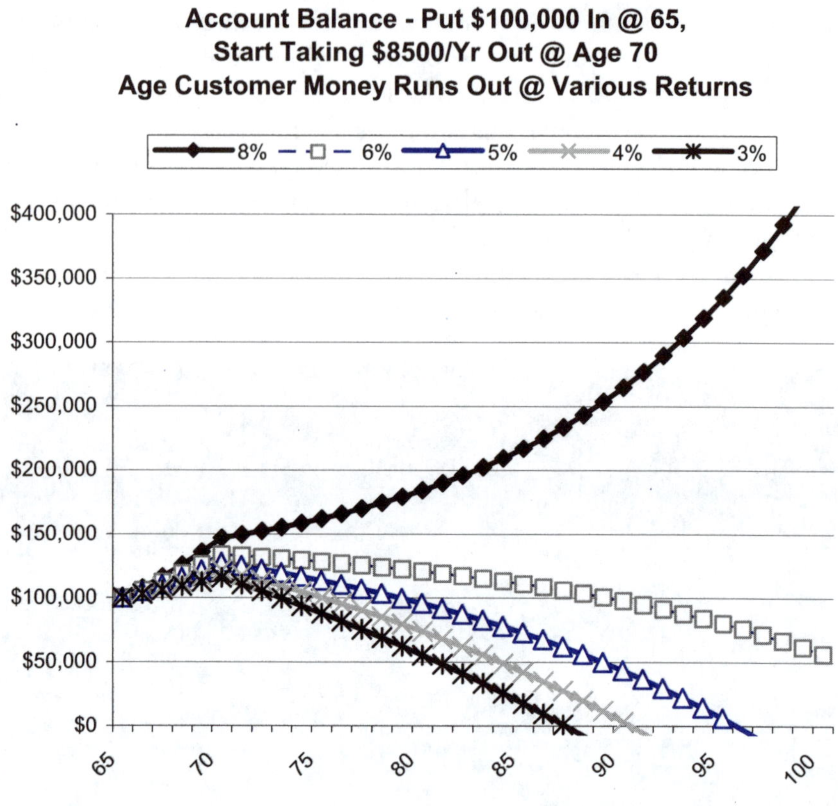

Most Consumers Will Never See Any Financial Benefit From Income Growth Guarantees

In general, consumers need to exceed life expectancy table odds and be winners in the "longevity lottery" to truly benefit from any GLWB. More specifically, <u>buyers of GLWBs receives no benefit from them unless they take maximum lifetime withdrawals</u>. Unless the buyer intends to take those maximum withdrawals, they are paying for what amounts to an insurance policy under which they will never make a claim. Is that bad? Not necessarily. We all pay homeowner's policy premiums, but very few of us want our homes to burn.

What Affects The Income Account Return

A higher guaranteed income growth rate decreases the years needed before which the real benefit of a GLWB guarantee can be realized (that is, the point at which income payments will represent the insurance company's money, not a return of the annuity owner's cash value) – an 8% income account growth rate will, in that sense, "pay off" quicker than a 6% rate, because it produces a larger annual payout. But if the annuity cash value return is really awful, the GLWB – and the growth rate guaranteed in it – becomes meaningful very quickly. If the annuity were to earn only 3%, a $12,000 payout at age 70 would start using the insurer's money by age 84 instead of 91. On the other hand if the annuity were to earn 6%, 7% or 8%, that same $12,000 per year payout would always consist of the buyer's own money (the account value), which one might take to mean that the buyer never needed the GLWB protection in the first place. Of course, the same thing could be said about fire insurance if one never has a fire or auto insurance if one never has an accident) We believe a GLWB is amply justified as longevity insurance – not as a way to get high returns.

Consumer Perceptions Are Part Of The Problem

Even if representatives fully explains how all of this works, consumers may still have a tough time understanding what they are getting. We are used to earning "cash on cash" and a yield or bonus that affects only the income payout, but never the cash account balance is a new and unfamiliar concept to most of us. The other problem that is consumers are used to receiving a return <u>on</u> money and not a return <u>of</u> money. A 6% payout consisting, at least partly if not entirely, of one's own principal is not a 6% return, yield or interest rate. The true yield on such an account can only be determined after the annuity owner dies. The problem with consumers not understanding the return <u>of</u> money resulted in lawsuits twenty years ago when Ginnie Mae mortgage bonds were all the rage, and the same disclosure problem exists with GLWBs today, except that the confusion is compounded by the fact that income account guarantees are not true yields.

<u>There Are Solutions</u>

We have noted that it is difficult for many consumers to grasp that a 7% income account growth factor is not the same thing as a 7% cash value account yield, and, indeed, cannot even be translated into an income payout yield. One solution to this problem would be for the marketing materials for these products to show only the payout percentages and the actual payout generated. This would be less likely to confuse annuity owners as to the cash value of their contracts. Another solution would be to require annuity representatives to use sales materials that show clearly what the income payout growth results really means. For example, a sliding card matrix that specifically translates the growth rate into the payout that would be produced by that rate would make it clear that growth of the GLWB "benefit base" will produce a higher GLWB benefit payment but not a higher cash value.

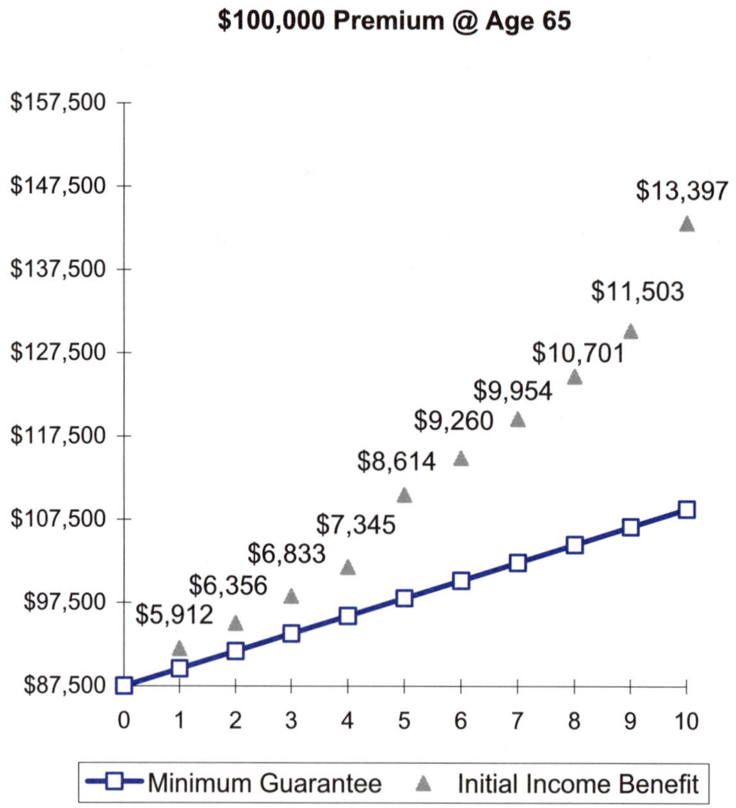

The GLWB Compliance Concern

Two problems with both VA and index annuity GLWBs are that the growth factor of the income account and resulting payout payout is often referred to as a yield, secondly that the bonus that may be applied, in an annuity, to the GLWB benefit base or to GLWB income factors may not work like a "bonus" that is applied to one's invested principal. The way a GLWB works is not fungible with other financial concepts .The problem is consumers think of income in terms of dividends and interest, and viewing the return of principal as income is a foreign concept. What can be done to avoid confusion on these points?

• Every GLWB disclosure could show a scenario in which GLWB withdrawals cause the account balance to fall to zero, so that the consumer understands that only *income*, and not *cash value,* is guaranteed.

• Focus on the dollar amounts of GLWB withdrawals, rather than upon the percentages of the benefit base that they represent making it easier to understand the real world impact of earning a rate of return less than the GLWB withdrawal rate.

• Presentation materials need to make a clear distinction between the cash account and the income account. It is easy for a consumer to confuse the two.

GLWB Annuity Alternatives

Fixed Immediate Annuities

Payments under an immediate annuity are composed of three sources: (1) return of principal. (A portion of each payment is the annuity owner's own money), (2) interest (at the rate of return assumed by the annuity payout factor in effect at the time of annuitization, and (2) a "mortality credit" (a distribution of gains realized by the pool of all policy owners from the earlier-than-expected death of some of them).

The payout from a GLWB includes a mortality credit ***or cost*** based on the actuaries' assumptions as to whether the insurer's money will ever be needed to make that payout.

At today's pricing, the payout from a single or joint life annuity (with no "refund element") is between 140% to 200% higher than the highest GLWB payout (for annuitants of the same ages), so could you do better by "building your own" GLWB? If you put 50% to 71% of the money you were considering investing in an annuity with a GLWB into an immediate annuity, you'd get the same income payout as the GLWB, and have cash left over, to invest in higher beta (risk-return) investments providing the potential for more ultimate cash. Which alternative would be better? It all depends.

The GLWB alternative produces significantly more cash surrender value in the early years. If you cash in an annuity containing a GLWB early – especially an index one – you get pretty much what you put in, less any surrender charges. But if you surrender the "immediate annuity plus growth investment" alternative, you'll have only the value of the "growth investment", because most "life only" annuities offer no "commutation" feature (that is, they have no surrender value). On the other hand, the "growth" component of the "do it yourself" alternative might, in later years, be larger than the surrender value of the annuity with the GLWB, especially, if the interest rate assumed on both is less than the GLWB withdrawal percentage.

Another advantage to the GLWB scenario is that the payout of most immediate annuities does not increase with inflation, whereas most GLWB annuities offer at least the potential for payment increases. Those immediate annuities that do include a "COLA" (Cost of Living Adjustment) feature provide a smaller (often, much smaller) initial benefit, per dollar of premium invested, than those with level payment amounts.

On the other hand, immediate annuities are taxed using the "regular annuity rules", in which a portion of each payment is considered non-taxable return of principal. Withdrawals made under a GLWB provision are, under current law, fully taxable until all "gain' in the annuity has been distributed (and included in taxable income).

However, if the premiums are identical and the GLWB offers a similar payout to the immediate annuity, the tax advantage of the immediate annuity would be more than offset by the realization that the annuity owner retains control of the asset with a GLWB and spends the asset in buying the immediate annuity.

The comparison changes significantly if the immediate annuity being considered is medically underwritten. These "substandard" contracts determine annuity payment amounts using an age-based *and health-based* life expectancy rather than the age-based expectancy used by non-medically underwritten annuities. Such contracts can offer income that may be significantly greater, for a "substandard risk" (an annuitant in worse than average health) than the amount a conventional immediate annuity would provide. Buying a substandard immediate annuity might mean you would need to allocate only 40% to 50% of your money to the SPIA to equal the GLWB payout. However, the payout that results from substandard underwriting recognizes that the annuitant is unlikely to live as long as a healthy person of the same age. Thus, the potential growth of the account into which the non-SPIA money is placed is limited by that shorter life expectancy.

An alternative to annuitizing an existing deferred annuity would be to *exchange* that contract for an *immediate annuity,* by using a *tax free exchange* (under Internal Revenue Code §1035 – a transaction usually called a "1035 exchange").

Why would one wish to do that, rather than to annuitize? *Because it might produce more income than annuitizing your existing annuity!* When you annuitize, you elect a "payout option". The amount of income you will receive will be the product of two factors: (A) the contract value (the number of dollars you place under that payout option) and (B) the "annuity payout factor" currently available, for that option, *for your particular annuity contract.*

Annuity "Payout Factors"

An annuity "payout factor" is t he amount that an insurer will pay, each month, per dollar annuitized. It varies with the type of payout. A "Life Only" payout (where payments cease upon the annuitant's death, no matter when that occurs) produces the most dollars/month per thousand dollars annuitized. If the payout includes a "refund feature" (where the insurer guarantees to pay for *the greater of* the annuitant's lifetime or a period of years) will pay less per month (because the insurer cannot stop paying if you die next month).

There are two kinds of annuity payout factors: (A) Guaranteed (those *minimum* rates specified in your deferred annuity contract, and (B) Current (those that the insurer is using *at the present time*). The Guaranteed rates are always lower than current rates because they're based on "worst case" assumptions. Current rates reflect current assumptions as to interest rates and longevity, and they change almost weekly. They vary, based on the annuitant's current age, sex, and the type of payout chosen, and they change almost weekly (although once you elect to annuitize, the payout won't change, unless it includes a "cost of living adjustment" (COLA).

The current rates also vary from insurer to insurer. The current "Life Only" payout for a 65 year old male may be $8.10 per month (per thousand annuitized) for Company A, while Company B may be paying $8.79 for the same option.

If you elect to annuitize your deferred annuity, your insurer will offer you the current rate for whatever payout type you wish. Let's say that's $6.79/month/thousand. But if another insurer, with the same financial strength, is currently offering $8.10, *why would you want to accept the lower rate?*

You wouldn't. It would pay you to *exchange* your existing deferred annuity for the other insurer's *immediate* annuity. Most annuity producers know that, which is why they'll "go shopping" in the immediate annuity marketplace for those clients with deferred annuities who are considering annuitization.

It is *very* common to find that the current payout rate offered by the issuer of a deferred annuity is less than the Single Premium Immediate Annuity payout rate offered by one or more other insurers.

The "Longevity Annuity"

A relatively new type of annuity offers a different way of managing the risk of outliving one's income. It works like this:

Joe, age 60, invests a small portion of his retirement portfolio in an annuity that will produce a guaranteed income to him, once he reaches an advanced age (say, age 85). The amount of that income may be greater, perhaps far greater, than can be assured by any alternative (including a deferred annuity, with or without a GLWB), and it will persist for his entire lifetime.

Example: Joe makes a single deposit of $50,000 at his age 60. If he lives to age 85, the annuity will produce, say, an income of $5,211 per month for life. He'll get back his entire principal in less than the first year, and he'll continue to receive that $5,211 per month for as long as he breathes, no matter what happens to interest or mortality rates in the future. How can this product do this?

It can do this because there's no benefit until the Annuity Starting Date. If Joe dies prior to reaching age 85, the annuity expires without value. Hearing this last point, many annuity representatives may ask "Why would anyone buy such a thing? My client buys a policy that won't pay him a penny for 25 years and if he doesn't make it that long, he loses his entire premium?" Sounds like a very bad investment".

It would be – if it were an investment. But it's not. It's a risk transfer instrument – a pure insurance play. The risk that the purchaser transfers to the issuing insurer is the risk he'll run out of money at an advanced age (when he cannot expect to earn income). That's the "covered peril", and if it materializes – if he lives past age 85 – the annuity will provide income in an amount that will never be reduced, no matter what happens to interest rates, for as long as he is alive.

<u>Transferring the Risk</u>

But what about the risk that he won't live that long? If he doesn't, the insurance company just keeps the money? Well, first of all, the insurance company doesn't "keep the money" in that scenario. It uses it to pay income to those policyholders who did live that long. That's how risk pooling works. But even if the insurer were to "keep the money," it shouldn't matter, in terms of the risk transfer agreement this client made. To put it bluntly, dead people don't need income. The risk transferred is that the policyholder will run out of income in old age. If he never makes it to old age, that risk will never materialize.

Some annuity representatives can't live with this, which is why those few insurers that now offer longevity annuities offer a variant that provides a death benefit if the annuitant does not survive to the payout commencement age. That seems a better deal to some, but it's not. The guaranteed annuity payment in a longevity annuity that offers a death benefit must be far less than that guaranteed by one with no death benefit. That's less leverage, and leverage is what insurance is all about. Moreover, a death benefit in a longevity annuity is like a "return of premium" provision in a term life or disability income policy; it offers protection against an outcome that is the direct opposite of the insured peril, which guarantees that one of the two protections will fail. (One is either disabled or not, alive or not; one cannot be both). Insuring against mutually exclusive outcomes destroys leverage.

In addition, if the dollars constituting the annual premium are so essential to the economic well-being of the insured or his family that he must insure against their "loss," he shouldn't be spending that many dollars on premiums in the first place. (This condition is sometimes known as being "insurance poor"). If our hypothetical client feels the obligation to leave those cumulative premiums to heirs as a legacy, that's an entirely different risk proposition, for which an entirely different type of risk transfer instrument — life insurance — serves well. But one cannot spend the same dollar twice.

Creating a "Back Door" for Retirees

A longevity annuity (without the superfluous death benefit) represents a remarkable opportunity for the annuity representatives to redefine the financial planning landscape. It can reduce, or even eliminate, its core uncertainty – the indefinite duration of the retirement income need – by providing a "back door," a point beyond which the retiree's retirement portfolio will not have to provide income because the annuity will do so. For investment advisors using stochastic modeling to manage the returns and sequence of returns risk, the job will become much easier and the results more credible, because the period of time over which those returns must be reckoned will become certain.

What does this mean, in practical terms? First, it means that having allocated a small portion (perhaps 5-15%) of our client's retirement portfolio to a longevity annuity, we can now manage the remainder differently (because the time horizon for that portfolio has changed). Even more importantly, it means that our client can now afford to engage in activities or behaviors that she might not normally be willing to consider. The assurance that a known income will be forthcoming, upon reaching a certain advanced age, may allow our client to spend more of her portfolio before reaching that age, and enjoy her wealth while she is able to do so.

Most insurers do not offer longevity annuities at this time. For those that do, sales have been meager. Both conditions are due to a simple, rather sad fact: Most investment advisors do not understand this new tool, so they do not recommend it. This is not a marketing problem; it's an education problem. The nature of this new device is not well understood, so the value it provides is not understood either.

The nature of the longevity annuity is simple: it is a risk transfer device, an insurance instrument. It is not an investment, and investment logic will not discover its value. We view a longevity annuity as most like a property and casualty insurance product. We insure our homes and automobiles because their loss would cause us hardship, but we don't expect a return on principal for those premium dollars. If our car and home aren't destroyed while we insured them, we've lost nothing, for we had the assurance that they would be restored with insurance proceeds. Similarly, if we "insure" our old age income, using only a small part of our total wealth, and die before reaching old age, that insurance will not have been in vain, for it gave us the confidence to spend the rest of our money while we could. The real value of the longevity annuity is not in the income it provides, but in the choices it makes feasible.

(The above article by John Olsen, appearing in the January, 2009 issue of Life Insurance Selling magazine, is reprinted here by permission).

Increasing Death Benefit Riders

The insurance aspect of a variable annuity initially was that you could always get back at least the original principal if the annuity owner died, even if the account value at time of death was lower. In the previous decade, this benefit was enhanced so that the death benefit often became the high water mark of the VA account value, while other versions had the VA death benefits steadily increasing by a minimum percentage each year.

An increasing death benefit rider was not used previously in the fixed annuity world because account values were already guaranteed to increase due to minimum returns and excess interest paid. A few carriers toyed with marketing "tax paying" riders that increased the annuity death benefit by 28% or so, with the idea that this could be used to pay the tax on the accumulated annuity interest due at death, but buyers of the tax rider were few.

The index annuity world also offers minimum guarantees, but, as these guarantees are often based on interest accumulating on less than 100% of initial principal, this means that, for many products, the guaranteed death benefit may remain the original principal, at least during the surrender period. Whether the actual death benefit involves only a return of premium or something more depends largely on the crediting structure used.

A Death Benefit Rider Analysis

Suppose a death benefit rider charges an annual fee of 0.4% based on the accumulated value. The death benefit grows at a *simple* -not compounded – rate of 6%. The rider does not require evidence of insurability.

Example: The premium is $100,000. The death benefit rider guarantees that if the annuity owner dies after contract year 1, the beneficiary will receive the greater of the annuity cash value or $106,000. If the annuity owner dies after year 2, the beneficiary will $112,000 (or the cash value, if greater). The cost of this rider is 0.4% of the accumulated value ($400 in the first year).

Minimum Returns

If there isn't a death benefit rider and the minimum guaranteed return on cash value is 1% interest, compounding on 87.5% of principal, the death benefit paid is still only the original principal after 5 to 10 years. If a 3% minimum rate is assumed, the death benefit is 101% of the premium in 5 years and 118% in 10 years. By contrast, selecting a rider with a 6% simple interest death benefit creates a death benefit equal to 130% of the original premium in 5 years – an annualized return of 5.4%, and 160% of the original premium in 10 years – an annualized return of 4.8%.

Death Benefit In	1% Min Intr on 87.5%	3% Min Intr on 87.5%	6% Simple DB on 100%
5 Yrs	100%	101%	130%
10 Yrs	100%	118%	160%
20 Yrs	107%	158%	220%

On an initial $100,000 premium this rider is producing a guaranteed death benefit of $130,000 in 5 years and $160,000 in ten years. If you contrast that with the $100,000 benefit produced by the 1% minimum return, you find that the rider gives the beneficiary $30,000 more after 5 years and $60,000 more after 10 years. If you compare the rider with the $101,000 in 5 years and $118,000 that a 3% minimum guarantee would produce, you find the net rider additional death benefit would be $29,000 in 5 years ot $42,000 in 10 years. All of this for an annual fee of $400. This assumes that no index-linked or fixed account interest is earned. However, based on actual historic returns, or even when using very pessimistic hypothetical assumptions on possible market returns, an annuity using an annual or biennial reset method would not need the rider, because the actual return should be greater than the simple death benefit rider under almost every scenario we analyzed.

Annual Reset: Is The Death Benefit Worth The Rider Fee?

An annual reset design looks at one year periods, calculates and credits interest, and then resets the index starting point. Because of this resetting, these methods have consistently produced actual average 5-year returns of 5% to 6%. The worst 5-year annualized return we have recorded for any annual reset product was 3.1% (a 16% period gain), and these returns were produced during terrible stock market periods.

When an annual reset design is used, the death benefit riders we have reviewed are, in our judgment, not worth even a small fee. However, they might be worth the cost when added to an annuity using a term end point method.

Term End Point: Is It Worth 40 Basis Points?

As discussed in earlier chapters a term end point design has the potential to pay higher interest than annual reset methods because more index participation can be purchased for the same amount of money. Indeed, the highest recorded returns over 5-year year periods were generated by term end point methods. However, since term end point designs do not reset until the end of a multiple year period, they are hammered by bad markets occurring near the end of the crediting period – the lowest recorded returns over 5-year periods were generated by term end point methods.

Roughly a quarter of the time over the last half century the S&P 500 would have recorded a loss over calendar year 5-year periods. Over two-fifths of the time, the total 5-year return would have been under the 30% earned by the 6% death benefit rider. The rider addresses a real problem of term end point designs, so we return to the question asked above – is it worth an annual cost of 0.4%?

Let's look at a term end point design with a five year term. On a $100,000 premium, the simple death benefit would be $6,000 at the end of one year and increase $6,000 a year thereafter. The cost would be $400 a year for each of the first five years because any index-linked interest would not be credited until the end of the term. If there was an initial 5% premium bonus, the death benefit growth would be based on $105,000 and the rider cost would be $420 a year ($105,000 x 0.4%). If there was an initial 10% bonus, the death benefit growth would be based on $110,000, and the rider cost would be $440 a year. So, this is what the cost and net insurance benefit would look like on the original premium, and if a 5% or 10% premium bonus was included (a bonus credited to the original premium would raise the death benefit whether the rider was purchased or not, but both the death benefit and rider cost would increase to reflect the bonus).

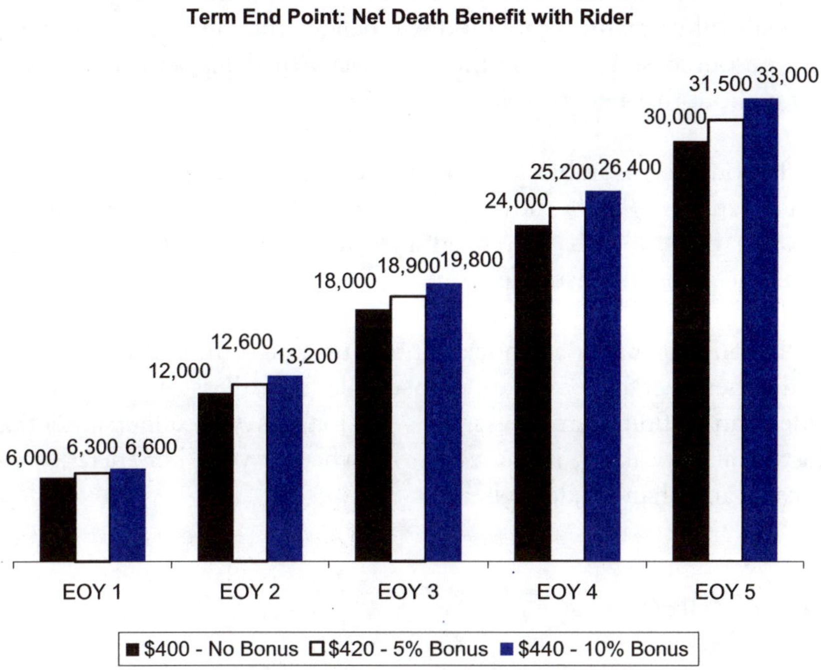

If you are insurable and are under age 65, you may well be able to find life insurance coverage providing a death benefit of at least $33,000 – the maximum possible death benefit produced by the rider – for a premium lower than $440 a year. If you are insurable and over age 65, it is a more difficult call, because although the "rider insurance premium" may well be less expensive than comparable separate life coverage, you'd have to consider that the annuity owner gets *the higher of* the account value or the death benefit rider. If the accumulated value is $133,000 in five years and the owner drops dead, the beneficiaries get $133,000, and the rider fees will have worked to reduce what would have been a greater accumulated value. Buying separate life insurance would provide a source of cash in addition to the annuity value.

A term end point method & an uninsurable annuity owner can justify buying the death benefit rider

Bottom Line

If a death benefit rider is offered on an index annuity using an annual or biennial reset method, we believe that, in general, it should not be purchased, because the probability of dying and being worse off without that benefit is low.

If you are insurable are under age 65, then it *probably* does not make sense to get the rider because true life insurance coverage will *probably* be less – if you need life insurance and qualify for life insurance, buy life insurance!

If you are buying an index annuity using a term end point design and either over age 65 or are uninsurable (regardless of your age), the rider can definitely make sense – so long as you understand that, historically speaking, it is a coin toss whether your beneficiaries will receive an enhanced death benefit.

Cheat Sheet

- It is, and will probably remain, difficult to combat the misperception that the payout rate is the return.
- Life expectancy is steadily increasing which lessens the attractiveness of self-insuring longevity risk.
- If you earn 5% and spend 5%, you could still run out of money early.

Chapter 7: "Tax Traps" In Annuity Planning

One of the greatest challenges to those who deal with annuities is the complexity (and, in some cases, uncertainty) of the tax laws governing these contracts. There are four parties to the annuity contract – *Issuer, Owner, Annuitant, and Beneficiary*. Several "tax traps" can be triggered when the owner and annuitant are not the same individual or when the owner or beneficiary is not a human being. And when the owner, annuitant, and beneficiary are all different individuals, the result is not so much a "tax trap" as a "tax disaster" – all because of how annuity contracts say death proceeds will be payable and how Federal tax law says they *must* be payable.

IRC § 72(s) – The Rules Governing Annuity Death Proceeds

Section 72(s) of the Internal Revenue Code provides rules governing how annuity contracts must be paid out upon the death of the contract owner. This section prescribes how the contract value must be distributed *only* when an annuity *owner* dies; it does not apply if a *non-owner annuitant* dies.

If Owner Dies *On Or After* Annuity Starting Date

If the owner dies on or after the "annuity starting date" (that is, after regular annuity payments, under an "annuity payout option" had begun), and before owner's entire interest in the contract has been distributed, §72(s)(1)(A) states that "the remaining portion of such interest will be distributed at least as rapidly as under the method of distributions being used as of the date of his death". If those death proceeds ("remaining portion of such interest") are received by the beneficiary either as a lump sum or in installments under the same annuity payout option elected by the deceased owner, those proceeds will be *excluded from income until the total amount received tax-free (by both owner and beneficiary) exceeds the owner's "investment in the contract"*.

What does this mean in plain English? It means that if the owner of an annuity that had already begun making annuity payments dies, any remaining value must be distributed *no less rapidly* than the owner had been taking payments. One curiosity of this rule (clarified by Treas. Reg. §1.72-11(c)) is that, although annuity payments received by the owner had been taxed under the "regular annuity rules" of Section 72(b) (where a portion of each payment was excludible from tax as a "return of principal"), any remaining "period certain" payments, made to the *beneficiary*, will be taxed much more favorably (excluded from tax *entirely*, until all of owner's "investment in the contract" has been received tax-free).

If Owner Dies *Before* Annuity Starting Date

If the owner of a *deferred* annuity dies before annuitizing the contract, Sect. 72(s)(1)(B) requires that all contract value must be distributed (to the beneficiary) "within five years after the death of the holder"[1], unless one of two exceptions applies.

The first exception applies when the annuity is payable to a "designated beneficiary", which term is defined as "any individual designated a beneficiary by the holder of the contract"[2]. Note the term "individual". It means *"human being"*. If a human being is the beneficiary, the annuity value may be distributed over a period not extending beyond the life expectancy of that beneficiary, so long as payments begin no later than one year after the owner's death[3].

The second exception applies *only* when the "designated beneficiary" is the *surviving spouse of the owner.* Where that is the case, that surviving spouse may elect to treat the annuity as his/her own, as if he or she purchased the annuity originally[4]. As *owner,* he or she may then continue the contract, and exercise all options within it as though he or she were the original owner. This is the so-called "spousal continuation" option, and most deferred annuity contracts issued today allow this option in their contract language.

1 "Holder" is *Internal Revenue Code "tax speak"* for "owner".
2 IRC §72(s)(4)
3 IRC §72(s)2)
4 IRC §72(s)2)

IRC §72(h) – The "Forgotten" Rule

One curiosity of annuity tax law is the presence of IRC Section 72(h). Unlike Section 72(s), this applies not only when an annuity *owner* dies, but whenever *any* death benefit is payable (including a death benefit payable by reason of the death of the *annuitant*). Under this subsection, any beneficiary given the right to receive "an annuity in lieu of" a lump sum benefit may elect that option and annuity payments will be taxable *as received* (under the "regular annuity rules" of Sect. 72(b)).

Sect. 72(h) requires that the election, by the beneficiary, to take proceeds as an annuity (instead of as a lump sum), must be made "*within sixty days after the day on which such lump sum first became payable*".

Why is this important? It's important because many annuity representatives believe that the beneficiary has *one year* to make such an election, because Sect. 72(s)(2) says that an annuity payout exception to the 5-year rule of Sect. 72(s)(1)(B) is available provided that payment commence *within one year of the death of the owner.* Thus, we have two Code provisions that specify *different time limits* for the beneficiary to elect an annuity payout. Which one is "right"? Some commentators believe that Sect. 72(s) "trumps" Sect. 72(h) because it's twenty odd years newer. But they're both *law*. And every annuity contract we've seen specifies that the beneficiary has *sixty days* to make the annuity election. But, *by company practice*, many insurers allow *one year.* This *may* be because insurers believe that the older Sect. 72(h) is no longer valid. It's almost never cited in recent Private Letter Rulings dealing with annuity payouts to beneficiaries. Or it could be because these insurers read Sect. 72(h)'s "*within sixty days after the day on which such lump sum first became payable*" to mean "sixty days after the beneficiary submits Proof of Death to the insurer" (before which date, it's arguable that no benefit was payable).

So what is the implication for us annuity representatives? We believe that the prudent representative will be aware of the 60-day limit of Sect. 72(h) and advise beneficiaries that they may need to make the annuity payout decision within sixty days of the annuity owner's death. Certainly, this should be the advice if the annuity issuer sticks to the 60-day rule (as it might not permit an annuity payout after that point). *Bottom Line: If you're not sure how long the issuer of an annuity you're dealing with will permit a beneficiary to wait before electing an annuity payout, find out!*

Let's return, now, to our discussion of "tax traps" that might result from an inappropriate or ill-considered ownership or beneficiary designation. Perhaps the most common "trap" occurs when the owner and annuitant are different individuals.

When The Owner And Annuitant Are Different Individuals

As discussed in Chapter 2, the *owner* of an annuity is the individual ("Individual", for purposes of annuity tax law, means a "natural person" – a *human being.*) or entity (it need not be a human being) that owns all rights to the annuity contract. The *annuitant* is the "measuring life" – that individual (it must be a human being) whose age and sex will determine, for "life contingent"[5] annuity payouts, the amount of each annuity payment. Most annuities are structured so that the owner and annuitant are the same individual. But where they're *different* individuals, problems can result when one of them dies. To avoid these problems, we *must* know, for any annuity contract about which we are giving advice, *whose death* triggers *which death benefit.*

With regard to the payment of death proceeds, there are two kinds of deferred annuity contracts[6].*(a) owner-driven* and *(b) annuitant-driven.* In an "owner-driven" contract, the death of the owner triggers

5 A "life contingent" annuity payout option guarantees that annuity payments will be made for the entire lifetime of one or more annuitants. By contrast, a "period certain" option guarantees that they will be made for, *and only for,* a specified period, irrespective of whether the annuitant dies during that period or survives beyond it. Some "life contingent" payouts include a "refund feature" that guarantees payments for a specified period, or totaling a specified total amount, even if the annuitant dies during that period (or before that specified total amount has been received).

payment of the contractually guaranteed death benefit (which, in contracts offering "enhanced" death benefits, may exceed the annuity's cash surrender value). In an "annuitant-driven" contract, it is the death of the annuitant that triggers payment of that contractually guaranteed minimum death benefit. These two facts would likely cause one to conclude that any deferred annuity is *either* annuitant-driven or owner-driven. That would make sense. But it's not the case, because *all* deferred annuities, issued since January 18th, 1985, *must* be "owner-driven"[7]. *Some* deferred annuities are *also* annuitant-driven. In other words, *all* deferred annuities *must* pay out a death benefit upon the death of the *owner. Some* will *also* pay a death benefit upon the death of the *annuitant.* And, if that were not complicated enough, the death benefits thus payable may be different. Let's look at some examples:

Annuitant-Driven Annuity: Annuitant Dies First

John owns a deferred annuity; his wife, Marsha, is the annuitant. If the contract is "annuitant-driven", Marsha's death will trigger payment of the death benefit. In many fixed annuities, that's the *cash surrender value.* But many variable or index annuities offer "enhanced" death benefits (also known as "guaranteed minimum death benefits") that may exceed the cash surrender values. If John's is such a contract, and that contract is annuitant-driven, it will pay that "enhanced" benefit on the death of the annuitant (in this case, that's Marsha).

Annuitant-Driven Annuity: Owner Dies First

But what if John predeceases Marsha? Because *all* deferred annuities *must* pay out on the death of the *owner*, John's death will trigger *a* death benefit. In this example, that's the cash surrender

6 This distinction of "owner-driven" vs. "annuitant-driven" contracts is applicable only to *deferred* annuities. *Immediate* annuities cease payments either at the expiry of the "period certain" (if the annuity is of the "period certain" type) or (if the annuity is "life contingent" and a "refund feature" is operative) upon the later of the death of the annuitant or the expiry of the period certain.

7 IRC §72(s)(1)(B)

value (because the contract, being annuitant-driven, provides that the "enhanced" death benefit is payable only on the death of the annuitant (Marsha).

Non-Annuitant-Driven Annuity: Owner Dies First

If John's contract is not "annuitant-driven", John's death will trigger the death benefit – an "enhanced" one, if the contract provides for one, or the cash surrender value, if it does not.

Non-Annuitant-Driven Annuity: Annuitant Dies First

If John's contract is not "annuitant-driven" and Marsha (the annuitant) dies, no death benefit will be payable. John can name a new annuitant and continue the contract.

When The Owner, Annuitant, And Beneficiary Are Different

The death benefit of an annuity is payable to the beneficiary. Suppose, in our example, John, in addition to being the owner of the annuity, is also the beneficiary. Marsha is the annuitant. If the contract is annuitant-driven, Marsha's death triggers payment of the "enhanced" death benefit to John (the beneficiary). John cannot continue the contract under the "spousal continuation" option, even though he is the surviving spouse and the beneficiary, because that option is available only when (a) the *owner* dies and (b) the beneficiary is owner's surviving spouse. John's death will trigger payment of the cash value, to the *contingent* beneficiary (if one is named in the contract) or to John's estate.

If Marsha had been named beneficiary (as well as annuitant) and the contract was annuitant-driven, Marsha's death would trigger payment to the contingent beneficiary or (if none) to Marsha's estate, unless the contract provided otherwise[8]. In that same scenario, the death benefit, if the contract was not annuitant-driven, would be payable, at John's death, to Marsha (as beneficiary).

8 Some annuity contracts provide that if a named beneficiary is not living at the time a death payment is payable, the owner or owner's estate becomes the beneficiary.

But what if someone other than John or Marsha had been named beneficiary of the annuity? In that case, too, the result would depend upon whether the contract was or was not annuitant-driven. If not, John's death would trigger payment to the beneficiary; Marsha's death would trigger no payment. *But in that scenario (owner = John; annuitant = Marsha; beneficiary = someone else), if the contract was annuitant-driven, Marsha's death would produce a tax disaster.* The annuity would pay out to the beneficiary, even though John, the owner, was still living. The beneficiary would be liable for tax on the annuity "gain", *plus 10% of that gain*, unless proceeds were received after beneficiary's age 59 ½ or over his or her life expectancy[9]. *And, as if that weren't bad enough, John would have made a gift of the entire death proceeds to the beneficiary[10]!*

If the owner and annuitant are the same person, all this complexity vanishes.

At this point, the reader may be forgiven for saying something like "Are you kidding? Is this stuff *really* that complicated?" Such a response is understandable, but the fact remains that this stuff *really is* that complicated – *if the owner and annuitant are different individuals.* If the owner and annuitant are the same person, all this complexity vanishes. The death of the owner/annuitant triggers payment of *the* death benefit to the beneficiary. Whether the contract is annuitant-driven or not doesn't matter. So, the obvious solution to these problems is to prevent them by *never letting the annuitant and owner be different individuals unless (a) there is a* **very** *good reason for doing so and (b) everyone involved knows what will happen if either party dies.*

9 The IRC 72(q)(2)(B) exception to the penalty would not apply because the death proceeds were not received as the result of the death of the annuity "holder" (owner).

10 This is the infamous "triangle trap" or "Goodman triangle", in which, if the owner, beneficiary, and insured/annuitant ("insured" for life insurance contracts, "annuitant" for annuities) are all different individuals, at the death of insured/annuitant, owner is deemed to have made a gift equal to the death proceeds, to the beneficiary. *Goodman v. Commr. 156 F.2nd 28, (2nd Circuit, 1946).*

When The Annuity Is Owned Jointly

If a deferred annuity is owned jointly, the death of either owner *might* produce unexpected results. If the joint owners are spouses and each names the other as his/her beneficiary, there's no problem.

Why? Because the death of *either* owner will trigger payment of death proceeds to the beneficiary, and the surviving spouse/ beneficiary will be able to take the annuity proceeds as a lump sum, over five years (IRC §72(s)(1)(B)), as an annuity for lifetime or a shorter period (IRC §72(s)(2)), or to treat the annuity as his/her own (IRC §72(s)(3)).

But what if the annuity is owned jointly and one or both of the owners have designated a third party as beneficiary. There, we could have a problem. At the death of the first owner, the annuity *must* pay out to the beneficiary, *regardless of the fact that the contract was owned jointly*[11]. Some contracts avoid this problem by either disallowing joint ownership entirely or permitting it only between spouses *and* stating, in the contract, that if the annuity is owned jointly, the surviving owner will be deemed to be the primary beneficiary, *notwithstanding any beneficiary designation to the contrary.*

But at this point, we might ask ourselves "What is to be gained by owning the annuity jointly (which usually means "Jointly with right of survivorship")? Some clients (and some attorneys and accountants) prefer this ownership arrangement because it "equalizes estate values" for death tax purposes, to preserve "marital property" status, because jointly held property (especially, property held jointly between spouses) receives, in many States, special creditor protection, or simply because the clients believe that "this is *our* money; not *his* or *hers*". Any or all of these reasons may be compelling in some

11 This may surprise many lawyers and accountants, whose understanding of Joint Ownership with Right of Survivorship is that such an ownership designation automatically passes the property in question to the surviving owner. That's true -when property passes *by law* (that is, by the provisions of State law relating to joint ownership). But the value of an annuity contract passes to the beneficiary, not by operation of law, but by operation of *contract*, and the *terms of the contract* control what will happen.

situations. However, the cash value of annuity contracts is, in many States, accorded special creditor protection that may be as strong as or stronger than the protection afforded jointly held property

But the desire of a married couple to own an annuity jointly because "it's *our* money and it should pass to whichever of us survives" does not require joint ownership. If A and B are married, and A is owner and annuitant, and B is beneficiary, A's death will give B the option to take the annuity proceeds or to treat the annuity as his/her own, and B's death will have no effect on the annuity.

Bottom Line: Before designating joint ownership, all parties should be aware of what (if anything) is gained by that arrangement.

When The Owner Is Not An "Individual"

When an annuity is owned by a "non-natural person" (any entity other than a human being), a different set of planning problems arise and a serious "tax trap" may be triggered. The source of the problems is Internal Revenue Code Section 72(u), which states that -

If any annuity contract is held by a person who is not a natural person—

(A) such contract shall not be treated as an annuity contract for purposes of this subtitle (other than subchapter L), and

(B) the income on the contract for any taxable year of the policyholder shall be treated as ordinary income received or accrued by the owner during such taxable year.

What's that mean? It means any annuity contract owned by a trust, corporation, or other non-human entity will not be treated as "an annuity contract" for income tax purposes and that the annual increase in cash value will be reportable as ordinary income received by that owner. There are exceptions to this rule. It doesn't apply to an annuity that is (a) acquired by a decedent's estate, (b) is held by an IRA or employer-sponsored retirement plan, (c) used to fund a "structured settlement", or (d) an *immediate* annuity[12]. It also doesn't apply to a deferred annuity that is owned by a non-natural person that is acting as "*the agent of a natural person*"[13]. Just what constitutes an entity's acting as the "agent of a natural person" is not defined in either the Internal Revenue Code or Treasury Regulations. However, various Private letter Rulings have held that trusts holding an annuity for the benefit of trust beneficiaries, *where all trust beneficiaries were human beings* were acting in that capacity. Revocable Living Trusts will generally qualify (because they're ignored for income tax purposes), and other grantor trusts may, too, but one should *never* assume that a deferred annuity owned by a trust will be entitled to tax-deferred treatment. Some insurers will, as a matter of policy, issue Forms 1099R, showing the annual increase in annuity value as taxable income to any trust (or other "non-natural person") holding their annuities. Moreover, even if an insurer does not do so, the entity owning the annuity has the responsibility of demonstrating that it is acting as "the agent of a natural person" should the IRS assert that the rule of Sect. 72(u) applies (and that annual cash value increases must be reported as income).

If you're considering naming a trust or other "non-natural person" as the owner of an annuity you're recommending (or giving advice about), make sure that you, your client, and your client's tax and legal advisors, are aware that the annuity may not enjoy tax-deferred treatment, and that where a non-natural person is owner, the *primary annuitant* will be deemed to be the "holder" for purposes of Section 72(s) – meaning that the annuitant's death will trigger distribution as prescribed by that subsection.

When The Beneficiary Is Not An Individual

We've been talking about the rules that apply when a non-natural person, such as a trust, *owns* an annuity. A more common scenario is where the annuity is *payable to* such entity – that is, where the entity (we'll call it a trust, for simplicity) is named as *beneficiary* of the

12 IRC §72(u)(3)
13 IRC §72(u)(1)

annuity. Here, there's no question of whether the annuity gets tax-deferral (unless the trust is also the owner), but there are other tax traps to watch out for.

As we noted earlier, Sect. 72(s) of the Internal Revenue Code prescribes how the value of an annuity must be distributed when the owner dies. The general rule is that it must be fully distributed within five years, but there are two exceptions to that general rule, *both of which require the presence of a "designated beneficiary"* – a beneficiary specified, in the contract, who is a *human being.* A trust is not a human being, for which reason nearly all insurers take the position that the two exceptions to the five-year payout rule *are not available.* In short, most insurers (we know of very few exceptions) will require a payout over a period no longer than five years.

Making a living trust the annuity beneficiary reduces your options

What are the practical implications of this for someone who sells, or gives advice concerning, annuities? Let's look at a "case study" –

George owns a non-qualified deferred annuity, of which his wife, Gracie, is beneficiary. If George dies, what are Gracie's options?

1. She can take the annuity value in a lump sum.
2. She can take the annuity value over five years.
3. She can take the value, as regular annuity payments, over a period not longer than her life expectancy. (Any "life-contingent" payout, regularly offered by the issuing insurer will qualify).
4. As George's surviving spouse, she can elect to treat the annuity as her own, and continue earning tax-deferred growth until she surrenders or annuitizes the contract.

Now, suppose that George changes the beneficiary of that annuity to his revocable living trust (perhaps at the suggestion of one of his advisors). What are the payout options now, when George dies? *The last two options are no longer available!*

Why? Because a trust cannot marry, so the "spousal continuation" exception cannot be claimed. And a trust doesn't have a life expectancy (because it's not a human being), so the "annuitization" option is also barred. The trustee of George's trust will *probably* be required to take (and pay tax on the "gain" in) the annuity within five years. And this will probably be the case even if Gracie is the trustee and beneficiary of George's revocable living trust[14].

We say "probably" because, although nearly all annuity issuers take the position described above (that the "annuitization" and "spousal continuation" options aren't available in this situation), *a few* insurers will permit the trustee to elect to take proceeds as an annuity, over the lifetime of the oldest trust beneficiary. This position is based on a belief that Congress *intended* to make the rules governing required post-death distributions from a non-qualified annuity" (IRC §72(s)) consistent with the rules for post-death distributions from IRAs or qualified plans. There is merit in that position. The legislative history of §72(s) shows that intent. But the fact remains that there is nothing in the *law* or Treasury regulations that specifically authorizes such a payout.

So, how does this affect an agent who sells an annuity? What if that agent had recommended that beneficiary change, or simply "went along with it" without suggesting to George's tax or legal counsel that they consider the consequences? And what if, after George's death, Gracie learns that she didn't need to pay taxes on all the profit in that annuity within five years, and, indeed, that she could have deferred paying taxes on it *indefinitely?* Can we say "E&O claim"?

Let's look at another "case study". Anne, a wealthy woman, has established a "non-grantor" irrevocable trust for her 9 year old son, Mike, to provide Mike with an income for Mike's lifetime, commencing after his graduation from college. Jack, Anne's insurance agent, explains to her that the only financial instrument

14 There is one Private Letter Ruling (Let. Rul. 200323012) that held otherwise, but the facts in that case were very unusual.

that can *guarantee* a set income to Mike for life, no matter what, is an annuity, that a deferred annuity will shelter the trust earnings from income tax until Mike graduates (in 13 years or so), and that the accumulated annuity value can then be converted to the lifetime income she wants for Mike. Anne likes the idea, and, as trustee, buys a deferred annuity, naming Jack as annuitant. Fifteen years later, Mike gets his Bachelor's degree. (He took partying very seriously). Anne then directs the insurance company to annuitize the contract, using a life-contingent payout option.

Mike is now assured of an income for life. He's also assured that he'll pay ordinary income tax on the "gain" portion of each annuity payment, *plus 10% of that amount!*

Whoa! Wait a minute! Why should Mike have to pay that 10% penalty tax when he's taking the proceeds over his lifetime? Doesn't the "substantially equal payments over life expectancy" exception to Sect. 72(q) apply? No, it doesn't. Because that exception applies only when the "taxpayer" takes those payments over the taxpayer's life expectancy. Mike isn't the taxpayer. The trust is. So, Mike ends up with an income for life, *but it's taxed in the worst possible way.*

Was this result unavoidable? No, it wasn't. Anne, as trustee, could have distributed the annuity to Mike (if the trust terms permitted) at his graduation, and he could have annuitized it over his lifetime, avoiding the 10% penalty. But, in this case, she didn't – because she didn't know she had to, because no one told her about this "tax trap". If Jack (remember Jack? He's the agent who sold the annuity) is still in business, might he now get a phone call?

Our point, here, is not that you, acting as an insurance agent, need to "practice law". Heaven forbid! It's simply that you might be *held responsible* for the tax consequences that result from ownership or beneficiary designations that you recommend. And that you should, therefore, understand the tax implications of those arrangements *before* helping to put them in force.

Borrowing Against An Annuity

Another "tax trap" that can ensnare an annuity owner occurs when that owner uses the annuity as collateral for a loan. *Direct* loans from non-qualified annuities aren't a problem because most (but not all) non-qualified deferred annuity contracts do not contain a loan provision[15], however, the owner of a deferred annuity might pledge that contract, *as collateral*, for a loan from a financial institution or individual. When that occurs, the borrower/annuity owner is deemed, by IRC Sect. 72(e)(4), to have "received", as ordinary income", the value of the annuity pledged as collateral, up to but not in excess of, the "gain" in that contract. This fact is *not* well known among annuity buyers. Those non-qualified annuities that *do* contain loan provisions *always* state that such loans will be treated as "withdrawals" for income tax purposes (because IRC Sect. 72(e)(4) requires such treatment).

Multiple Deferred Annuities: The "Anti-Abuse" Rule

One method of reducing the impact of the "interest first" tax treatment of deferred annuities, for purchasers who may wish to make partial withdrawals, is to buy more than one contract. For example, John purchases a single deferred annuity for $100,000. Five years later, it is worth $120,000. If John withdraws $15,000 at that point, the entire withdrawal ($15,000) is taxable (because his "gain" is $20,000). Moreover, if he is under age 59½, he will have to pay the 10% penalty tax for "premature distributions" (unless an exception to that penalty applies). But if John were to purchase ten separate deferred annuities for $10,000 each, and each annuity is worth $12,000 five years later, a surrender of one contract (for $12,000) and a withdrawal of $3,000 from a second contract would

15 Some deferred annuities issued to fund "qualified plans" (including Sect. 403(b) plans) may contain policy loan provisions; however, these contracts are not subject to the rules governing non-qualified annuities (including IRC §72(e)(4)).

produce a taxable amount of only $4,000 (all of the $2,000 gain in each contract). Moreover, the penalty tax would be $400, instead of $1,500, as the penalty applies only to the taxable portion of early distributions.

Congress considered this technique to be abusive, and passed legislation that treats all annuities issued during a single calendar year and issued by the same insurance company as one annuity, for purposes of taxing withdrawals[16]. This provision does not apply to partial withdrawals or surrenders of deferred annuity contracts issued in the same calendar year by different insurance companies. Bottom Line: If your client intends to make partial withdrawals, you may wish to consider recommending multiple contracts from different companies. Of course, you'll want to ensure that this client understands that withdrawals in excess of the "free withdrawal" percentage (often, 10%) will trigger surrender charges, if made during the surrender charge period.

Exchanging One Annuity for Another

An annuity policy may be exchanged for another in a like-kind exchange under IRC Sect. 1035 and "no loss or gain shall be recognized on the exchange". The new annuity acquires the cost basis of the original one. These "1035 exchanges" can be very valuable to policy owners, but they need to be done properly. If the rules aren't followed, the transaction will be considered a taxable distribution from the original policy. Let's look at the requirements for a valid 1035 exchange.

What kinds of policies may be exchanged under IRC §1035?

The following are allowable exchanges under §1035:
1. A life insurance policy for a life insurance policy, endowment, annuity, or qualified long term care policy.

16 IRC §72(e)(11)

2. An endowment policy for another endowment policy (which provides for regular payments beginning not later than payments would begin under the original policy), or annuity policy, or qualified long term care policy.
3. An annuity policy for an annuity policy or qualified long term care policy.
4. A qualified long term care policy for another qualified long term care policy.

Note that while a life insurance or endowment policy can be exchanged for an annuity, an annuity cannot be exchanged for anything other than another annuity or a long term care policy.

The IRS has ruled that the following transactions qualify under §1035 (if all requirements described below are followed:
1. Multiple life insurance policies for a single annuity[17]
2. A policy plus cash for a new annuity[18]
3. Surrender of an existing annuity, where the surrender value was deposited into another existing annuity[19]
4. A *partial exchange*, in which the original contract is retained by the taxpayer and the proceeds of a *withdrawal* from that contract is deposited into a new annuit[20]. Under current rules, the taxpayer (owner of both annuities) may not make any withdrawals from either contract for 12 months from the date of the exchange[21].

17 Let. Rul. 9708016. Note that this is a *Private Letter Ruling*, which has no precedential value and may only be relied upon by the taxpayer to whom it is issued.
18 Let. Rul. 9820018. This, too, is a *Private Letter Ruling*. It should be pointed out that this Ruling permitted the taxpayer to exchange an annuity plus cash to a new annuity without current tax consequences. Had the taxpayer exchanged an annuity for another annuity plus cash, that cash would have been considered "boot" and would have been taxable as income in the year of the exchange.
19 Rev. Rul. 2002-75
20 Rev. Rul. 2003-76
21 Rev. Proc. 2008-24

What requirements must be met for the exchange to be qualified under §1035?

1. The original policy must be *assigned* to the issuer of the replacement annuity[22]. The taxpayer may not receive a surrender check and endorse it to the new annuity issuer[23].
2. The owner and annuitant of the new contract must be the same as under the original contract[24].
3. The requirements of the issuer of the original annuity *and* of the issuer of the replacement contract *must* be followed. Many insurers have "their own forms" for Sect. 1035 exchanges and the prudent agent will make sure that he or she completes all of them – as the consequences of not doing so are a "busted exchange" and, almost certainly, a very angry client.

It should be mentioned that Sect. 1035 exchanges are currently, and have been for some time, under special scrutiny by regulators, insurers, and Compliance Officers. The prudent agent will be able to *document* that the exchange is *clearly* to the benefit of the policy owner *and* that any *adverse* consequences of the exchange (e.g.: imposition of surrender charges in the original annuity, a new surrender charge schedule in the replacement annuity, a new contestable period, etc).

22Rev. Rul. 2002-75

23 Rev. Rul. 2007-24

24 Treas. Reg. §1.1035-1 states that "*section 1035 does not apply to such exchanges if the policies exchanged do not relate to the same insured. The exchange, without recognition of gain or loss, of an annuity contract for another annuity contract under section 1035(a)(3) is limited to cases where the same person or persons are the obligee or obligees under the contract received in exchange as under the original contract*". Clearly, the *owner* of both the original and replacement annuities must be the same taxpayer. Moreover, while this Regulation does not state, specifically, that the *annuitant* of both contracts must be the same, most commentators believe that both the *owner* and *annuitant* of both contracts must be the same individual or entity.

Surrendering An Annuity

Tax Due On "Gain" When An Annuity Is Surrendered

As discussed earlier, distributions from a deferred annuity that are not "amounts received as an annuity" are taxed as "all ordinary income" (if the contract was issued after 8/13/82). However, the method used to determine the amount of gain (the amount taxable as income) depends upon whether the distribution is a *partial withdrawal* or a *complete surrender.*

In the event of a partial surrender (anything less than the full value of the contract), the amount of gain is determined as the excess of the contract value over the owner's "investment in the contract" (AKA "cost basis"), "*without regard to any surrender charges*". But in the case of a full surrender, the taxable gain is equal to the amount received, less "investment in the contract". This can produce *very* different tax results.

Example: Alice's deferred annuity is now worth $54,000. She paid $50,000 for it, and she's made no withdrawals. The surrender charge this year is 8% of the amount withdrawn (we're ignoring any "free withdrawal" provision for simplicity). A partial withdrawal of $4,000 or less will be fully taxable (because her gain is $4,000). But if she surrenders the contract, she'll receive only $49,680 ($52,000 times 92%). As her investment in the contract exceeds the amount she *actually receives,* she has no taxable gain. In fact, she has a deductible *loss* of $320 (see below).

It should be noted that some insurance companies do not agree with this analysis. Those companies will compute the taxable gain in *both* cases by ignoring surrender charges. If the issuer of Alice's annuity is such a company, it will issue a 1099R for $4,000 - the cash value of the annuity before surrender, *without regard to surrender charges* ($54,000), less her investment in the contract ($50,000). This is simply *wrong,* and the IRS has recognized it as such (in Private Letter Ruling 200030013). We suggest that you confirm, with the Home Office of any annuity carriers you deal with, how that company handles this issue.

Deducting A Loss On An Annuity

Many annuity owners (and more than a few agents) are surprised to learn that a taxpayer who surrenders an annuity contract for less than his or her "investment in the contract" (which is basically the total amount contributed, less the *non-taxable* portion of all prior distributions) can claim the difference as an itemized deduction, so long as the loss is incurred "in a trade or business" or "in any transaction entered into for profit[25]". The loss is an *ordinary loss,* not a *capital loss*, and is taken on the taxpayer's income tax return as a "miscellaneous deduction", subject to the 2% of Adjusted Gross Income hurdle. There are folks out there who claim that it's *not* subject to that 2% limitation, but we think that's overly aggressive tax planning. So does the IRS.

Transfer Of An Annuity

The *transfer* of an annuity from the owner to someone else, during the owner's lifetime, may have both *income tax* and *gift tax* consequences.

Gift Of An Annuity

The transfer of an annuity for less than full and adequate consideration is a *gift*, subject to *gift tax*. It is also an *income tax* event, and the tax treatment depends upon when the annuity contract was issued.

If the annuity was issued after April 22, 1987, the income tax consequences are pretty simple. The *transferor* (the party making the gift) must report, as ordinary income, the amount of gain in the contract in the year of the gift. The cost basis ("investment in the contract") of the *transferee* (the party receiving the gift) will be transferor's adjusted basis (the adjusted basis prior to the gift plus the income reported by transferor as a result of the transfer - i.e.: the contract gain at the time of the gift).

25 IRC §165

"You call *that* 'pretty simple?'", we hear you ask. Well, it's simpler than if the annuity in question had been issued before April 23, 1987. In that situation, there is no tax consequence until the donee surrenders the contract. At that point, the gain in the contract *at the time of the gift* will be taxable to the *donor* and any subsequent gain, to the *donee.* The IRS hasn't provided guidance as to how the tax on the gain in such a partial withdrawal by donee will be allocated between donor and donee. However, the normal rules for determining the amount of gain will apply, as will the "return of principal first" rules, if the annuity had been issued prior to 8/13/82.

Transfer Of An Annuity To A Trust

As noted above, the transfer of an annuity is generally a taxable event for income tax purposes, and, if the transfer is for less than full and adequate consideration, a *gift tax* event as well. When the transferee is a trust, the tax consequences depend upon the nature of the trust.

1. Transfer of an annuity (or any other property) from a taxpayer to that taxpayer's *revocable* trust is not a taxable event.

2. Gift of an annuity to an *irrevocable* trust that is not a grantor trust (of which transferor is grantor) will trigger recognition, by the transferor, of all annuity gain in the year of the transfer (because the new owner, the trust, is a different taxpayer)[26].

3. The tax consequences of a *gift* of an annuity to the annuity owner's *irrevocable grantor* trust are not clear. Some commentators believe that because the trust is a grantor trust, and because the grantor is the same individual who owned the annuity before the transfer, the transfer is not a taxable event. The logic here is "you cannot make a taxable transaction with yourself". This *may* be true, with regard to the gift of an *annuity* to the transfer's irrevocable grantor trust, but it's not a sure thing. Section 72(e)(4)(C) clearly states that the recognition of gain occurs

26 IRC §72(e)(4)(C)

whenever there is a transfer of an annuity "without full and adequate consideration". And if the trust doesn't pay for the annuity, that's clearly the case.

It comes down to whether or not the IRC provision dealing with the gift of an annuity (Sect. 72(e)(4)(C)) "trumps" the *grantor trust rules* that, according to some commentators, make *any* gift to one's own grantor trust a non-event for tax purposes. Maybe it does; maybe it doesn't. The bottom line here is this: *The rules aren't clear and the prudent agent will not try to "practice law" by offering an opinion on the tax treatment of such a gift* (or any other point of law, for that matter).

4. If an annuity is transferred by means of a *sale,* the tax treatment is not clear (and this is the case whether the buyer of the annuity is a trust or an individual or other entity). The "profit" to the annuity owner (the difference between what the amount received from the buyer and the seller's adjusted basis) will clearly be taxable, but it is unclear what the character of that profit will be, for tax purposes. If the sales price equals the annuity's surrender value, that profit is probably ordinary income, although some might assert that it ought to be treated as capital gains. If the amount received in the sale exceeds the cash value, it may be that some of the profit is capital gains and the balance is ordinary income. There is, regrettably, no clear answer, as neither the Internal Revenue Code, nor the Treasury Regulations provide any specific guidance on this issue.

Another point to bear in mind, with regard to *any* transfer of an annuity to a trust, is that, because the new owner (the trust) is not a "natural person", the annuity may no longer be treated as "an annuity contract" and be eligible for tax-deferred treatment (see "When The Owner Is Not An Individual", above).

Cheat Sheet

- Determine whether the annuity contract is owner driven or annuity driven.
- If the owner and annuitant are different parties, problems – perhaps very serious ones, can result.
- Even if you are not giving tax advice, you can still be sued if something goes wrong. Be aware of annuity tax consideration.

Chapter 8 – Suitability

What are the suitability rules that sellers of annuities must observe? Regrettably, there is no simple answer to that question – for at least four reasons.

1. There is not one set of rules. Annuities, and those who sell them, are subject to regulation by multiple regulatory entities.

2. The existing rules, from those various regulatory authorities, are not always perfectly consistent.

3. The existing rules are not always clear.

4. The rules ***keep changing!***

Regulators – those responsible for overseeing the activities of financial advisors – have their own tests for determining appropriateness *and advisors subject to their oversight may be held accountable for the results of those tests.*

The Current Environment

Registration and Regulation Of Variable Annuities As Products

Variable annuities are *securities*, subject to regulation by the Securities & Exchange Commission (SEC) and by the securities regulatory agencies of the various states. They are also *insurance products*, and, as such, are regulated by the departments of insurance of the various states.

Registration And Regulation Of Sellers Of Variable Annuities & Registered Index Annuities

Sellers of securities must be properly licensed at both the Federal and State levels. A representative who wishes to sell mutual funds and/or *commissionable* variable annuities or life insurance policies, must first have passed at least the Series 6 exam, regulated by the Financial Industry Regulatory Authority (FINRA), *and* be registered to sell such contracts with the state department regulating securities. As variable annuities are also *insurance* products, those who sell them must be properly licensed with, and be subject to the regulatory authority of, the various State Departments of Insurance.

FINRA Rule 2330 (formerly, NASD Rule 2821) imposes particular duties upon sellers of variable annuities and those who exercise compliance oversight over those sellers.

Variable annuities (and variable life insurance policies) that pay *commissions* may be sold only by a *registered representative*, affiliated with a *Broker/Dealer* that is a member of FINRA. Contrary to popular belief, this <u>does not</u> mean that one who is not a registered representative may never sell *any* variable annuity or variable life insurance policy. That's because there are numerous variable contracts out there that pay no commissions. These contracts are designed to appeal to (and be sold by) *Registered Investment Advisors* (who are not required to be registered representatives of a Broker/Dealer member of FINRA). These individuals are subject to a different regulatory regime and are held to a different, and higher, standard of duty.

Securities registered index annuities are typically not registered as variable annuities but as modified single premium deferred annuities. These are essentially securities versions of index annuities with reset features and protection of principal from market risk. Because they pay commissions, they also may be sold only by a registered representative, and because they are insurance products, that representative must hold the required insurance licenses.

Many advisors are "dually registered", as *both* registered representatives of a FINRA-member Broker/Dealer and as either a Registered Investment Advisor or "Associate" of a Registered Investment Advisory firm (affiliated with that Broker/Dealer). This "hybrid" registration allows these advisors to act *either* as a registered representative (and receive commissions) or as a Registered Investment Advisor (or Advisory Associate) (and receive *fees*). Such advisors must comply with the rules applicable to "whichever hat they are wearing". The *standard of duty* applicable to Registered Investment Advisors is a form of the *fiduciary standard*, which is "higher than" (more stringent than) the standard applying to registered representatives acting as "product sellers".

All sellers of securities, whether Registered Investment Advisors (or Associates) or registered representatives, are subject to rules promulgated by the SEC, and to numerous Federal laws relating to securities and securities sales. These laws include:

Securities Act of 1933
Securities Exchange Act of 1934
Trust Indenture Act of 1939
Investment Company Act of 1940
Investment Advisers Act of 1940
Sarbanes-Oxley Act of 2002

Moreover, sellers of all securities are required to comply with the "Know Your Customer" (KYC) rules contained in the Patriot Act and other Federal statutes and/or the seller's Broker/Dealer, and/or any State KYC rules. (Essentially, these boil down to a requirement that the identity of the customer be clearly established and that recommendations of products be appropriate and suitable for that customer).

Regulation of Fixed Rate Deferred Annuities

"Fixed Rate" deferred annuities are not "securities", and, thus, are not subject to regulation by either the SEC or FINRA. These contracts are regulated by State insurance departments, and the regulations, and definitions and conditions used to determine "suitability" of annuity transactions, vary from state to state (and one should consult the rules in those states where he or she does business).

NAIC Suitability In Annuity Transactions Model Regulation

In 2010, the National Association of Insurance Commissioners (NAIC) adopted a model regulation for suitability of annuity transactions that included an expanded definition of "suitability" (information that is reasonably appropriate to determine the suitability of a recommendation), and identifies twelve factors that *must* be taken into account *prior to* any recommendation of any annuity. These factors are:

(1) Age;
(2) Annual income;
(3) Financial situation and needs, including the financial resources used for the funding of the annuity;
(4) Financial experience;
(5) Financial objectives;
(6) Intended use of the annuity;
(7) Financial time horizon;
(8) Existing assets, including investment and life insurance holdings;
(9) Liquidity needs;
(10) Liquid net worth;
(11) Risk tolerance; and
(12) Tax status.

These factors are typical of those found in many discussions of suitability and are not by any means exclusive to NAIC, so it is absolutely vital that annuity representatives address all these issues with the purchaser before making any recommendations.

1. Age

The proposed annuity buyer's age is one of the most important factors in determining the suitability of an annuity. One question that should be raised immediately is *whose age*? Will the buyer of the annuity (the proposed *owner*) also be the *annuitant*? If not, a number of other, very serious, questions are raised. The *owner* of an annuity is the person (or entity) that owns all rights to that annuity. The *annuitant* is the person (and it must be a human being) who is the "measuring life" – whose age (for annuities that will pay income for the annuitant's entire lifetime [so-called *life-contingent annuities*]), sex (except for *unisex annuities*), and (for *underwritten* annuities only) health condition will determine the amount of each annuity payment. Contrary to popular belief, the annuitant is not "the person who will receive annuity payments". In fact, annuity payments will be made to the contract owner unless that owner directs the insurer to make them directly to the annuitant. Moreover, the tax liability for that annuity income is that of the owner, not of the annuitant.

If the annuitant and owner are different parties, problems can result. Both the amount of the death benefit and the tax treatment of that benefit when an owner dies may be different from the amount and tax treatment when a non-owner annuitant dies (see (see *The Rules Governing Annuity Death Proceeds* in Chapter 7.)

If the annuitant and owner are the same individual (which is almost always the right way to do it), the appropriateness of an annuity recommendation, given that individual's age, must still be considered.

The suitability of adding a guaranteed lifetime withdrawal benefit (GLWB) rider to the index annuity being purchased is also highly sensitive to age. The point of having a GLWB is it guarantees an income for as long as you live – even if you use up your annuity cash value. A 7% withdrawal rate means that the withdrawals are guaranteed to last for 14 years, even if zero interest is earned. Is there an age at which adding a GLWB to an annuity become unsuitable?

Many regulatory authorities have increased their scrutiny of annuity sales to senior citizens. The NAIC and insurance regulators in many states have issued "Consumer Alerts" warning seniors of "deceptive sales practices. Some states impose special restrictions upon the provisions that annuities sold to seniors may contain (e.g.: a maximum term and/or initial amount of surrender charges).

2. Annual Income

The annual income of the annuity buyer is a factor that should be considered (and, certainly, known) by the representative recommending that annuity. Why? Well, if the annuity is a "flexible premium" contract and ongoing contributions (premiums) are contemplated, the question of whether the annuity buyer can afford to make those ongoing contributions is clearly relevant. But what if the annuity is of the "single premium" type?

Existing client income is still relevant if there is any expectation that distributions from the annuity may be required to augment that income.

3. Financial Situation And Needs, Including The Financial Resources Used For The Funding Of The Annuity

This one should be obvious. If the annuity is a tool to meet financial needs, the nature and extent of those needs *must* be known in advance. Moreover, the *source of funds* is of vital importance, not only because it's a part of the client's "total picture", but also because it must be ascertained before the agent can be sure that he or she holds the licenses and registrations required by the regulators of the state in which the sale is made. (discussed later in the chapter).

One aspect of this "sources of funds" issue that frustrates many agents is that when the funds the client wishes to invest in an annuity are currently invested in securities. Some annuity issuers will not approve the sale if those funds represent more than a certain percentage of the client's total wealth or liquid assets – even if that client's goal in purchasing the annuity is to reduce market risk and even if the client does not intend to touch those funds for many years. (This is often the case when the funds are invested in the client's IRA or qualified plan). When presented with this situation, agents should consider that the sale need not be "all or nothing" and can recommend moving only a portion of those funds to the annuity and re-allocating the remainder to less "risky" options available. *However, any such re-allocation advice may very well be construed by regulators as "investment advice".*

4. Financial Experience

The financial experience of the client is arguably more important if the annuity being recommended is a variable or indexed product than if it's a conventional fixed annuity, because the former products are more complicated. Moreover, if the annuity is a variable one, the familiarity of the client with the types of investments offered in the separate accounts is essential.

5. Financial Objectives

This one comes down to "what are we trying to accomplish with this annuity?" If the annuity is the *tool*, the financial objectives are the jobs to be done. The better everyone's understanding about those jobs, the better their appreciation of whether the annuity in question is the right tool. "Everyone" here, means not only the annuity buyer and annuity representative, but, arguably at least, the beneficiaries – especially if the annuity buyer is of an advanced age. Putting the beneficiaries of a senior citizen client in the information loop, up front, can greatly reduce the risks of misunderstanding (and, possibly, litigation) later on.

6. Intended Use Of The Annuity

Here, again, we're talking about the "tool" and the "job". The appropriateness of any annuity is hugely dependent upon the job it's intended to do. Is the annuity expected to serve as an accumulation instrument? As a source of income? As a mechanism for deferring income taxes? Is *creditor protection* an issue? Is providing a legacy for heirs a major concern? (If that's a major intended use, has life insurance been considered?) We believe that a detailed discussion of this subject ("what are you going to do with this money?") will enhance client confidence in the annuity representative, increase client satisfaction with the purchase, and go a long way towards eliminating future misunderstandings.

7. Financial Time Horizon

"Time horizon" can be a confusing term. It might mean the maximum period during which this annuity will be held. Or it might mean the number of years before which distributions (income) will be needed. We've seen it used both ways. Both are relevant to a determination of suitability, and we suggest that both should be discussed, and the client's estimates for both be documented.

8. Existing Assets

Why are the annuity buyer's *other* assets of relevance to the suitability of the annuity being proposed? For several reasons. First, because the type and total value of those other assets shed light on the extent to which the financial objectives identified in concern #5, above are likely to be met. Second, they serve as a "check" on the annuity buyer's responses in several of the other concerns. For example, if he claims substantial financial experience (concern #4), little need for liquidity (concern #9), a high tolerance for market risk (concern #11), and a high marginal tax bracket, yet all, or nearly all, of his existing assets are certificates of deposit and money market accounts, a discussion of how the risk and reward characteristics of a savings instrument can "match up" with the consumer's goals and concerns is probably in order.

9. Liquidity Needs

The *liquidity* of an asset refers to how quickly and cheaply it can be converted to cash. While a deferred annuity that imposes surrender charges (as most do) can be surrendered for cash relatively quickly, the cash received might, because of those charges, be significantly less than the annuity's value just prior to surrender. In a few index annuities, surrender charges never expire, and may even apply to death proceeds taken in a lump sum. But even those contracts whose charges do expire after a term of years may have a high cost for early liquidity during that surrender charge period.

Surrender charges are the subject of many, if not most, complaints to regulators by annuity buyers. Annuity sellers who want to avoid litigation (and make appropriate sales) should take great care that the buyer fully understands how, when, and to what extent, surrender charges are imposed, and accepts the "liquidity risk" that they represent.

10. Liquid Net Worth

If liquidity is a concern that must be addressed on every annuity sale (and it is), liquid net worth is a vitally important factor, because it's the value of the annuity buyer's assets that are liquid – that can be converted to cash quickly and cheaply. If Mr. Jones has, say, $100,000 in a money market account (which is highly liquid) and his *financial objectives, time horizon*, and *liquidity need* are such that the $100,000 will almost certainly not be required while surrender charges of the proposed annuity apply, liquidity, for the money to be invested in the annuity may not be of great concern – *so long as that $100,000 will remain liquid after the annuity sale.*

11. Risk Tolerance

Risk tolerance is a concept absolutely vital to any determination of whether an annuity sale is (or is not) "suitable" because *annuities are risk management instruments.* Unfortunately, this simple fact is not widely – or well – understood by many financial advisors (or, sad to say, regulators). Moreover, the very notion of "risk" is largely misunderstood or misapplied.

What is "risk"? Textbooks in Finance tell us that there are many different kids of "risk", including *market risk, interest rate risk, inflation risk, currency risk, credit risk, liquidity risk*, etc. Yet many "risk tolerance questionnaires" used by financial advisors (and often required by insurers and/or broker/dealers to be completed prior to the sale of an annuity – especially a variable annuity) focus only on one of these – market risk, which is commonly defined in either of two very different ways. One definition says that "market risk" is "the risk that market pressures may cause the value of an investment to fluctuate". In that sense, "market risk" means "volatility". Another, equally widely-held, says that "market risk" is the possibility that market pressures will cause the value of an investment to decline. In that sense, "market risk" equals "principal risk". Both involve uncertainty, which is arguably the central element of "risk", as to the future value of one's capital.

Certainly, that's an important consideration to any consumer; but it's not all-important. The widespread use of a risk tolerance assessment tool (such as a questionnaire) that identifies "risk" *only* as the possibility of losing one's capital (or principal) focuses attention only on the "capital preservation" and "wealth accumulation" potential of the product being considered (concerning which the tool is employed). Why can that be a problem when such a tool is used to determine the suitability of an annuity? Because the risk that is of greatest concern to the consumer may not be "that I might lose some principal", but that "I might run out of income". Moreover, principal risk is not really a factor when an *immediate annuity* is being proposed (because an immediate annuity amounts to an exchange of capital (principal) for income). And it may not be a factor when the product proposed is a fixed deferred annuity, because all fixed deferred annuities guarantee principal (except to the extent that surrender charges or a market value adjustment may erode principal if the contract is surrendered early). Indeed, principal risk may not be a great concern even when the proposed product is a variable deferred annuity if a *guaranteed living benefit* has been chosen (because the income guaranteed with such benefits is often immune to adverse market performance.

Our point here is not that market risk shouldn't be a concern when one is determining the suitability of a proposed annuity, but only that many "risk tolerance" measurement tools focus only on market risk – and, in doing so, marginalize, or ignore completely, the annuity buyer's tolerance for other risks that may be of far greater concern. We believe that a discussion of "risk tolerance" should be informed by the consumer's responses to other suitability factors – especially, financial objectives, intended use of the annuity, financial time horizon, and liquidity needs.

12. Tax Status

An annuity buyer's tax status is obviously important in any reckoning of the suitability of a proposed annuity because different financial vehicles get different tax treatment, and the utility of a given tax treatment depends largely on the taxpayer's existing tax situation *and on the type of account in which the vehicle will be held.* With a deferred annuity, "tax status" acquires special significance, because deferred annuities enjoy tax deferred growth. The value – or, to put it more precisely, the utility – of that tax deferral is the subject of much debate. In the following section, we'll examine some of the issues in that debate, in the context of when a deferred annuity may or may not be suitable.

Issues Relating To The Value Of Tax Deferral (As Enjoyed By A Deferred Annuity)

Is the tax-deferral worth the costs?

This is a particularly tricky question. It's tricky because it asks for an assessment of "worth" (which is bound to be a matter of opinion) and because it doesn't define what it means by "costs". Some critics of deferred annuities insist that the contracts themselves impose charges ("costs") for tax deferral. That one's easy. *It just ain't so!* No deferred annuity that the authors are aware of imposes any charge – explicitly or implicitly – for tax deferral. Moreover, tax deferral is granted, not by the issuer of an annuity, but by Section 72 of the Internal Revenue Code. But if you're looking for "where it says that", don't bother; there is no text in that (or any other section) of the Code that specifically grants this benefit; it's granted by implication. Section 72 prescribes the tax treatment for distributions from an annuity and specifies that all distributions are either (a) "amounts received as an annuity" or (b) "amounts not received as an annuity" (see Chapter 2). The growth of the account value of an annuity is neither; nor is it a "distribution", and that growth is not subject to tax until it actually is distributed – with one exception. Section 72(u) states that an annuity held by a "non-natural person" (that is, an entity other than a human being) will not be considered "an annuity" for income tax purposes, and, thus, the annual growth of such an annuity will be taxed as earned. The point here is that there is no contractual cost (imposed by the terms of the annuity contract) for the benefit of tax deferral. But that doesn't mean that this benefit comes at no cost.

The *real* "cost" of tax deferral of a "non-qualified" deferred annuity is twofold: First, all distributions from any annuity, whether made to the contract holder or to a beneficiary, are taxed as Ordinary Income. *No distribution, of any kind, from any annuity, ever gets Capital Gains treatment under current law.* Second, all distributions, from any "non-qualified" annuity are subject to a penalty tax, equal to 10% of the amount of such distribution that would be includible in the taxpayer's income (IRC Section 72(q)), *unless an exception to the penalty applies* (These exceptions are listed in Chapter 2).

Those are the *real* costs of tax deferral, as enjoyed by a *non-qualified* annuity. But why do we specify "non-qualified"? What does that mean? "Non-qualified", as applied to an annuity contract, means that the contract is not designed for, or held in, a "qualified plan", such as an employer-sponsored pension or profit sharing plan or an IRA. (Technically, an IRA is not a *qualified plan*, but it shares many of the same tax treatments and restrictions that apply to employer-sponsored plans, including mandated "Required Minimum Distributions"; moreover, many of the provisions described in Chapter 2 and above, that pertain to "non-qualified" annuities, *do not apply to annuities held in IRAs*. For those reasons, an annuity held within an IRA is usually called a "qualified annuity").

So, the "costs" of tax deferral for a *non-qualified* annuity are (a) All Ordinary Income treatment and (b) the possible 10% penalty imposed on distributions by Section 72(q). Now that we've got that straight, let's return to the original question. *Is the benefit of tax deferral worth those costs?*

Any answer will necessarily be a matter of opinion. First, because there's more than one way to examine this issue and, second, because the relative importance of the variables involved in any reckoning of cost/benefit are also a matter of opinion. But we'll give it a try.

If the annuity in question is a variable one, we believe that it's arguable that the benefit of tax deferral is not worth the costs we just described. We've performed hundreds of comparisons of a hypothetical variable deferred annuity versus a hypothetical mutual fund portfolio, and the result has usually favored the mutual funds – especially where the difference between the taxpayer's marginal Ordinary Income Tax rate and his Long Term Capital Gains rate is large and where the asset allocation of the instrument is heavily weighted toward equities. That said, the annuity sometimes "won", especially when the accumulated value of both instruments was taken as an *income for life* (which payout avoids the Section 72(q) penalty).

Where the (non-qualified) annuity in question is a fixed annuity, the cost/benefit equation is very different. Why? Because the "All Ordinary Income" treatment of distributions applies to both sides of the comparison – to the annuity, because all distributions from an annuity are always taxed that way, and to the alternative being considered, because financial instruments properly comparable to a fixed annuity (e.g.: CDs, bonds) are also taxed that way. The 72(q) penalty is still a disadvantage of the annuity, of course.

What if the annuity is "qualified"? If the annuity being considered will be held in a qualified plan or IRA, the *cost/benefit calculation will have nothing whatever to do with taxation.* All distributions from an IRA (or qualified plan) are always Ordinary Income and the early distribution penalty of Section 7(t) (which is similar, but not identical, to Section 72(q)), which applies only to non-qualified annuities) is a factor – *regardless of the type of instrument.* Some critics of annuities claim that funding an IRA with a variable deferred annuity amounts to "putting a tax shelter inside a tax shelter" or "wasting the tax deferral" that would apply to the annuity if it were held outside the IRA".

That's simply wrong. To show why, let's suppose that, instead of an annuity, we're considering a "small cap", non-dividend paying stock, or a mutual fund investing in such stocks. If we buy it outside the IRA and hold it for at least a year and sell it, all our profit will (under current tax law) be taxable at Long Term Capital Gains rate – which is a lot better (lower) than the rate for Ordinary Income. Indeed, even dividends from stock, or a stock mutual fund, if they're "qualified dividends" would (as we write this) receive such preferential treatment. But if we buy that same stock (or fund) inside an IRA, all our profit will be taxed at Ordinary Income rates. We would, by the strange logic that says that funding an IRA with an annuity "wastes" its tax deferral, "waste" the Capital Gains treatment that stock (or fund) would have received, had we bought it outside the IRA. By such "logic", one should conclude that funding any qualified plan or IRA with stock is a mistake.

That's nonsense. *The tax treatment that would apply to a financial instrument* (an annuity, a share of stock, or whatever), *if held outside an IRA is totally irrelevant to the question of that instrument's suitability for inclusion in that IRA.* The annuity or stock might be suitable or unsuitable for a variety of reasons, but the tax treatment it would get if it weren't in the IRA isn't a factor.

To conclude our discussion of this topic, let's assume, once again, that the annuity under consideration is "non-qualified". We said, earlier, that it's arguable that the tax deferral it gets isn't worth the costs, for which reason it might be unsuitable. But what if it's an indexed or variable annuity and it includes a *guaranteed living benefit* provision. Once again, the reckoning of suitability must be different, especially if the annuity is variable. Now, there are additional costs (the charge for the "living benefit" rider) and, in a variable annuity, there may be additional asset allocation restrictions (which might be viewed as a "cost"). But those "costs" aren't simply a "drag on performance", *because they're not investment costs.* They're *insurance costs* – imposed on the buyer in exchange for the benefit of transferring a specified risk (that the income derived from the annuity might be reduced or even eliminated by adverse market performance) from that buyer to the annuity issuer.

How can one determine if this annuity with its guaranteed living benefit is worth the costs (which include the tax treatment)? We believe that one simple and easy way of doing that is to show the annuity with the benefit and without it, highlighting the differences in costs, and asking the buyer the question with which we began this discussion. "Are the benefits we just reviewed the costs I just explained?"

Once the NAIC Suitability In Annuity Transactions Model Regulation is adopted by the state in which an annuity is being proposed, or if the insurer issuing that annuity has adopted the suitability guidelines of that regulation, the twelve factors that we've just reviewed must be discussed with the annuity buyer; this applies to any annuity – deferred or immediate, variable, fixed rate, or indexed. It's our belief that they ought to be reviewed anyway (even if not required to), because they're all important, and because a thorough discussion of these factors will greatly reduce the chances of a "bad sale" – and of its consequences.

Regulation Of Index Annuities

Index annuities have, in recent years, been subjected to increasing regulatory scrutiny. In August, 2005, the National Association of Securities Dealers (NASD) issued **Notice To Members 05-50**, which detailed the responsibility of member firms for supervising sales of *unregistered* index annuities (that is to say, index annuities that were not registered as securities with the SEC). The Notice began with a section entitled "Investor Protection Issues Presented By Equity-Indexed Annuities", and noted, in the opening sentence, that "EIAs are complex investments". After detailing some of the complexities of these products, the Notice declared that, "NASD is concerned about the manner in which associated persons [individuals engaged in the sales of securities, including "Registered Representatives", in NASD member firms] are marketing and selling unregistered EIAs, and the absence of adequate supervision of these sales practices". In other words, the NASD was sufficiently concerned that registered representatives of NASD member firms, over which it had regulatory authority, might have been marketing these unregistered products (over which it did not have authority) in ways that "could confuse or mislead investors". "Moreover", it continued, "because of the product's complexity, some associated persons might have difficulty understanding all the features of the product and determining the extent to which those features meet the need of the customer".

The next section of the Notice was entitled "The Uncertain Status of Unregistered Equity-Indexed Annuities", which addressed the crux of the problem – that index annuities, although being sold both by unregistered insurance agents and by registered representatives (over which the NASD had authority) were not clearly "securities", within the purview of the NASD. The Notice acknowledged that "The question of whether a particular EIA is an insurance product or a security is complicated and depends upon the particular facts and circumstances concerning the instrument offered or sold".

In the next section, the Notice outlined the *supervisory measures* that it deemed necessary for NASD member firms to implement with regard to index annuities, citing its Rules 3030 and 3040. It began by acknowledging that many Broker/Dealers treat the sale of unregistered index annuities as "outside business activities", beyond the reach of their supervision. It declared that these firms "run certain risks" by assuming that the annuity is not a security and that that question was unclear.

This was the justification used by NASD in 05-50 to why broker/dealers should require their registered representatives to submit all index annuity business through them. However the ***Dodd-Frank Wall Street Reform and Consumer Protection Act*** removed this uncertainty. Congress has ruled that index annuities are not and cannot be treated as securities as long as they follow the rules. Rule 3040 cannot be applicable because you can't have a private securities transaction if the transaction involves a product that the law says is not a security. Whether or not FINRA changes their treatment of index annuities in recognition that the questions raised by NASD NTM 05-50 have now been answered is up to FINRA.

Source of Funds

SCENARIO: The insurance licensed producer makes a balanced presentation on the pros and cons of an index annuity. The consumer weighs the information and decides the annuity will do a better job of meeting his or her needs and sells a mutual fund to get the cash and then buys the annuity. Does the annuity producer need to be securities registered? No! No securities registration is needed by the annuity producer for this sale in any state of the union, including Arkansas.

On 18 September 2009 the Arkansas Insurance Department and the Arkansas Securities Department issued Joint Bulletin No-14-2009 ***Sales Or Investment Advice Related To Securities Products By Insurance Producers.*** This bulletin has quickly become perhaps the most noted and misquoted piece of annuity regulation of recent times. Apparently many agents think it says is that you can't use the proceeds from a securities sales to buy an annuity unless you are securities registered. The bulletin does not say that. It does not come close to saying that. What is says is this:

"The recommendation to replace securities such as mutual funds, stocks, bonds and various other investment vehicles defined as securities under the Arkansas Securities Act is the offering of investment advice. It is unlawful to offer investment advice unless one is registered (licensed) with the Arkansas Securities Department as an investment adviser or investment adviser representative."

EVERY STATE say you must be securities registered to recommend selling securities. NO STATE says a securities license is required <u>if the consumer decides</u> to liquidate securities and use the proceeds to buy an annuity from a non-securities registered agent.

In the enforcement actions we reviewed relating to source of funds, the non-securities registered agents were either specifically advising consumers to sell securities or presenting themselves as experts in investments and investment advice.

If a consumer looks at their personal situation and makes his or her own decision to sell securities and uses the proceeds to buy an annuity, then no violation has occurred. Even Arkansas alludes to this, saying in case (S-08-029) that the reason for the Consent Order is because the agent didn't merely recommend an annuity but instead provided advice on securities matters.

Assuming the agent does not put the recommendation to sell in writing, it could come down to the consumer's stating that there was a recommendation to sell and the agent denying this. The non-investment registered insurance agent might want to consider having the annuity purchaser sign, at the time of application, a form attesting that no recommendation was made by that agent to sell or replace any instruments defined by state law as a security. We know of at least one agency that requires a form with such an attestation to be completed, and signed by the annuity buyer. Of course, we are not offering this as legal advice.

We have found that state regulators tend to look at several things to determine whether an insurance agent is acting as an investment advisor. One is a pattern of fixed annuity sales in which the money came from the sales of securities. Another is the language used by the agent. Does the agent talk about repositioning funds, allocating assets, or advising the consumer? Those are "red flags". Still another red flag is if the agent helped the consumer to complete the securities transfer or sales forms. However, there are no absolute guaranteed ways to avoid an accusation by the state that an agent is offering investment advice in a fixed annuity sale.

Compliance Issues

Balancing Language

We recently found a sales training piece from a decade ago that talked about the benefits of averaging. Here are some of the positive points mentioned on the front page:

1. Averaging saves you if the index plunges right before the anniversary

2. When markets go up and down in a year, the averaging design can register a positive when others register a zero.

3. Averaging reduces downward volatility.

The sales piece also included easy to understand index calculation that probably looked fair to the customer.

We then flipped it over to the back and it was blank. Apparently the writer did not feel there were negative aspects of averaging...but there are. Here are a few:

1. Averaging does help if the index plunges right before you calculate the movement. By the end of February 2008, the S&P 500 was showing a loss if calculated from a start point to end point for the past 12 months, but some averaging methods were still crediting over 4% for same period due to a higher end point calculation value (resulting from averaging ending values). However, by April 2008 averaging methods were crediting zero interest (because the averaged ending values had dropped). Averaging can result in a positive return

for a negative period if the fall in the values is concentrated at the end of the period, but the positive result is temporary.

2. While averaging does reduce downward volatility, it also reduces the effects of upward movements. As discussed in Chapter 3, the return of a monthly averaged structure averaged roughly 57% of a point-to-point structure. This means that a 10% index return reported in the financial pages could be 5% or 6% when averaged. Such reduction is offset, to an extent, by the fact that averaging methods typically have higher rates and/or caps. It is important that we understand that a 100% index participation rate, when applied to a contract using averaging, will never credit precisely the same return reported for that index in the newspaper. Occasionally it will be higher, but usually it will be lower.

3. Averaging does sound fair, which is why both averaging positives and negatives need to be explained.

A time period often used in sales materials showing the wonders of averaging is the year 1987. In this calendar year, the S&P rose 2% from 1 January to 31 December, but if you measured it using daily or monthly averaging the index rose 18%! We believe that if you're going to show 1987, you really ought to show 1982 – where a point-to-point look at the year reveals a 15% gain, but an averaging calculations results in a loss.

Index annuities offer consumers a vehicle with the potential for a higher return than they might realize from other conservative alternatives. However, an index annuity is not an index mutual fund or any other form of equity investment. No index annuity realizes gains from reinvested dividends and capital gains. On the other hand, all index annuities offer principal protection.

The annuity representative proposing an index annuity should present a balanced picture of its strengths and weaknesses. You could say that an index annuity, unlike a mutual fund, preserves the principal if the market declines, but you should also say that the index annuity does not normally have the same upside potential of a fund. You could say that an index annuity has the potential for higher interest than a CD, but you also need to state that the annuity return could be as low as the minimum guarantee.

"This is a fixed index annuity. Because it is a fixed annuity, it provides minimum guaranteed interest. Because the annuity's interest calculation is linked to an index, additional interest may be earned. What will your interest be? I don't know, because it depends on how the index performs and how much of the performance you are able to participate in. Some years will be good and some years could be zero."

Balancing language needs to disclose the positives and negatives of both index annuities and the interest crediting structures and product features. For example, it is fair to say that averaging methodologies eliminate the risk of locking in a period's lowest value, however you also need to say that averaging prevents you from getting the highest value.

Fair Disclosure

The compliance and suitability regulations talk about "full disclosure" but we feel that this phrase can be misleading. A securities prospectus may attempt to disclose every possible risk or issue, but the odds of a potential buyer finding the information he needs to make a decision are low when the prospectus is written in "lawyerese" and runs some 300 pages (and even worse, when important information is relegated to footnotes). Unclear language and sheer length don't just make it hard for consumers to understand; they discourage many from even trying.

The answer isn't to ensure that the reader is presented every single item that could, in any conceivable circumstance, have anything to do with the subject. That approach is what created monstrous prospectuses in the first place. We believe that a better outcome – *fair disclosure* – occurs when the consumer is presented with all *relevant* and *material* information in *clearly understandable* language and when all descriptions and "sales points" are both accurate and balanced (the latter meaning that both positive and negative aspects to the thing discussed are presented fairly).

Minimum Guarantee Not Credited Each Year

With the exception of a very few products, an index annuity minimum guaranteed return will not be credited until the end of the surrender period, and will be credited only if the index-linked interest is less than the guarantee. Most products currently base the minimum guarantee on 87.5% of the premium.

You could try to explain that the minimum interest rate is 1%, 2% or 3%, or that it floats, and then go on to say that in reality, the effective minimum rate may be 0.75% or even zero, and then say that this rate is not even credited each year, and it is not paid in addition to the index-linked interest earned. We don't recommend this.

Or, you could say "At the end of x years (or however long the surrender period is), the insurer guarantees that you will have an account value of at least $1.10 (or $1.07 or $1) for each $1 of premium, and, if, at that point, the index crediting hasn't produced that much, the insurer will go back and RETROACTIVELY credit you the additional interest required to produce that guaranteed minimum value."

The key word here is "retroactive." When you tell consumers that they will probably see years with zero interest credited and then add that last explanation, they will understand that they will, by the end of the term, get at least the minimum return – because retroactive means that the minimum interest isn't lost, for those years when zero interest was earned; it is merely delayed.

Why Surrender Charges?

Surrender charges serve two functions. The first is to encourage the annuity owner to keep the annuity for at least a minimum number of years so that carrier can match up the maturity of the investments supporting the annuity. In other words, if the carrier issues an annuity that they expect will be cashed in after seven years, they probably do not want to back that annuity with a pool of bonds having a 15 year maturity. Why? Because, while the value of those bonds after 15 years is assured, the value at any time before that is not known (or knowable). The insurer cannot adequately back its liability to pay the surrender value of the annuity with assets that may, at the time, be worth less.

Another factor is that longer maturity bonds tend, in most situations, to pay higher yields than bonds of shorter duration, to compensate the buyer for the time element risk. If an annuity's surrender charge is longer, the carrier can invest in longer maturity bonds, typically producing higher yields, and this extra yield can be passed along to the annuity owner. The surrender charge helps the carrier to buy the appropriate supporting investments.

The second function of a surrender charge is to pay the costs associated with acquiring the annuity, including account set-up costs, sales commissions, and premium bonuses. These costs are generally amortized over the surrender charge period of the annuity. However, if the policy is cashed in before the initial costs can be recouped the surrender charge works to complete the recapture of the costs.

Fair disclosure requires that the annuity owner be informed, clearly, what it will cost to get out of the contract at any given time. This, in turn, requires disclosure of the actual surrender charge (that is, how it is calculated),the amount to which the surrender charge is applied, and the point after which no surrender charge is applicable. Regrettably, not all annuity sales literature provides all this information in clear, understandable English.

Premium Bonus Are Not Free

Chapter 4 ends with the observation that "a premium bonus is never free." A bonus is a cost to the contract, just like commissions and policy expenses, and these costs are amortized. If you are comparing two annuity contracts, that are identical, except that one has an upfront bonus and the other does not, the one with the bonus will earn less interest during future renewal periods until the cost of the bonus is recaptured.

Does this mean an up-front bonus is bad? Not necessarily. A consumer may prefer to have a "bird in the hand", in the shape of a tangible bonus today, rather than trust those bonus bucks to the future uncertainties of the financial markets. An index annuity with an up-front bonus may be better positioned to take advantage of periods of index growth in the early years of the policy, thus earning more index-linked interest, than would a contract without an initial bonus. However, a problem can arise if the terms of the bonus are not fully explained, such as when the bonus is "recapturable" upon early surrender, or when transfers from existing annuity contracts are involved and the bonus has been described as an "offset" to the surrender charges imposed by those existing contracts. (As we have noted earlier, bonuses should not be characterized that way).

How Bonuses Affect Contract Value

Let's suppose that an existing contract has a remaining surrender penalty period of five years and that a tax-free exchange of that contract for a new one (under Internal Revenue Code Section 1035) will result in a 5% surrender charge. If the new contract has a 10% premium bonus, it might appear, at first blush, that a transfer to the new annuity would pay off the old 5% charge and leave the consumer with 5% "found money". However, the cost of that 10% bonus on the new contract is amortized under that contract. It will result in either longer or steeper surrender charges than would have been applicable without that bonus or a reduction in the renewal interest rate (compared to the renewal rate that would have been credited without the bonus) or both. In essence, not only does the consumer still feel the effect of the old 5% surrender charge, but also the effect will impact future earnings longer than the 5 years left originally.

All of this does not mean that it is bad to do an exchange from an existing policy to a new annuity paying an up-front bonus. It means only that there should be other, solid, financial reasons for making that exchange. These might include a stronger minimum guarantee on the new policy, the presence of *guaranteed living benefits* in the new policy that are not available in the existing one, or a different – and more preferable, from the consumer's perspective – method of earning interest (index-linked interest for example). But even these reasons may not be enough if the old policy still imposes surrender charges. The costs and benefits of an exchange, compared to the costs and benefits of continuing the existing annuity, must be fully understood by both the annuity owner and the agent recommending such an exchange.

One reason for understanding these realities of up-front annuity bonuses is that they are the subject of very serious regulator attention. On the variable annuity side, the SEC has expressed concern for several years over the way VA bonus products are presented to consumers, and both the SEC and FINRA have gone after producers whom they felt were engaging in abusive transactions. State insurance regulators are also beginning to show concern about the use of bonuses in fixed annuity exchanges. While all annuity transfers should always be in the best interests of the consumer, it would be prudent for agents to take extra care if a bonus is involved, and to ensure that the consumer understands a reality of life that the late Robert Heinlein called "TANSTAAFL! – There Ain't No Such Thing As A Free Lunch!"

Required Annuitization (Two-Tier)

One definition of "annuity" is "a regular income paid for a set period of time or as long as an individual lives". Annuitization provides several distinct benefits: a certainty of regular, predictable income, possible tax advantages, and peace of mind from investment volatility. The income you get is determined by the insurance company (using conservative assumptions, because the insurance company is taking the risk of having to provide that income, no matter what). When you annuitize you are saying that you are comfortable with exchanging the amount of capital you're annuitizing for the amount of income that will surely be paid. You're also hoping, , in the case of a "life only" annuitization, that you will live long enough to enjoy that income.

Fixed Annuitization – Good

- Income Guarantees
- Some Tax Advantages (Possible Relief From Income & Social Security Benefit Taxation)
- Portion Of Income Is Excluded From Taxes (Your Own Money Coming Back To You)
- Asset Protection Vehicle In Some Instances

Fixed Annuitization – Not So Good

- Insurer Credit Risk – Your continued income is dependent on the survival of the insurance company
- Perception Of Lousy Returns (The Higher The Exclusion Rate The Worse The Return)
- Rigid Inflation-Insensitive Income (if no "COLA" feature)

Annuitizing "Two-Tier" Index Annuities

Most annuity owners do not convert the money they have built up in their annuity into a guaranteed income stream. And 99% of index annuities on the market do not require policy annuitization to receive the index-linked interest earned. The handful of annuities that do require annuitization to receive index-linked interest earned have a minimum payout period of usually 5-years, but the minimum may be as long as 10-years, and the minimum interest credited during payout can be as low as 1%. In return for these restrictions, these contracts may offer the potential for higher index-linked returns during the accumulation period than are offered by contracts that do not require annuitization. This is often done with a 'two-tier" crediting model.

When the annuity owner annuitizes a 'two-tier" contract, using the required annuitization payout, the amount annuitized includes interest calculated using the contract's "normal" interest calculation and crediting formula. However, if the annuity owner wants to surrender the policy for a lump sum (and not take proceeds using the required annuitization), the cash value will be re-calculated, using a less generous (lower) interest rate calculation and crediting method.

If you intend to annuitize the annuity, to create a future guaranteed income stream, and you feel you can trust the insurance company to provide a fair annuitization return, then required annuitization will not be a detriment. But make very sure that you want to annuitize, because the penalty for not annuitizing can be severe.

What if your intent is not to turn the annuity into an income stream that you will spend, but rather to reclaim the money you'll receive under the forced annuitization for use someplace else? Would a "two tier" annuity (that requires annuitization to earn the higher interest) make sense? Our admittedly vague answer is: it depends on the interest you earn with that strategy, compared to the interest you might have earned using another strategy.

For example, say that your "two-tier" annuity averaged an 8% a year index-linked return for the first five years and then only received a 2% annual return when you annuitized it for the next five years? Your true overall return for the entire ten-years would be 4.92%. If you could have found a fixed rate annuity with a ten-year 5% rate guarantee you would have been ahead by buying that fixed rate annuity. But if the best ten-year guaranteed rate available was 4%, then you were better off using the forced annuitization product. Would an index annuity not requiring annuitization have been better? Again, it depends. If its average ten-year return had been higher than 4.92%, yes. If not, no.

Key Points On Annuitization

- Required annuitization may not be an issue if you intend to annuitize anyway
- 99% of index carriers don't require annuitization to receive index-linked interest
- Annuitization products amplify the "trust me" relationship with the insurance carrier
- Annuitization products usually severely limit any index-linked interest credited if the policy is surrendered and not annuitized
- Annuitization provides certainty of income and return

GLWBs Must Be Used To Get A Benefit

As discussed in Chapter 6, all index annuities with lifetime benefits guaranteed some type of withdrawal income growth, but these income account bonuses or annual growth guarantees are only realized if the annuity owner uses up all of his own money and the GLWB payout steadily dips into the pocket of the carrier. As we have noted earlier, the consumer needs to realize that a 7% or 8% withdrawal income growth rate is not a return on capital.

GLWBs are a wonderful retirement income tool but to benefit from them, the annuity owner must 1) live a long time, 2) earn a relatively poor return on the annuity cash value, and – most important of all – 3) actually take those withdrawals available from the GLWB.

Cheat Sheet

- The annuity representative may be regulated by differing standards of suitability from various regulatory authorities, that are not always consistent, and the rules keep changing!

- Once the NAIC Suitability In Annuity Transactions Model Regulation is adopted by the state or the carrier, the twelve factors must be discussed with the annuity buyer.

- The suitability of an annuity for a particular individual's IRA or "qualified plan" account depends upon how well that particular annuity fits the investment objectives, income needs, and risk tolerance of that particular client. It has absolutely nothing to do with the tax treatment that it would receive if it were not held in such an account.

- Source of funds does not mean a non-securities registered insurance agent cannot sell an annuity simply because the money for the purchase is coming from the sales of securities. It means that the non-securities registered insurance agent cannot recommend the sales of securities.

- "Balancing Language" means that both the good and bad must be disclosed, but practicing "fair disclosure" means that the emphasis is on disclosing information that is meaningful for the consumer.

Chapter 9: When Is An Index Annuity (or any annuity) Appropriate?

One of the questions that any annuity representative must determine, when considering an annuity for a client, is whether that annuity is appropriate. The answer will depend, not only upon the "facts and circumstances" (the client's age, goals, income, net worth, risk tolerance, etc.), but also on what is meant by "appropriate". There is not a single standard. One standard is that of suitability, which is used by regulatory agencies such as FINRA, state insurance departments, broker/dealers, insurance companies that issue such contracts, and in the previous chapter we discussed at length the NAIC Suitability In Annuity Transactions Model Regulation. However, there are additional standards as well.

The *fiduciary standard* is considerably stricter than most regulatory definitions of suitability, but it applies, at present, only to certain situations. And, as with the standard of "suitability", there is not merely one variety, but for the moment, let's return to the general question. When, in what circumstances, is an annuity "OK", such that an annuity representative may recommend it?

We suggest that the best approach is a utilitarian one. It begins with recognition that an annuity, like any financial instrument, is just a tool, and that its utility (its usefulness) depends upon how well it is suited to the task.

How does one determine that? We should begin with a close examination of the job to be done. What is required? What is not required? What is merely desired? Or not desired? We then examine the tool, evaluating its characteristics in terms of how well they fit with the requirements and desiderata of the job. Let's look at some examples of tasks and tools (in this case, types of annuities and see how they match up. You should bear in mind that these are merely exercises, not the authors' recommendations – much less, prescribed solutions. You may disagree with our suggestions. That's OK. Although there are surely some "wrong" answers (where the characteristics of the tool clearly do not fit well with the job requirements), there is, just as surely, more than one "right" answer.

Tasks and Tools

We'll begin with some typical planning tasks and evaluate how appropriate each of five annuity types, or tools, will be for each task.

Tasks

1. To provide the greatest possible fully-guaranteed income, commencing immediately, which must continue for as long as the client lives, and where no value need remain at the income recipient's death.

2. To provide an income, commencing immediately, that will keep up with inflation, and which must continue for life and where no value need remain at the income recipient's death.

3. To provide the greatest possible fully-guaranteed income, commencing immediately, which must continue for as long as the client lives, and where some value must remain at the income recipient's death.

4. To provide an income, commencing immediately, that will keep up with inflation, and which must continue for life and where some value must remain at the income recipient's death

5. To accumulate as much wealth as possible in 20 years, with no risk of principal.

6. To accumulate as much wealth as possible in 20 years, with the possibility of losses in some years.

7. To pass as much net, after-tax wealth to heirs as possible.

Tools

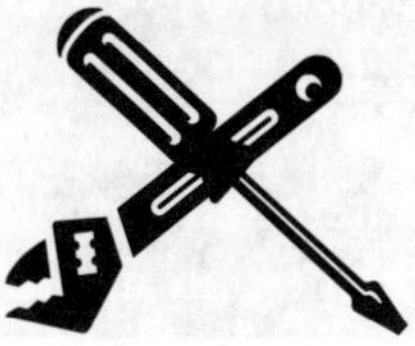

Immediate fixed annuity
Immediate variable annuity
Deferred fixed annuity
Deferred fixed index annuity
Deferred variable annuity

Task 1: To provide the greatest possible fully-guaranteed income, commencing immediately, which must continue for as long as the client lives and where no value need remain at the income recipient's death

How well do the four types of annuities match up with the first task? Well, as the income must commence immediately, the deferred annuities are out of the running. Why? First, because most deferred annuities do not permit annuitization during the first contract year. A fixed deferred annuity wouldn't make much sense anyway, even if it did permit annuitization in the first year, because interest is generally credited to such contract annually (which means that any interest earned in the first year prior to annuitization would be lost).

Some variable deferred annuities offer a *guaranteed lifetime withdrawal benefit (GLWB)* that may be activated in the first year. However, except for annuity buyers in their early forties or younger, the maximum withdrawal under that rider is less than a typical payout for a single life annuity (even with a Cash Refund option). Of course, the GMWB rider, because it does not involve annuitization, offers the opportunity to "undo" the income stream and surrender the annuity for its remaining cash value, something that is generally not possible with immediate annuities. Moreover, some GLWB riders provide that if any amount of the "benefit base" (from which the GLWB income payments are calculated) remains at the death of the income recipient, that remainder will be paid to the beneficiary named in the contract. However, in this task, there is no requirement that any value remain at the income recipient's death (to be paid to a beneficiary).

Conclusion: Where the planning goal is to provide the greatest income possible, on a fully-guaranteed basis, and for life, and where no value need remain at the end of the income period, an immediate fixed annuity is not only the most appropriate tool; it's arguably the only appropriate tool.

Task 2: To provide an income, commencing immediately, that will keep up with inflation, and which must continue for life and where no value need remain at the income recipient's death

This task is identical to the first, with one very important difference. The amount of income is to "keep up with inflation". An immediate fixed annuity without a "COLA" (Cost of Living Adjustment) feature won't work here. Many insurers offer a COLA option in their immediate fixed annuities; very few, however, link the amount of annual increase to an external index of inflation such as the CPI. Typically, the annuity buyer is permitted to choose from a few fixed rates of increase (e.g.: 3%, 4%, 5%) and that choice will apply to all future payments, regardless of actual inflation experience.

An immediate variable annuity is sometimes recommended in this situation. Here, the amount of each year's income payment(s) varies with the unit values of the investment sub-accounts chosen. If one believes that those chosen investments will increase in value at or above the rate of inflation, an immediate variable annuity might be a good choice. But it might not, because the amount can go down as well as up (because the value of variable investment accounts can). An immediate index annuity might serve as an appropriate tool for this task, but, as we write this, no carrier offers one.

Task 3: To provide the greatest possible fully-guaranteed income, commencing immediately, which must continue for as long as the client lives, and where some value must remain at the income recipient's death

For this task, no immediate annuity is ever appropriate, because, even with a "refund" feature if the annuitant lives long enough, no value will remain at his or her death.

A "refund feature" is a guarantee that, if the annuitant dies before receiving either a specified number of payments ("period certain" refund) or the amount originally invested ("cash refund" or "installment refund"), the beneficiary will receive either the remaining number of guaranteed payments or the remaining principal.

Task 4: To provide an income, commencing immediately, that will keep up with inflation, and which must continue for life and where some value must remain at the income recipient's death

Again, no immediate annuity is suitable here (for the reason stated above).

Task 5: To accumulate as much wealth as possible in 20 years, using annuities that protect principal from market risk

Now, deferred annuities enter the picture (as income need not commence immediately). The problem is now one of accumulation of wealth. A deferred annuity can serve as an instrument for wealth accumulation. Indeed, many annuity buyers buy them solely for that purpose. However, it should be noted that all deferred annuities must (as a matter of law) contain annuity payout options based on annuitization of the contract Some critics maintain that these guarantees are of little (or no) value. Two reasons given for this position are:

First, that the "payout factors" (the number of dollars that will be paid per year (or month), for each $1,000 placed under the specified annuity payout option, regardless of future changes in longevity or interest rates) guaranteed in deferred annuity contracts are not nearly as attractive (as high) as those available in the immediate annuity marketplace.

This is quite correct. In the nearly forty years we have been in this business, we've almost never seen a time when immediate annuity rates were not higher (often, much higher) than the payout rates guarantees in deferred annuity contracts. You could, in the past, have simply invested in some alternatives, and when the time came to "convert" one's accumulated wealth into income, have bought an immediate annuity.

But will that be the case in the future? Who knows? Americans are living longer with each passing decade. If, decades hence, we're living (on average) to age 90, or even 100, will immediate annuity rates not reflect that? (All other factors being equal, the longer the insurance company expects you to live, the less it will pay you, each year, if payments must persist for your lifetime).

Second, "few annuities are ever annuitized". Simply because a deferred annuity is not placed under an annuity payout option does not mean that it cannot be – or will be – "converted" to a lifetime income. Many investment advisors have never recommended annuitization to any client, because when a client has wanted to "turn on the income stream", they have "gone shopping" in the immediate annuity marketplace, for an immediate annuity with higher payout factors.

As the owner of a deferred annuity can exchange that contract for an immediate one on a tax-free basis, nearly always without any cost, and because there has always (up to now) been a time when payout rates from at least one immediate annuity (issued by an insurer with financial strength at least as high as that of the deferred annuity issuer) were more attractive, one might argue that investment advisors are ethically obliged not to recommend annuitization.

But to return to the task at hand, what sorts of deferred annuities might be appropriate here? Well, we can rule out variable deferred annuities, with a few cautious exceptions. To the extent that a variable deferred annuity is invested in the insurer's "fixed account", its owner bears no risk of lost principal. Indeed, there is nearly always a positive interest rate guaranteed on these accounts. And a variable annuity with a "guaranteed minimum accumulation benefit" ensures that the owner will be able to surrender the contract for no less than the amount invested (less withdrawals). However, many insurers have stopped issuing these "riders", and those that still do typically impose a waiting period before the guarantee is operative. One might argue that a variable annuity with a "guaranteed minimum withdrawal benefit" also eliminates "principal risk", as this rider does assure its owner that no less than the original principal may be taken, regardless of investment performance, but only in the form of periodic withdrawals over many years.

If variable deferred annuities are inappropriate tools for this task (because they present principal risk) and all immediate annuities are as well (because they serve to distribute wealth, not to accumulate it), what's left? We're left with fixed deferred annuities offering a stated rate or stated participation in an index. Which type is the most appropriate tool? The answer depends upon whether one believes that the wealth created by interest declared in the conventional way is likely to be more or less than that created by interest linked to the performance of an external index.

Task 6: To accumulate as much wealth as possible in 20 years, using annuities with the possibility of losses in some years

In this task, the chief goal remains the accumulation of as much wealth as possible, but the requirement of no principal risk has yielded to an acceptance of "the possibility of losses in some years". Now, a variable deferred annuity may be appropriate, as the potential gains in a VA (especially, if largely invested in equities) are greater than those realistically achievable in a fixed annuity (either conventional or index). Of course, that increased upside potential is offset by the very real possibility of losses. Indeed, the annuity buyer considering a VA for this task should clearly understand that the possibility of loss is not limited to "some years" and that, except for funds invested in the "fixed account" and absent any "guaranteed living benefit" rider, money invested in a variable annuity is entirely subject to the market risks of the investment accounts chosen.

Variable annuities, unlike fixed annuities, are both securities (subject to regulation by the SEC, FINRA and state securities regulatory departments) and insurance products (subject to regulation by state departments of insurance). They also get heightened scrutiny by both Federal and State regulators and are subject to special rules.

Task 7: To pass as much net, after-tax wealth to heirs as possible

This task is very different from the first six. Instead of an immediate income or maximum wealth accumulation for the consumer, the goal here is maximizing the wealth that will pass from the consumer to his or her heirs. How well do the various kinds of annuities perform that task?

The answer is: Generally speaking, not well at all.

No immediate annuity can do the job. As was noted above, an immediate annuity is a device for distributing wealth, in the form of income. No immediate annuity can guarantee that any value will remain, in the annuity contract, after the end of the annuity payout period.

A deferred annuity can serve to pass wealth to heirs, but the tax treatment that applies to all deferred annuities is not favorable, compared to the treatment enjoyed by most types of property.

Most property owned by a taxpayer receives a "step-up in basis" at his or her death (as of this writing). Thus, property purchased by a taxpayer for $10 that has grown in value to $50 by the time of that taxpayer's death, will have an adjusted cost basis of $50 when it passes to heirs. A deferred annuity does not enjoy this treatment. The annuity must be paid out to beneficiaries at the owner's death and all previously untaxed "gain" will be taxable to those beneficiaries.

All distributions from any annuity are taxed, under current law, as "Ordinary Income"; Capital Gains treatment is never available.

Approaches to the Problem

The above approach (viewing the various types of annuities as tools and matching them with the planning tasks for which they might be recommended) is a good way to begin to answer the question of "When is an annuity appropriate?" It might be called a utility-based approach. But there are other ways to evaluate the appropriateness of annuities. There is the rules-based approach, in which one constructs specific directives as to when the recommendation of an annuity will or will not be deemed appropriate. Another is the principles-based approach, in which the determination rests, not upon "do the rules say I must not do this?", but upon "is my doing this inconsistent with principles which I have agreed [as a condition of my licenses and credentials] to follow?"

Both of the latter two approaches are employed by regulators, as we discussed in Chapter 8 and will continue to talk about in the next chapter. However, in the remainder of this chapter, we'll stick mostly with the utility-based approach, seeking to answer the question of "when does an annuity make sense?" Thus far, we have, in matching annuity tools with planning tasks and examined a few facts situations in which a particular type of annuity either clearly is or clearly is not appropriate. We've seen that, where immediate income is a planning objective, an immediate annuity is often appropriate (and may be the only appropriate solution). And that, where a future lump sum is required (either for the use of the consumer or to pass as an inheritance), an immediate annuity is never appropriate. These are clear rules of thumb that might amount to what attorneys call "bright line tests"* - a "rules based" approach. While this approach has obvious limitations (any rule worth using must avoid both being so specific that it addresses only rare situations and so general that its application must be accompanied by "but it depends upon…"), we believe that there are several "bright line" rules that can be applied to the question of when an annuity is or is not appropriate. But, before listing these rules, let's look at two issues that almost always come up in discussions about "suitability" or "appropriateness", and are often elements in complaints about "mis-sold" annuities – the relative tax advantages of annuities and the surrender charges that many deferred annuities impose.

* A "bright line test" is "a clearly defined rule or standard, generally used in law, composed of objective factors, which leaves little or no room for varying interpretation. The purpose of a bright-line rule is to produce predictable and consistent results in its application.

Tax Treatment of Annuities Versus Alternatives

All annuities receive tax-favored treatment, but the treatment of immediate annuities is very different from that of deferred annuities.

Immediate Annuities

The income payments under an immediate annuity are taxed according to a "cost recovery" rule, in which part of each payment is deemed to be a return of principal (and, thus, not taxable).

Readers can find a detailed explanation of this treatment in chapters 2 and 3 of The Annuity Advisor (National Underwriter Co., 2nd ed., 2009), by John Olsen and Michael Kitces.

Deferred Annuities

The earnings in deferred annuities are, generally speaking, not subject to tax as earned. Tax on those earnings is due only when earnings are distributed, which is why these contracts are sometimes called "tax deferred annuities". All distributions from any annuity are, under current tax law, either (a) amounts received as an annuity or (b) amounts not received as an annuity. This is a source of considerable confusion for many people, so let's clear it up now.

How can a distribution from an annuity contract consist of "amounts not received as an annuity"? This seeming contradiction stems from the fact that "annuity" has different meanings. When paired with the word "contract", the result ("annuity contract") refers to a specific type of legal agreement, a "contract for income", between an issuer (usually, an insurance company) and a purchaser, guaranteeing the latter the right to convert (immediately or at a future date) the amount(s) invested to an income that is guaranteed to last for a specified period of years or for life. Those payments of income are what the Internal Revenue Code and Treasury Regulations refer to as "amounts received as an annuity". In the latter sense, "annuity" refers, not to a contract for income, but to the special nature of the income itself (that it consists of part principal and part earnings, guaranteed for a specified duration).

In nearly all immediate annuities, the only payments possible are these regular annuity payments (payments made under an annuity payment option). But in a deferred annuity, the contract holder may defer "turning on" the stream of such regular payments and use the contract to accumulate wealth. Prior to annuitization, distributions may be taken either as partial withdrawals or by surrender of the contract for its entire value. Such distributions are, in tax parlance, "amounts not received as an annuity".

So, regular annuity payments, under an "annuity payout option" are "amounts received as an annuity" and any other distributions (including "deemed" distributions such as the pledging of annuity cash value as collateral for a loan) are "amounts not received as an annuity". The annual earnings in a deferred annuity, until received via annuitization or withdrawal, are neither, which is why such earnings are not taxed as earned.

This tax deferred growth is often cited as a chief advantage of a deferred annuity (over investments which do not enjoy such tax treatment). But that tax treatment comes at a cost, which is often not well understood and is frequently an issue in determinations of annuity suitability.

The "Cost" of Tax Deferral in a Deferred Annuity

The "cost" of tax deferral is not a charge imposed by the annuity contract. Contrary to the assertions of some ill-informed critics, no annuity ever imposes a charge for tax deferral. However, the Internal Revenue Code does. In fact, it imposes three costs:

1. All taxable distributions from any annuity are taxed (under current law) as Ordinary Income. No distribution from any annuity is eligible for Capital Gains treatment.

2. All previously untaxed earnings (including any guaranteed death benefit in excess of cash value) in any annuity will, at death, be taxed (as Ordinary Income) to the beneficiar(ies). "Tax deferred" does not mean "tax free".

3. All distributions from an annuity are subject to a penalty tax (equal to 10% of the taxable amount distributed) unless an exception to this penalty applies. The exceptions are listed in the appendix, but those that most often come into play in a discussion of annuity suitability are –

a. §72(q)(2)(A) – distributions taken on or after the contract owner reaches age 59, and

b. §72(q)(2)(D) – distributions taken in the form of "substantially equal periodic payments" over lifetime (strictly speaking, such payments must be "made for the life expectancy of the taxpayer or the joint lives of such taxpayer and his designated beneficiary".

If an annuity owner takes distributions before reaching age 59 ½, the penalty tax will apply unless those distributions are in the form of an income that will persist to that ower's life expectancy. (As noted in the Appendix there are other exceptions, such as the annuity owner's disability, but the point here is that, in general, the benefit of tax deferral is that no money can be withdrawn from an annuity before age 59 ½ unless in the form of a lifetime income.

How do these "costs of tax deferral" affect the question of whether a deferred annuity is "appropriate" (or "suitable")? The third "cost" mentioned (the 10% penalty tax) is, like surrender charges, a restriction on the liquidity of the deferred annuity. The second "cost" reduces the effectiveness of a deferred annuity as an instrument for transferring wealth to heirs. The third (that all earnings are taxed as Ordinary Income) impacts the effectiveness of a deferred annuity as a device for accumulating wealth during lifetime. "Deferred annuities convert Capital Gains into Ordinary Income" is a charge often leveled by critics of annuities, who seem to believe that this criticism is both valid and applicable to both fixed and variable annuities. We agree that it is valid, but it does not apply to fixed annuities – or even to variable ones, when those contracts are used to fund IRAs or qualified plans.

The "Cost" of "All Ordinary Income" Treatment of Variable Deferred Annuities

Variable deferred annuities are securities – instruments that allow the purchaser to allocate her investments into a variety of investment sub-accounts that are, in many respects, similar to mutual funds. These sub-accounts, like mutual funds, may invest in stocks, bonds, real estate, commodities, or other asset classes. Thus, a variable annuity may be fairly and reasonably compared with a mutual fund portfolio where the investment objectives (and asset classes chosen to achieve those objectives) are similar.

If earnings in the asset classes chosen would qualify for Long Term Capital Gains treatment if mutual funds were used (or if those asset classes were purchased directly, as individual stocks, real estate properties, etc.), it is entirely reasonable to observe that gains in variable annuity sub-accounts invested in those same asset classes would not get such treatment. In that sense, it is at least arguable that, by electing to purchase these assets in a VA, one ends up "converting" the Long Term Capital Gains treatment, that would have applied to most (or all) profit had one bought the assets directly (or via mutual funds), to Ordinary Income (because all gains in all annuities is always taxed that way).

But that reasoning does not apply when the variable annuity is held in an IRA or qualified plan, because all earnings in such plans are taxed as Ordinary Income. And it does not apply when the deferred annuity in question is not a variable one.

The "Cost" of "All Ordinary Income" Treatment of Fixed Deferred Annuities

The reason why there is no "All Ordinary Income" cost to a fixed deferred annuity is that earnings in those financial alternatives to which a fixed annuity may properly be compared are taxed – mostly, if not entirely – as Ordinary Income. We noted that a variable annuity allocated to equities (such as stock or real estate) may reasonably be compared to a mutual fund portfolio allocated to those same asset classes. A fixed annuity (of either the declared rate or index type) is a very different kind of financial instrument. It offers guarantees, both of principal and of a minimum interest rate. Its "comparables" are certificates of deposit, money market accounts, bonds, and the like. And earnings on those instruments are taxed, mostly or entirely, as Ordinary Income.

Thus, from the standpoint of "appropriateness" or "suitability", the benefit of tax deferral that annuities enjoy must be reckoned along with those "costs" that such treatment imposes, but only with those "costs" that actually apply to the type of annuity under consideration.

Surrender Charges in Deferred Annuities

When liquidity is a major concern (that is, the consumer requires access to the invested dollars immediately, or within the surrender charge period, a deferred annuity that assesses surrender charges may be inappropriate. Most such contracts offer a "free withdrawal" feature, whereby a percentage of the account balance (typically, 10%) or (in some contracts) all interest already credited may be withdrawn without surrender charges. Often, this degree of liquidity is sufficient. But what if greater access turns out to be needed? The surrender charge in the first few contract years may be substantial – quite possibly, greater than cumulative interest credited.

Surrender charges are the subject of many complaints about annuity sales. We suggest that one way of forestalling such complaints is for the annuity representative to ask the proposed annuity owner, before recommending a deferred annuity with surrender charges, something like this: "Is there any chance that you'll need any of this money [the money being considered for placing in the deferred annuity] during the surrender charge period we just discussed?" Asked that way, the question is very likely to elicit a "yes" response. The annuity representative can then confirm that the consumer realized that the question related only to the money being considered for placement in the annuity, and ask the question again – as in "So, even though you'll have access to this other money [referencing other liquid capital not being considered for the annuity], you might still need some of this money? If the answer is still "yes", the annuity representative can recommend reducing the proposed annuity premium, putting part into some other, very liquid, instrument, and then asking "Now, with the knowledge that you'll have access to this [the new liquid asset] money, is there any chance that you'll need any of these [the annuity] dollars?"

If the answer is always "yes", then a deferred annuity is probably not suitable, even if it allows penalty-free withdrawals. But, in many cases, the consumer's answer will eventually become "no" (that is, that the consumer, realizing that she has access to other funds during the surrender charge period, is willing to state that she does not need to tap the annuity during that period). At that point, surrender charges cease to be a concern – or reasonable grounds for a customer complaint. The annuity representative can then point out the "free withdrawal" feature as an additional benefit without having to wonder if its provisions are adequate.

Why Have Surrender Charges In The First Place?

One reason why surrender charges are so commonly cited in complaints about deferred annuity sales (apart from the fact that few annuity representatives include, in their sales presentations, the liquidity discussion just described) is that most don't explain why such charges exist in the first place. Let's look at why they do.

The insurer wishing to sell a deferred annuity must make a profit by doing so (else it would never develop the product in the first place). It knows that, in "acquiring" business through sales, it will incur "acquisition costs". These include sales commissions, premium bonuses, costs of product development and policy issue and setting aside reserves to meet statutory requirements. If that buyer surrenders that annuity within the first few years (before the insurer has earned enough on that invested premium to offset the costs), the insurer will lose money. The carrier knows this and also knows that there are essentially only three ways it can hedge that risk:

1. It can impose a front-end sales charge, sufficient that it will offset the loss produced by early surrender (and, perhaps, produce at least the minimum level of profit required) No index annuity does this because most annuity buyers dislike "front end loads".

2. It can charge annual expenses or reduce credited interest to accomplish the same objective. And carriers do this until expenses are recaptured.

3. It can assess surrender charges, typically reducing over time (because the potential loss to the insurer from early surrender declines with each year the annuity remains in force). The principal advantage of this is that the loss to the insurer wrought by early surrenders is offset by charges borne only by those who made those early surrenders.

Buyers of contracts that impose surrender charges are far less likely to complain about those charges when they understand that they're (a) contingent (that is, they only apply to buyers who surrender early) and (b) are in lieu of a "front end" sales charge.

Having dealt with two of the most commonly cited elements in complaints as to the "suitability" of an annuity, let's now look at some rules of thumb – "bright line tests" – that annuity representatives can use to make quick initial judgments on that subject.

"Bright Line" Rules for Annuity Suitability

1. If wealth accumulation or wealth transfer to heirs is a planning goal, an immediate annuity is never appropriate (for the dollars in question).

2. If wealth transfer to heirs is a planning goal, a deferred annuity may not be appropriate, chiefly because (a) it is not eligible for the "step up in basis" that is enjoyed by many types of investments and (b) the earnings are taxed at Ordinary Income rates, either to the contract owner or the beneficiar(ies). That said, the guaranteed death benefit "riders" in some deferred annuities (both fixed and variable) may be attractive to buyers who are uninsurable (or whose insurance would be extremely expensive), notwithstanding the fact that those benefit amounts would be taxed to the beneficiaries in the same manner as other contract earnings.

3. If immediate income is a goal and that income must keep place with inflation, the only immediate annuity that makes sense is one with a "cost of living" (COLA) feature. Few such contracts offer an annual increase tied to an external inflation rate, but a fixed COLA might work. An immediate variable annuity might also, as its offers the opportunity for an increase in annual annuity payments due to good investment performance. But it also offers the prospect of a decrease in such payments (due to adverse investment performance). Some index annuity GLWBs have options that increase the payout by a certain percentage each year or where payout changes are based on changes in the Consumer Price Index.

4. If safety of principal is a requirement, no immediate annuity will serve, as an immediate annuity is designed to distribute principal. Moreover, no variable deferred annuity will work, unless (a) it contains a "guaranteed living benefit" rider that guarantees a return of principal and (b) the conditions under which the rider guarantees principal are acceptable. Most such riders do not guarantee that the contract holder may surrender the contract in a lump sum for no less than the amount invested (less withdrawals, of course); they generally guarantee return of principal only in installments. Thus, only a fixed rate or index deferred annuity will generally satisfy this requirement.

5. If safety of principal and a guaranteed minimum rate of return are the goals, any fixed annuity will serve (and no variable one will, unless its cash value is allocated entirely to the "fixed account" which we feel is generally a very poor idea).

6. If safety of principal and a minimum rate of return and the opportunity for potential interest linked to movements of an external index is desired, an index deferred annuity is clearly appropriate. An index annuity provides a potentially higher interest rate while protecting principal and credited interest from market loss.

7. During every extended bull market, some investors enter an investment world for which they are psychologically or financial unsuited. They became investors because they misjudged the risk of loss. These are the often the investors hurt most by bear markets because they panic and sell at market bottoms. Index annuities may be suitable for these investors, because (to put it bluntly), they protect these investors from themselves.

8. An index annuity may be especially appropriate for a buyer who wants both an assurance of a minimum lifetime income and guarantees of principal. A GLWB guarantees to the purchaser a payout for life. However, if that purchaser wishes to surrender the contract for cash, he or she can calculate a "worst case" outcome upon surrendering the index annuity.

9. For some buyers, a fixed-rate annuity is simply too "boring", (but a variable annuity is too "scary"). Many years ago psychologists discovered that no person is completely risk-averse or risk-oriented because they both buy insurance AND lottery tickets. An index annuity solves this fundamental risk-return quandary by giving the buyer both protection and power.

Helping Seniors Make Wise Annuity Decisions

That mental skills decline as we become aged is not something newly realized, and many theories have been advanced over the years to try to explain why this happens. It is interesting work, but this is not about asking why, or even if, the decisions of senior citizen are negatively impacted by aging. Instead, our goal is to examine things that may help seniors arrive at better decisions regarding the purchase of an annuity.

We have outlined the problems in senior decision-making that research has uncovered and suggested ways that these problems may be minimized and possibly avoided. It should be noted the proposed solutions assume seniors are not afflicted by dementia, Alzheimer's, or anything else beyond normal aging that would hurt the decision-making ability. Dementia not only affects the person's actual ability to make an informed decision but the ability to determine whether additional help is needed. Coupled with this is the problem that if the dementia is mild, the senior may still be able to process information and respond to some financial decisions without seeming impaired. These solutions assume the senior is not legally impaired.

Who Is A Senior Citizen?

Although the U.S. Senate Committee on Aging describes senior citizens as anyone age 60 or older, most of the state regulatory laws and proposals seem to define a senior as a citizen age 65 and beyond.

Problems In Decision-Making

Declines In Working Memory

There have been numerous studies that conclude our working memory gets worse as old age progresses. Making decisions requires the use of working memory.

Working Memory Declines – Seniors can hold less new data in their heads at one time and the speed of processing the data slows. This means

- Seniors get overwhelmed by too many choices
- Don't multitask well) and
- Seniors use mental shortcuts that often do not result in good decisions. They mistake quantity for quality, they ignore the true risk of a situation, and they tend to choose what they recognize instead of what is best.

During the decision-making process, our minds are fed streams of data consisting of words, numbers and pictures. We need to store that data temporarily, while determining the extent to which different parts of that data are useful to our decision. We need to make comparisons and rankings between the different types of data, accessing our stored knowledge, to determine whether the data is consistent with what we know. We then need to coordinate it all, to put it in a form that we can process. Finally, we need to sift and sort through our past knowledge, to see if it and what we've just examined supports or contradicts a past decision reached. All of this is involved in our making new decisions. It is an extraordinary process.

Two related factors affecting senior decision-making are the slowing of reaction time in processing, comparing and coordinating all of these pieces, and a decrease in the total data we are able to hold in our heads. Seniors process decisions more slowly than young adults and decision accuracy also declines.

A comparison of the differences in decision-making between young and old could be made by looking at a recent computer with a Pentium chip and an earlier one with an 8086 processor. Both can solve problems, but the early processor can only take in so much data at a time, which is why it processes the data more slowly than a computer with the Pentium chip. If the old processor received too much data at one time, it often went into a "data loop freeze" and could not generate an optimal solution. It appears that normal aging eventually downgrades our mental hardware in an analogous fashion, while still allowing us to compute. This analogy can be taken further. The 8086 processor can still provide good answer, provided that the data is presented simply and that more time is given for computation. These same steps should be taken to improve seniors' capability.

Seniors Suffer From Too Many Choices

Many studies have concluded that too many choices result in worse decisions or no decision, regardless of age, which is why the more choices you offer to old consumers, the worse they do in making a good decision.

Seniors Don't Do Multitasking Well

Although studies show that multitasking hurts decision-making accuracy for both young and old, the inaccuracy of seniors while multitasking is greater. The implication is all adults, but especially seniors, should focus solely on the decision at hand and not attempt to do additional things at the same time.

This means that, while everyone can suffer from the negative effects of too much information, seniors are more likely to make decision errors when given too much information and offered too many choices.

Seniors Look At Quantity, Not Value

Seniors tend to choose the product with the greatest number of benefits instead of the product with the greatest value, even when some of those benefits are not important to them. For example, a senior strongly interested in an annuity in which surrender charges are waived upon death might be more likely to choose an annuity that waives surrender charges for critical illness, nursing care needs and unemployment – but that does not waive charges for death – over an annuity that waives charges only at death. Why? Because three benefits are more than one benefit. Seniors tend to ignore information on the importance of the benefits and make selection based on quantity of benefits.

Seniors Ignore The Odds Even When Disclosed

In a similar vein, in decisions where the odds are presented, younger consumers tend to look at the odds and choose payoffs based on the best odds; by contrast, seniors treat all choices as having equal probability - even when the odds are presented. This could be the reason why seniors congregate at the slot machines instead of enjoying the better odds at the blackjack tables.

Seniors Use More Rules of Thumb

Rules of thumb are often good because we rely on a favorable past decision to guide the current one, but they may also produce poor decisions.

As an example, if a senior is trying to decide which annuity will pay the highest return, and the annuities being considered are issued by Fidelity, MetLife, and XYZ Life, he or she might choose the Fidelity or MetLife annuity, inferring that those companies will offer a better deal simply because they are more familiar. This rule of thumb can backfire if the recognition is negative. If one had a bad experience with a known choice they would be inclined to try their luck with the unknown choice.

Consequences

Seniors select decision-making strategies that are less mentally demanding than young adults do. However, these less intensive strategies often result in good decisions because seniors have more knowledge than young adults and they can often use this knowledge to offset capacity and processing declines.

Being Too Positive

As people age their motivation changes from learning new things to maintaining a positive emotional state; seniors work hard to keep themselves in a positive frame of mind. A possible problem exists if the senior works so hard to remain positive that he or she creates false memories.

Seniors may subconsciously block information about surrender charges

Although the stereotype of seniors is often the "complaining curmudgeon", seniors are likely to be in a good mood more often than young adults (because seniors work hard to keep themselves in a positive frame of mind). They are more affected by appeals to emotion than logic, and react positively when asked to recount life experiences. All of this may mean, for example, that a senior does not comprehend the possible impact of surrender charges because they are viewed as a bummer on their positive outlook. Moreover, if this senior does not intend to surrender the policy, he or she may not anticipate (or wish to anticipate) feeling the emotion of regret.

Improving Decision-Making

Give Seniors Enough Time To Make The Decision

When seniors are given more time to study and remember new data, they perform as well as young adults. That said, seniors may have trouble learning new data, so learning may take repeated exposure to get new data. Ongoing questioning is called for, to determine if the new data is being processed.

To improve their decisions, seniors should be given all the time they need without feeling pressured or rushed.

Give Seniors Choices, But Sort The Data

In November 2005, Part D Medicare made available what eventually became a menu of 55 prescription drug plans. Of the 43 million eligible Medicare customers, roughly 10 million – less than a quarter – actively decided to select one plan. What about the other three-quarters of eligible retirees? We believe that these consumers were subjected to "choice overload". Given so many choices, they became so fearful of making a bad decision that they refused to make any decision.

This does not mean the senior to whom you're proposing a annuity should be denied the opportunity of selecting from amongst the 96 variable annuity sub-accounts, or among the six different crediting methods on the five different indices with the three different premium bonus levels. It means simply that you should present the information as clearly and simply as possible, and to help him or her sort through all that information, so as to make the decision manageable.

Data Sorting

In the annuity world, the process could begin by determining whether the annuity will be used to generate an income now or in the near future. If the answer is now, the presentation could then focus on comparing immediate annuities and annuities with lifetime payout/withdrawal benefits. If the answer is "later" (that is, that the annuity will be used for growth), the presentation could focus on the risk/reward aspects of variable, index and fixed rate annuities. If the senior clearly wants no market risk to principal and a yield guaranteed for the surrender charge period, the presentation could compare the yields on multi-year annuities with varying terms. If a five-year term is chosen, the presentation could then focus on choosing from among the three highest yielding annuities from carriers rated by A.M. Best as "A+, A, or A-".

By sorting the data in this fashion, the senior is not faced with the need to pick the "one perfect annuity" out of the thousands available.

The greatest number of choices encountered at any one time, here, is four, and each step involves one small aspect of the overall decision process, to keep working memory from being overwhelmed. The idea is not to deny choices to the senior, but to create a strategy that simplifies the processing of the choices.

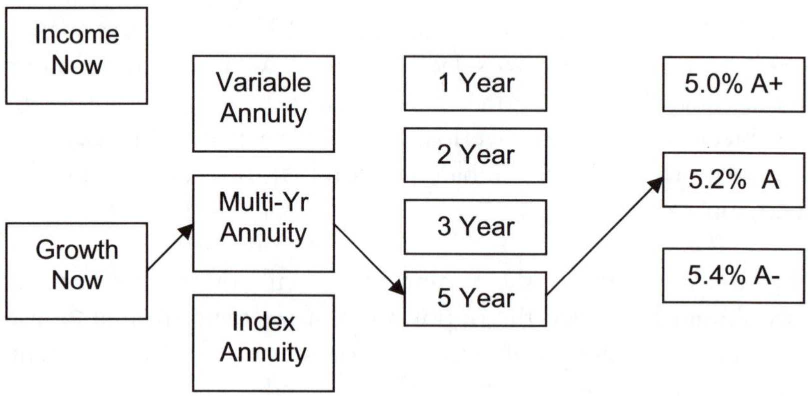

Give the senior choices, but present a series of bite-sized choices rather than entire buffet.

Training Seniors

A 2003 study took college educated young and senior adults through six financial planning problems. A group of both young and senior adults received six hours training on retirement planning concepts; another group of young and old received no training. Although the untrained young and senior (average age 69) adults did worse than either trained group the untrained seniors did much worse. On the other hand, the trained young and senior (average age 73) adults performed at much high levels – at times the seniors outperformed the youngsters.

Financially inexperienced seniors need to rely on help, because their own decisions may not be good. Therefore, the representative needs to determine how savvy a particular senior is, in order to determine how much help is needed.

Connect Emotionally With The Senior

In the case of seniors, it has been found they respond better to, and remember more of, information when it is emotionally charged. The message here is that when emotions are tied in with goals seniors remember the message.

The other element mentioned earlier is that seniors focus on positive information over negative or neutral data. This positive focus could mean that as soon as a senior connects a decision with a positive emotion, he or she quits processing any new information. It also indicates how information should be presented to enhance decision-making.

If the emotional tie-in is presented first, the senior may stop looking for new information. This suggests that factual information should be presented first, followed by the emotional link to the senior's goal.

This is a balancing act. Seniors need to know the facts so they can make good decisions, but they will not be motivated to remember and process the facts unless they feel an emotional connection. However, if the emotional link is built up too quickly, seniors may make a premature decision that is not optimal.

Help Seniors Process Information

The correct amount of data disclosure depends on the need for what is and is not disclosed. In the index annuity world, the senior needs to be able to determine whether 1) an annuity is the right decision, and, if so, 2) which annuity product is the right one. Unfortunately, this process is hampered by the fact that disclosure is not uniform across products or states.

Standardized Disclosure

Annuity representatives do not need to wait for insurance companies to create forms in order to help standardize the disclosure of information. They should try to be consistent in references and definitions they during the annuity presentation. The senior needs a frame of reference to process the annuity information and the representative often provides that frame. There are a few "rules of thumb" in this regard.

1. Never use an acronym or technical term without first having defined it in clear English.

2. Confirm that the senior actually understands your definition. You can do that by watching for body language (confused looks, for example) or by simply repeating the definition when you're in doubt.

3. Never assume that the client knows the meaning of a term or a concept just because you do.

4. Confirm understanding of a key concept or term by asking the consumer (especially, if it's a senior) to tell you what he or she thinks it means. This need not appear to be patronizing or rude. You might say, for example, "I'm so used to these terms that I sometimes forget to explain them properly. What does [that term or concept] mean to you?"

Conclusions

There are things that can be done to help seniors make better decisions about buying an annuity. The easiest way to help the decision process is to take it slowly. Do not rush through the presentation, probe for understanding, and if possible, schedule the appointment for the morning.

Seniors need to be aware of choices, but pre-sort the choices into manageable sizes. Disclose all relevant facts but only relevant and material facts. Seniors (or any consumers, for that matter) do not need to know everything; they need to know everything meaningful for their decision. When the information is disclosed, it should be done in stages, so that working memory can process and digest the data, make a series of small decision, which can then be used to make the final decision.

Seniors process information better if they have an emotional attachment, and they respond more strongly to a positive message. This means one should not simple recite facts, but show how the facts relate to their emotional needs because this leads to greater concentration in making the decision. However, seniors can also use finding a positive emotion as a stopping point and not give the decision their full consideration. This may result in seniors' "tuning" out the negative aspects of the annuity because they've found one or two positive emotional points to attach to.

When we read seniors' complaints about the annuities they purchased, they often claim they were unaware of the surrender penalties when they bought the annuities, even though the evidence shows that they signed disclosures at time of purchase stating these penalties. The research suggests that this result is possible – that these seniors simply ignored any discussion of surrender penalties - because a positive emotion, generated during the sales interview, created a mental shortcut to the decision. This may mean that representatives need to spend more time covering surrender penalties with seniors, and perhaps increasing the prominence of the surrender penalties, and any other negative facts, on sales materials and disclosures.

Although standardized definitions and disclosure forms would aid in senior decisions, it would probably take regulatory action for this to happen. This does not mean carriers and agents cannot standardize their own approach by creating disclosures and product benefit descriptions that are similar in appearance and meaning, or when presenting different annuities to the senior using similar terms and comparisons.

Someday we may find out exactly why decision-making powers decline with age, and, if we can identify the specific problem, we may be able to find a specific solution to prevent age-related decline. Until then, there are many things that can be done to assist seniors in making wise decisions.

Cheat Sheet

- An annuity is just a tool, and that its usefulness depends upon how well it is suited to the task.
- Annuity buyers of contracts are far less likely to complain about surrender charges when they understand that they (a) only apply to buyers who surrender early and are (b) in lieu of a "front end" sales charge.
- If safety of principal and a minimum rate of return and the opportunity for potential interest linked to movements of an external index is desired, an index annuity is clearly appropriate.
- To help seniors make wise decisions give them all the time they need, make choices bite-sized, and try to standardize the information so that decision powers are used to determine the best choice

Chapter 10 – Case Studies In Annuity Planning

In this chapter, we will look at a series of case studies where we describe different financial situations and objectives of hypothetical consumers ("prospective clients", if you will), who have asked our hypothetical annuity professional, Matt, for recommendations. We'll assume, in each case, that Matt is acting (a) as an *insurance agent* and, alternatively, (b) as an "*investment advisor*", "wealth manager", "financial consultant" or in any other capacity that would subject Matt to some form of *fiduciary standard.*

We'll do it this way for two reasons: First, to point out that the factors that Matt must consider, when acting solely as an insurance agent may (but not necessarily will) be different from those factors he must consider when he's acting as an investment advisor. And second, to point out the potential differences in the obligations and duties he must assume in each scenario. Let's get started.

Case One: "I'm Tired of Paying Taxes!"

Jubal is a single 45 year old physician. He currently earns $220,000 per year (net of expenses), and expects his income to increase each year by at least 8%. Jubal contributes the maximum amount permissible to the 401(k) plan at his practice (Tanstaafl Medical, LLC) and still manages to put away $4,000 per month into a "moderately aggressive" portfolio of mutual funds. Jubal has very little debt (other than his home mortgage) and his health is quite good, but he doesn't want to continue working "forever". In fact, he'd like to retire in ten years or so. Jubal's one main gripe is *taxes.* Not only does he pay substantial income taxes each year on his earnings, but he expects that the taxes he'll have to pay when he sells his practice to his partners (pursuant to a buy-sell agreement) will be "downright confiscatory". He's asked Matt to recommend something that (a) will give him some income tax relief, (b) offers "decent growth", but isn't "risky" (he feels he's already taking a lot of market risk), and (c) will give him an income in retirement. What factors should Matt consider, when developing a recommendation and what annuity products (if any) would be most appropriate for Jubal?

Scenario A: Matt is an insurance agent, but not a registered representative or "investment advisor"

As an insurance agent with no securities registration, Matt is limited, not only with respect to the investment types he may sell, but also with respect to those he may even discuss. He cannot discuss *variable* annuities. Moreover, he cannot offer advice regarding Jubal's mutual fund portfolio. He's limited to talking about *fixed* insurance products. Let's assume that Matt wants to recommend a fixed annuity. What factors should he take into account prior to making any such recommendation? If Matt is subject to the NAIC *Suitability in Annuity Transactions Model Regulation*, Matt must take into account the twelve factors listed in that Regulation (see Chapter 8) These are:

(1) Age
(2) Annual income;
(3) Financial situation and needs, including the financial resources used for the funding of the annuity;
(4) Financial experience;
(5) Financial objectives;
(6) Intended use of the annuity;
(7) Financial time horizon;
(8) Existing assets, including investment and life insurance holdings;
(9) Liquidity needs;
(10) Liquid net worth;
(11) Risk tolerance; and
(12) Tax status.

Let's look at some of these: Note: The fact that we may not address every one of these 12 factors in every scenario should not be interpreted to mean that only those factors we address should be considered.

Age. Jubal is 45 years old. He doesn't need more income currently, so an immediate annuity clearly isn't called for. But what about a deferred annuity? Any distributions Jubal takes from a deferred annuity, prior to his age 59 ½, will be subject to a 10% penalty tax (unless one of the exceptions noted in Chapter 1 applies). Moreover, he plans to retire in "ten years or so". Even then, he'll be under age 59 ½. Does this rule out the appropriateness of a deferred annuity? Not necessarily. If Jubal were planning to use the annuity to produce income via "partial withdrawals", it might. But consider that (a) if that income is in the form of a "life contingent" annuity, that penalty will not apply and (b) Jubal has other funds (Factor #8). He's contributing to a 401(k) plan. He can take his money from that plan at age 55 without any early distribution penalty (so long as he's leaving Tanstaafl Medical). Moreover, he's got quite a lot of money in non-qualified mutual funds. Thus, if Jubal intends not to "tap" a deferred annuity except as a life income or commencing after he's reached age 59 ½, the early distribution penalty that might otherwise suggest that a deferred annuity is inappropriate may not be a factor at all.

Annual Income. Jubal's income does not appear to pose a suitability concern.

Financial Situation and Needs. As Jubal has expressed a desire for an instrument to produce "decent growth" and, ultimately, to produce an income, a deferred annuity appears to be consistent with these goals. But *what kind* of deferred annuity? Consideration of the remaining factors should help Matt to make that determination.

Financial Experience. If Matt is considering an indexed annuity, he'll need to have a good sense of Jubal's investment sophistication. Why? Because indexed annuities can be complicated and someone who is financially unsophisticated may require additional explanation of the annuity's structure and benefits.

Liquidity Needs. This should always – *in every case* – be addressed in *every* deferred annuity presentation, and every agent who is thinking of recommending one should have a *very clear* understanding of this factor, and of the prospective buyer's *Financial Time Horizon.* Why? Because as we noted in Chapter 8, surrender charges are the subject of many, if not most, complaints to regulators by annuity buyers. In

Jubal's case, a need for liquidity, *with respect to the funds that may be invested in an annuity*, does not appear to be a concern, but Matt can make that determination only by addressing the Liquidity and Investment Time Horizon factors, and the others we're highlighting here.

Tax Status. Jubal's desire to reduce his current income tax liability would certainly suggest that a deferred annuity may be appropriate. As we noted above, the early distribution penalty that might be a factor for someone else of Jubal's age may not be a concern here.

Intended Use of the Annuity. This is *always* a factor that deserves close attention, because a deferred annuity can serve both as an accumulation instrument and a tool for the production of a guaranteed income. A variable deferred annuity offers greater potential for growth, but also the potential for capital *loss*. A non-variable annuity (either fixed-rate or indexed) offers less growth potential, but guarantees both principal and a minimum rate of return. Which appeals more to Jubal? Matt cannot know (without asking Jubal) *and should not guess.*

If Matt decides (after considering all twelve factors, in the light of Jubal's responses to his questions about those factors) that a deferred annuity is most appropriate, should that annuity include a guaranteed living benefit rider? Both variable and indexed annuities offer these, but variable annuities and indexed annuities are *very* different beasts and are generally not alternatives for the same set of client needs and wants.

Scenario B: Matt is an insurance agent and a registered representative, but not an "investment advisor"

As a registered representative with a Series 6 or 7, Matt can sell, and offer advice concerning, *variable* annuities. If Matt recommends a variable annuity, he must adhere to the suitability rules applying to sales of variable annuities, including FINRA Rule 2330 (formerly, NASD Rule 2821). He must also follow the rules of his Broker/Dealer – all *in addition to* the rules listed earlier (because he is both a registered representative *and* an insurance agent recommending an annuity).

If Matt is considering a variable annuity, he will want to ask Jubal for details of his existing mutual funds portfolio. *What kinds* of funds are represented? *How long* has Jubal been investing in those (or any) mutual funds. (He'll almost certainly need to answer that last question on the "investor experience" section of his broker/dealer's "New Account Statement", but even if that question isn't on that form, Jubal needs to know the answer if he's going to recommend variable annuity sub-accounts).

Risk Tolerance will certainly come into play in that determination. A variable deferred annuity presents *market risk* (although a *guaranteed living benefit rider* may reduce that risk, with respect to the *income* guaranteed under the rider, it does not eliminate it). Matt will certainly want to discuss this factor with Jubal, to determine how comfortable he is with the level of investment risks (including market risk) he's already taking and whether he wishes to take more or less investment risk with respect to the money that will fund an annuity.

The other suitability factors are, of course, no less relevant or important in this scenario (where Matt holds a securities registration) than in the first one (or the one following).

Scenario C: Matt is an insurance agent and a registered representative, and an "investment advisor"

What additional considerations come into play if Matt is either an *investment advisor* or *investment advisory associate*? (The quick and easy answer to that one is "Ask your supervisor" or "Contact your Compliance Department *immediately*!") A more thorough (and, one hopes, more nearly accurate) answer would be a combination of "it depends" and "nobody knows for sure". There are several reasons for that:

- Compliance policies and requirements differ among financial institutions.

- Is Matt *acting* as a "financial advisor" in his dealings with Jubal? Does Matt's advisory status determine the requirements that apply to him *even when he is not acting as an advisor*? (Example: What if Jubal asks Matt to sell him a $500,000 term life policy? Will advisory status – and, perhaps, *fiduciary duty* – attach in that situation?) These factors affect which rules may be applicable.

- Finally, *The Rules Are Never Quite Clear*! The regulators will reinterpret existing rules or create new ones.

- We can be reasonably sure of one thing: The rules regarding when an annuity recommendation is or is not acceptable ("suitable") are not going to become more lax; they're going to get tougher. The prudent agent will make adjustments to his or her marketing strategies and procedures to accommodate those tougher rules – and not wait until the last minute to do so.

Case Two: "I'm About to Retire, I Need Income, and This Market Scares Me!"

Harriet is a 64 year old widow, planning to retire in nine months (when she reaches age 65). Her parents and grandparents all lived into their eighties or beyond, and Harriett's greatest concern is that she might outlive her income. She knows that her existing portfolio of a 401(k) plan (invested about half in bond funds and half in "growth and income" stock funds), plus some bonds and CDs, might not produce the income she feels she'll need in addition to Social Security, but she's very leery of increasing her exposure to "the market". Harriett has two children, but her Number One planning priority is her own financial security. Harriett has told all of this to our agent, Matt, and asked him for recommendations.

Scenario A: Matt is a licensed insurance agent, but does not hold a securities license, and is not an investment advisor

What factors must Matt take into account? Well, for openers, we suggest that the 12 factors cited in the NAIC Model Regulation mentioned earlier are all relevant and that Matt should gather enough information to enable him to consider each one properly. But what else should he be on the lookout for? *Sources of Funds*, for sure. Every state says you must be securities registered to recommend selling securities to fund a fixed annuity purchase, but no state says a securities license is required if the consumer decides to liquidate, say , a mutual fund and buy an annuity from a non-securities registered insurance agent. As Matt is not securities registered, he cannot suggest selling securities. But what if the consumer decides entirely on his or her own to sell securities, buy a fixed annuity, and someone tells the state regulator they think Matt was behind the securities decision?

We have found state regulators tend to look at several things to determine whether an insurance agent is acting as an advisor. One is a pattern of fixed annuity sales whereby the money came from the sales of securities. Another is the language used by the agent. Does the agent take about repositioning funds, allocating assets or advising the consumer? Still another red flag is if the agent helped the consumer complete the securities transfer or sales forms. It might be helpful for the agent to have a letter signed by the consumer saying the agent did not suggest selling securities as a source of funds for the fixed annuity. However, there are no clear cut answers.

As Matt is not securities registered, it should go without saying that Matt cannot sell, or give advice regarding, variable annuities, because he's not legally entitled to do so. One implication of this (which seems to have escaped some of the more ardent "consumerists") is that Matt cannot be held responsible for failing to consider a variable annuity for Harriett.

Scenario B: Matt is a licensed insurance agent and registered rep, but not an "investment advisor"

In this scenario, Matt is not only authorized to consider a variable contract when he's examining annuity alternatives for Harriett, but is arguably duty-bound to do so. Moreover, the 12 factors mentioned earlier must, in a variable annuity recommendation, be taken into account, even if Matt's state or the issuer of the variable annuity Matt proposes hasn't yet adopted the NAIC Model Reg, because FINRA Rule 2330, dealing with suitability recommendations in variable annuity, requires consideration of those exact same 12 factors.

In either scenario, some of those factors will be of greater importance than others because some are more important to Harriett. Clearly, the assurance of income is vital. This might suggest an *immediate annuity* (as Harriett plans to retire within a year). It might also suggest a deferred annuity with a *guaranteed living benefit rider* (either a guaranteed lifetime withdrawal benefit, or, if Matt can sell variable contracts, a guaranteed minimum income benefit). Certainly, liquidity is a factor. To what extent will the annuity be required to produce income during the surrender charge period – (a) if a guaranteed living benefit is chosen and (b) if it is not chosen?

Risk tolerance should be given serious consideration in this case, especially if Matt is a registered rep and a variable deferred annuity is being considered, and, perhaps especially, if a guaranteed living benefit is being considered (because the income guarantees of that benefit might permit Harriett to allocate her investments in that variable annuity more aggressively than she would otherwise be willing to do.

Age. How important is the age factor in this case? Harriett is 64. Some states impose special suitability restrictions upon sales of annuities to "senior citizens". Although most states define senior citizens as those age 65 or older, Harriett's state may include 64 year olds. Even absent such additional state restrictions, many insurers give special scrutiny to sales of annuities to seniors.

Financial Experience. If Matt intends to recommend either an indexed annuity or a variable one (especially, if it includes a living benefit), he should make certain that Harriett understands how the recommended contract works and how it does not work. The mechanics of these contracts can be complicated and misunderstandings are common.

Scenario C: Matt is an agent, a registered rep and an investment advisor

Do additional concerns as to appropriateness of recommendations come into play in this scenario? Yes! As we've noted, investment advisors must adhere to a higher standard of duty than registered reps or insurance agents. Even if the standards applying to the latter are increased (as appears likely at the time of this writing), it is possible (even likely) that the resulting standards for registered reps will be less stringent than those now applying to investment advisors (but probably, substantially more stringent than those applying to non-securities licensed insurance agents). Matt, as an investment advisor, must be able to demonstrate that the annuity recommended is in Harriett's "best interest" and that he has disclosed any conflicts of interest.

Case Three: "I May Be Young, But This Market Scares Me!"

Ken is an unmarried 32 year old computer programmer. He's just recently managed to pay off his college loans and purchase a home. He earns $45,000 per year and contributes 6% of this salary to his employer's 401(k) plan (which is the maximum level at which the employer will provide matching funds). He's told Matt that he can invest $300 per month for "retirement", because, other than his 401(k) plan and about $4,000 in a non-qualified growth stock mutual fund, he has no long term savings. Ken has heard about annuities, and likes the idea of not having to pay income tax on his earnings each year, but he doesn't know if an annuity would be appropriate for someone of his age. Wouldn't he be better off putting more money into his mutual funds? How should Matt proceed?

Scenario A: Matt is a licensed insurance agent, but holds no securities license or advisory status

Right up front, Matt needs to be very careful about how he answers Ken's question about the relative merits (for him) of "an annuity" versus mutual funds. He cannot offer advice about either mutual funds or variable annuities, so what can he say? *Does Matt need to duck the question?*

A reasonable, educated, and ethical-minded person might well argue that, if Matt is to serve as a responsible advisor to Ken, he can't ignore Ken's concerns. (Besides, that's really *awful* salesmanship!) Matt should (in this view) tell Ken something like "that's a darned good question, and I'll be happy to discuss it with you, but you need to know, up front, that I do not hold a securities license, which means that I cannot make recommendations of, or offer advice about, specific mutual funds – because they're securities. But we can talk about how mutual funds and annuities work, in general."

Matt should (in this view) then discuss the basics of mutual funds – how they work, what they can be invested in, etc., and, in the process, discover how much Ken knows about these instruments (that he already owns). Matt could even include a *basic* discussion of how variable annuities work, all without making any specific recommendations, and after having made very clear the restrictions that bind him.

That may strike one as eminently reasonable, and just plain good practice. We have considerable sympathy for that view, because it strikes us that way too. But here's the rub: *If Matt does that, he may end up in serious trouble!* Some regulators may regard the *mere mention* of mutual funds and variable annuities (which are indisputably "securities") as "*offering advice about securities*" – or even that Matt, by mentioning those instruments, has acted as an "*investment advisor*". Either conclusion, by a regulator having authority over Matt, is bad news.

So what *can* Matt do (without running the risk of putting himself out of business)? He could say, "Ken, I simply cannot discuss mutual fun s with you, because I'm not permitted to do so under the law." That is not, in the authors' experience, what many non-securities licensed agents do. A *lot* of them will attempt some explanation such as the one we offered above, and they may do so with the very best of motives. And they may not have gotten in trouble for doing so – yet. But the sad fact is that doing that can get you in real trouble, which is why we say (with great sadness) that Matt – and other people in that same situation – should stick with "I am not permitted, under the law, to discuss that, and I follow the law".

Can Matt refer Ken to someone else, who *can* lawfully discuss mutual funds and/or variable annuities with him? Yes, *but he cannot share in any compensation that may be earned by that other advisor on any securities product. Moreover, he cannot receive a "finder's fee" from that other advisor, where the finder's fee is related to any securities sale that other advisor makes to Ken.*

In practical terms, this may be a moot point, as few insurance agents are likely to want to "hand off" a "live prospect" to a competitor, but it's worth emphasizing that if that is done, the agent cannot profit from any securities sale made as a result. But can Matt refer Ken to a colleague who is securities licensed, but who doesn't sell insurance, in consideration for that colleague's willingness to refer clients needing insurance to Matt? Yes, provided that...

1. Matt never receives any compensation related to securities sales and

2. Matt's colleague does not receive any part of insurance commissions made by Matt unless that colleague is also licensed to sell the type of insurance sold, and

3. Any "commission split" conforms to the rules of the insurance agency Matt works for (if applicable) and the state insurance department(s) involved and the rules of the issuing insurer, and

4. That colleague's Broker/Dealer or Investment Advisory Firm has approved the arrangement in writing.

Let's suppose that Matt, aware of all of this, tells Ken that he cannot discuss mutual funds and that Ken says "OK, what can you recommend?" Can Matt proceed to make an annuity sale? Yes, *provided that he has assured himself that the sale of that annuity is "suitable",* under the suitability rules that apply to Matt. We believe that both Matt and Ken would be much better off if Matt takes into consideration the 12 factors we've been talking about, even if the NAIC suitability guideline are not in effect.

Scenario B: Matt is an insurance agent with a securities license

"Whew!" This one's much easier, because Matt *can* talk about both mutual funds and variable annuities without getting himself in trouble. (It should be noted that, in the previous scenario, Matt's non-registered status might indicate that he knows very little about mutual funds or variable annuities – in which event, he should not discuss same, *if only for that reason*).

Does Matt bear a greater duty as a registered rep than he does as a non-registered insurance agent? If he recommends a variable annuity, that's clearly true, because FINRA Rule 2330 (among others) governs that recommendation. (To reiterate, the 12 suitability factors in that Rule are the same 12 factors cited in the NAIC Model Regulation). Moreover, he must comply with any suitability rules imposed by his Broker/Dealer on the sale of the annuity. Those rules will apply if the annuity in question is variable, and may apply if it's an indexed contract. (Some B/Ds require all indexed annuity sales by their reps to be made through them, subject to the same suitability rules as govern variable contracts. In that situation, the registered rep might be viewed – if only by a Compliance Officer – as acting as a registered rep, even when the product being recommended isn't a registered product [i.e.: a security]). It may even be that his B/D imposes the same rules on sales of non-indexed fixed annuities.

Scenario C: Matt is an agent, a registered rep, and an investment advisor

As we saw in our earlier examples, Matt's obligations here are substantially greater than in the other two scenarios. As an *investment advisor* (or *advisory representative*), he bears a fiduciary duty. He must make *full disclosure* of all pertinent information about the product he recommends, including charges, fees, restrictions, etc. (That duty applies in all three scenarios). In addition, as an investment advisor, he must put his client's interest first, which means that he must subordinate his compensation interest to the question of whether the product he ultimately recommends is superior to those he rejected (especially if they paid a lower commission). He must reveal his compensation and any conflicts of interest.

The very best defense against a charge of making an "unsuitable" recommendation of an annuity is threefold:
(1) Know what rules govern that recommendation before you make it;
(2) Follow those rules; and
(3) Be able to prove that you did so

Case Four: "I'm Not Happy with my Portfolio's Performance; Can You Do Better For Me?"

Lucy is a married 40 year old attorney. Recent economic troubles (and the attendant decline in the stock and bond markets) have caused the balance in her portfolio of mutual funds and stocks to plummet by over 20% in the past year. She's not happy, either with the performance of that account, or with the investment advice she's been getting from Jim, her financial advisor, and she's come to Matt for a "second opinion". "Can you do better for me?" she asks. What are some of the issues that Matt must consider and what "suitability" factors must he take into account prior to making a recommendation of an annuity?

Scenario A: Matt's an insurance agent with no securities license

Right off the bat, Matt needs to decide whether he should be working with Lucy, and, if so, in what capacity. What does she mean by "Can you do better for me?" If she's looking for a "better" *investment advisor*, Matt's not qualified (or authorized) to give investment advice. Does that mean that Matt must tell Lucy that she must look elsewhere for help? Not necessarily. It depends upon her *Financial Objectives* and what she expects Matt to do to help her realize them. He can only determine that by asking her about those objectives – and that's a good place for him to start.

Matt can (and should, and must) determine whether an annuity is clearly suitable for the client, whether that client will, *in the light of all relevant factors*, be better off with an annuity than without it.

Does Matt need to determine if something else (such as mutual funds) – something that he cannot legally offer or render advice about – would be "better" for the client than an annuity? Some "consumerists' will say "yes". But that position rests upon at least two unspoken assumptions: First, that Matt has an ethical obligation to recommend *only* "the best" product for a client in each and every circumstance, even if that means that he cannot profit from doing so *and* that it can be determined objectively, by Matt, or *a regulator, jury, or arbitrator*, just what the "best" product is in every given situation. The second unspoken assumption is that Matt is both *qualified* and *legally permitted* to make that assessment. As an *insurance agent* without a securities license, Matt may neither recommend securities nor discuss their pros and cons, versus an annuity. As we noted earlier, he can be punished if he does either. Moreover, Matt's non-registered rep status means that he is deemed, under the law, not to have the expertise to do so.

So what can he do? He can – and must - restrict his discussion and recommendations to those financial products – solutions – that he is both qualified and legally authorized to talk about. And he can – and must – determine which of those solutions makes the most sense for the client, *when all relevant factors are taken into account.*

That's where Matt needs to start – with Lucy's *Financial Objectives* (What are you trying to accomplish?). Lucy is upset at the performance of her mutual fund portfolio. OK, what does she expect that portfolio to do for her? Does she want capital appreciation? Any deferred annuity offers that benefit. Is that portfolio expected to provide retirement income? A deferred annuity can do that, and with greater certainty than alternatives. Once he has discovered her financial objectives, time horizon, etc., Matt can explain how an annuity can serve as an instrument for capital accumulation, a source of income, or both, and explain the tax deferral available with an annuity. As part of his discussion of Lucy's *Risk Tolerance*, Matt can discuss the growth potential of a fixed annuity (including an indexed one), in the light of the guaranteed principal and minimum return that it offers.

In short, Matt can match the potential advantages of those financial products he is permitted to discuss and sell with Lucy's objectives and concerns. Not only is he not allowed to compare those products with those he cannot sell (including mutual funds), but *it is not necessary for him to try.*

Scenario B: Matt is licensed to sell both insurance and securities

In this scenario, Matt is not only allowed to compare fixed annuities with mutual funds, but is arguably obliged to do so when he recommends an annuity (because that's what Lucy asked him to do). But he must be very careful to be both accurate and fair in his comparisons. If he discusses the advantage of tax deferral of the annuity gain, he should make sure that Lucy understands that all taxable distributions from the annuity will be Ordinary Income, and that profit from mutual funds may receive Capital Gains treatment. He must avoid making unfair or misleading comparisons. This is particularly important as Lucy has asked "can you do better for me?" Matt mustn't fall into the trap of suggesting that her portfolio *would have performed better if Matt had been managing it.* (Hypothetical comparisons of actual past performance are permissible, but they must be hypothetical).

Scenario C: Matt is an insurance agent, registered rep, and investment advisor

As we saw in earlier examples, Matt is now under a higher, *fiduciary*, standard of duty. He must consider all factors mentioned in the other scenarios, put Lucy's interests ahead of his own, and disclose compensation and conflicts of interest.

Case Five: "I Need To Roll Over My 401(k). Where Should I Put It?"

Milo is taking early retirement (at age 55) and wants to know what he should do with the $500,000 in his 401(k) plan. He's unmarried, owns his home outright, and has about $200,000 in other investments (mutual funds, mostly). He got Matt's name from Alex, a mutual friend and has arranged to meet Matt to discuss "retirement planning".

Scenario A: Matt is an insurance agent, with no securities or advisory license or credentials

As noted before, if Matt expects to recommend an annuity – *or is even considering making such a recommendation* – he needs to consider the 12 factors we've been talking about. Moreover, as we have noted, that consideration is always an *individualized* one, colored by the "facts and circumstances" of the individual client. Does Milo's situation call for special attention to any of these factors? If so, which ones and why?

Milo is 55. Does his *age* present any special concerns with regard to what he can, should, cannot, or should not do with the money he's asked Matt about (i.e.: his 401(k) balance)? Yes, it does. The 401(k) is an employer-sponsored retirement plan, subject to the distribution rules of IRC §401(a)(9), which makes the factor of *Tax Status* of particular importance. There are some things that Milo *may* do with this money and some things that he *must* do.

- He can keep the money in the 401(k) plan and begin taking distributions whenever he wishes, commencing no later than his age 70 ½.
- He can "roll over" this money to a traditional IRA (or to another employer-sponsored plan if he becomes a participant).
- He can "roll over" this money to a Roth IRA.

- He can take a cash distribution of all or part of this money.

Let's suppose that Matt is not highly familiar with the rules and requirements applying to each of these options. What should he do? Let's start with what he *should not do.* He should not attempt to discuss these options as though he has expertise concerning them. Unless he knows – really knows – what the rules are, he should either enlist the help of a colleague who does or refrain from offering opinions. Even if he does have a solid understanding of the rules governing each of those options, he must refrain from giving "legal" or "tax" advice (e.g.: how the tax rules will affect Milo's individual situation or what Milo's "best tax option" would be) – for several reasons: First, because a life insurance agent who gives legal or tax advice may be violating the laws of his state; second, because he will almost surely be violating the rules of the insurers he represents; third, because doing so will expose him to far greater risk of a lawsuit than would acting solely as an "insurance agent", and, last but not least, because it's simply the wrong thing to do. Incorrect advice offered with the best of intentions can be just as damaging as advice offered through malice.

For example, does Matt know that if Milo begins taking distributions from the 401(k) plan upon retirement, the "early distribution" penalty of IRC §72(t) will not apply (IRC §72(t)(2)(A)(v) but that if he "rolls over" that 401(k) to an IRA and begins taking distributions immediately, that penalty will be imposed (unless one of the exceptions of IRC §72(t)(2) applies)? Does Matt know how Milo can make that "roll over", take distributions immediately, and still avoid that penalty? Clearly, the factors *of Time Horizon* and *Financial Objectives* are of special relevance here, as is that of the *Intended Use of the Annuity.*

What if some of Milo's 401(k) money represents "employer securities" (e.g.: employer stock)? Does Matt know that a "qualified lump sum distribution" of such stock in kind can let Milo pay the tax on the appreciated portion of such stock at long term capital gains rates (IRC §402(e)(4)(A) but that, if Milo "rolls over" the 401(k) to an IRA, that opportunity is lost forever?

Does Matt know enough about "Roth IRA rollovers" to describe the pros and cons, and what factors need to be considered by anyone contemplating that strategy?

We're not suggesting that Matt, as an insurance agent, has the obligation to be expert in these subjects or even that he must discuss each of them with Milo. Indeed, as we've mentioned, Matt is not allowed to hold himself out as an expert in these areas unless he has genuine expertise (e.g.: he is a CPA or Enrolled Agent). We're simply saying that Matt should be very careful to confine his comments to general principles (e.g.: "distributions from IRAs are taxable as ordinary income"), to avoid applying general rules to Milo's specific situations (which can be construed as "tax advice"), and, above all, to refrain from discussing things he doesn't fully understand.

The other 12 factors not yet mentioned in this scenario are, of course, still important. They're important whenever any annuity is recommended.

Scenario B: Matt holds insurance and securities licenses

In this scenario, Matt can address both the mutual funds Milo already owns (including any within the 401(k)) and the relative advantages and disadvantages of a variable annuity. He's also held to a somewhat higher standard than in the first scenario, although the specifics of that higher standard are not at all clear at this time – chiefly because the standard of duty to which registered reps will be held in the future has yet to be finally determined. That said, Matt needs to avoid presenting his analysis and recommendations as being part of a "financial plan" and himself as a "financial planner", "financial consultant", or as being "independent and objective", as these are held, by some regulators, to be elements of an advisory relationship above that of "salesperson to customer" – one to which *fiduciary duty* must attach.

One final note on this "Milo case": Because Milo is asking Matt for advice concerning "qualified money" (i.e.: money in an employer-sponsored plan) and Matt is considering recommending an annuity, some regulatory authorities (including Compliance Departments at both insurance companies and Broker/Dealers) have published special caveats to be taken into account. Ignore them at your peril! Moreover, as we noted in earlier chapters, there is a persistent, and rather widespread, belief that annuities are *ipso facto* inappropriate for use in IRAs or qualified plans. Sometimes, this belief is grounded in mere nonsense. For example, the notion that the tax treatment that would apply to a deferred annuity held in a non-qualified account is somehow relevant to the question of whether the annuity is suitable when held in a tax-deferred account makes no sense.

By the logic that declares that one "wastes" the tax deferral of an annuity when buying it within a tax-deferred account, a small-cap, non-dividend paying stock (or mutual fund investing in such stocks) would be equally inappropriate for such an account. Why? Because the gains that such a stock (or fund) would receive, if held in a non-qualified account, would be chiefly, if not entirely, taxed at long term capital gains rates. Thus (by this contorted logic), one would "waste" that more favorable tax treatment by buying the stock in an IRA or qualified plan. But would any reasonable person suggest that no one should ever fund such an account with such stock? Of course not. There are certainly reasons why that stock (or fund) – or variable annuity - may be inappropriate in an IRA or qualified plan, but they have nothing whatever to do with taxation, *because any investment held in such account always gets ordinary income treatment.*

The prudent agent will be aware of the factors that truly do make an annuity suitable or unsuitable in a given situation as well as the fallacious arguments that seek to declare an annuity to be flatly unsuitable, so as to be able to educate clients as to the facts.

Case Six: "I've Got This Annuity…"

Parker has a deferred annuity that he purchased six years ago. He's disappointed in its performance and has approached Matt for advice. Should he cash it in? Keep it? Exchange it for another annuity?

This is a situation that almost everyone has encountered or will encounter. Many see it as an opportunity for a sale, and it may be that. But it's also an invitation to serious problems if not handled correctly.

- The agent who recommends the surrender of an existing annuity will, if that agent proposes another product for the surrender proceeds, be subject to the replacement rules of the state in which the new sale takes place (and of the issuer of the new product and of the agent's Broker/Dealer [if applicable]).

- If the existing annuity is to be exchanged for another annuity, in accordance with the rules of IRC §1035, the requirements (of the Dept. of the Treasury and of the issuers of both the original and replacement annuity and of the agent's Broker/Dealer [if applicable]) must be followed precisely. Even a minor mistake could invite regulatory scrutiny (and possible sanctions) or cause the transaction to fail to qualify as a "tax free exchange" (in which case, the gain in the original contract will be taxable to the annuity owner in the year of the surrender). Moreover, a "failed" exchange of contracts can be very difficult to "undo".

- Every issuer of annuity contracts has its own requirements (and, often, special forms) for "1035 exchanges". The prudent agent will ensure, before recommending an exchange, that he or she understands and can comply with those requirements.

"1035 exchanges" are subject to special scrutiny by regulators, Broker/Dealers, and insurers themselves. The specific rules vary from jurisdiction to jurisdiction, but the trend has been from "show that the policy owner is not harmed by this exchange" to "show that the policy owner clearly benefits from it".

What factors (in addition to the 12 factors mentioned earlier) should be considered by any insurance agent recommending such an exchange of annuity contracts?

1. Surrender charges. What charges will the policy owner incur as a result of surrender of the existing annuity? What new surrender charges will be imposed as a result of the exchange? Matt must make very certain that Parker understands both and that Parker is willing to incur them in exchange for the additional benefits offered by the new annuity.

2. Death benefit of existing annuity? Does the existing annuity have a guaranteed minimum death benefit that exceeds its surrender value? If so, and if that additional death benefit will be lost as a result of the surrender, Matt must ensure that Parker is willing to accept that loss.

3. Death benefit of new annuity. Is the exchange partly or wholly to obtain a guaranteed *minimum death benefit?*

4. Loss of any unvested "bonus" interest in the existing annuity. Will surrender of the first annuity cause a loss of any "bonus" interest?

5. Interest rates. If the exchange is of a fixed annuity for another fixed annuity, is the guaranteed minimum interest rate on the new contract different from that of the existing one? If it's lower, Matt should consider (and discuss with Parker) why Parker should accept the lower rate. The same caveat applies to the non-guaranteed ("current") interest rate.

6. Living Benefit Riders. Does the existing annuity contain a "living benefit"? If so, it is "in the money"? (That is, is the "benefit base" of that rider greater than the cash value?) Does the replacement annuity contain such a rider? If so, is it better? Does it cost more, or less, than the rider on the existing annuity?

7. Insurer financial solvency. If the new annuity is issued by a different insurer, the relative financial strength of the two insurers should be addressed.

8. If either contract is an indexed annuity, Matt must ensure that Parker understands how interest is calculated and credited and the term of the annuity.

9. If either annuity is a variable contract, there are additional caveats. Each Broker/Dealer has established guidelines and rules (pursuant to FINRA's requirement that they do so) for 1035 exchanges of variable annuities, and no agent should even think of recommending such an exchange without a clear understanding of those rules.

These are not the only factors to be considered, of course. Essentially, a *suitable* recommendation for an exchange of annuity contracts requires that *all relevant factors* be disclosed to, and understood by, the policy owner. This is the case whether Matt is acting solely as an insurance agent, as an agent and registered rep, or as agent, registered rep, and investment advisor. As in earlier case studies, the more registrations Matt has, the higher the level of duty that regulators – or litigators – may apply to his actions.

Does Matt's perceived duty vary with the credentials he holds and how he "holds himself out"? The answer, here, is "it depends upon who is doing the perceiving". State insurance regulators may or may not hold an insurance agent who holds professional credentials such as CLU®, ChFC®, or CFP® to a higher standard than an agent without such credentials, but, when litigation is involved, possession of such credentials often comes at a price. In a court case or arbitration, a plaintiff (complaining of an allegedly bad sale by an agent) will often include, in the Complaint, that the agent "held himself out" as having "special expertise". This is also true when the agent's business card lists him as a "Counselor", "Advisor", or by some other title that may suggest *independent and unbiased judgment.* It's especially true when the agent possesses professional credentials and employs a title such as those just mentioned. For this reason, some insurance marketing organizations forbid their representatives to advertise certain credentials and/or to use certain titles. If you intend to do either (assuming you're permitted to do so), be aware that you are very likely raising the standard of duty by which you may be held accountable.

This is especially true when one acts in multiple roles (e.g.: sometimes, as a "pure insurance agent", sometimes, as a registered rep, and sometimes as an investment advisor", depending upon the products being sold and/or services being performed). If this describes your practice (or what may become your practice), make very, very sure that your client understands, not only what you are recommending and why, but the *capacity in which you are acting*. It is far easier, and far less costly, to explain these things to a client, up front, before making any recommendation, than to a jury or panel of arbitrators.

Cheat Sheet

- The suitability factors may changes depending upno whether one is acting as an insurance agent, registered representative or financial advisor

- Professional certifications such as CLU®, ChFC®, or CFP® may cause regulators to hold an agent to a higher standard

- The consumer needs to fully understand the capacity in which you are acting

Glossary

Accumulated Value – the original premium plus any interest credited.

American-style option – may be exercised at any time before it expires. A European-style option may only be exercised on its expiration date.

Annual Reset (annual ratchet, cliquet) – crediting methods measuring index movement over a one year period. Positive interest is calculated and credited at the end of each contract year and cannot be lost if the index subsequently declines. *Say that the index increased from 100 to 110 in one year and the index annuity had an 80% participation rate. The insurance company would take the 10% gross index gain for the year (110-100/100), apply the participation rate (10% index gain x 80% rate) and credit 8% interest to the annuity. But, what if in the following year the index declined back to 100? The individual would keep the 8% interest earned and simply receive zero interest for the down year.* An annual reset structure preserves credited gains and treats negative index periods as years with zero growth.

Annuitant – the person upon whose life expectancy a life income is based upon annuitization.

Annuitization – converting an annuity's value into an income.

Averaging – index values may either be measured from a start point to an end point (point-to-point) or values between the start point and end point may added up, divided by the number of periods used, and this average becomes the end point. Index values may be averaged over the days, weeks, months, or quarters of the period.

Balanced Allocation (Balanced Allocation Annuities) – a fixed rate component is combined with an indexed component. At the end of the period gains from the fixed rate and index-linked components are totaled and credited. An annualized asset fee (yield spread) may be deducted from the combined return.

Blended (Multiple) Indices – this crediting method adds up the returns from different indices and applies a participation rate to the overall index gain or loss. This is not a rainbow method because the allocation of the indices is fixed and does not change based on index performance.

Bright Line Text – a clearly defined rule or standard, generally used in law, composed of objective factors, which leaves little or no room for varying interpretation.

Call Option (also see put option) – gives the option buyer the right to buy an underlying security or index at a specified price on or before a given date.

Cap – the maximum interest rate that will be credited to the annuity for the year or period, or the maximum index growth upon which interest will be calculated. The Cap usually refers to the maximum interest credited after applying the participation rate or yield spread. *If the index methodology showed a 20% increase, the participation rate was 60% and the maximum interest cap was 10%, the contract would credit 10% interest.* Other annuities use a maximum index cap instead of a maximum interest cap with the participation rate or yield spread applied to the lesser of the gain or the cap. *If the index methodology showed a 20% increase, the participation rate was 60% and the maximum gain cap was 10%, the contract would credit 6% interest.*

Cash Value (contract value, surrender value) – the minimum amount the annuity owner receives if the contract is surrendered.

Certificate of deposit – a bank investment derivative product without a minimum guaranteed interest rate, tax-deferral or life income options.

Cherry Picking – strengthening a hypothetical illustration by picking time periods that make a particular crediting method look better than it really is by using extreme examples.

Commercial Annuity – a contract for income between an issuing insurance company and a purchaser.

Compound Interest – interest is earned on both the original principal and on previous interest. If you're only looking at a few periods there isn't a lot of difference between the effects of simple and compound interest. However, the effects of compound interest become proportionately greater with each passing period.

Crediting Method (also see methodology) – the formula(s) used to determine the excess interest that is credited above the minimum interest guarantee.

Commercial Annuity – a contract for income between an issuing insurance company and a purchaser.

Death Benefit Rider – an optional annuity feature that guarantees the annuity death benefit will increase by at a least a minimum percentage each year.

Deferred Annuity – an annuity whereby at least a year will elapse between when the premium or premiums are paid and the annuity is annuitized with a stream of income produced.

Defined Liquidity – Unlike stocks or bonds, index annuities have defined liquidity. Regardless of how the market performs you usually know exactly what your surrender value is at any time.

Dynamic hedging – mimicking the behavior of options by building a small portfolio of other equity instruments.

Equity Index Universal Life – shares the coverage and premium flexibility of other universal life policies, but the crediting of interest is linked to an equity index.

European-style option – may only be exercised on its expiration date. An American-style option may be exercised at any time before it expires.

Excess Interest – interest credited to the annuity contract above the minimum guaranteed interest rate. In an index annuity the excess interest is determined by applying a stated crediting method to a specific index or indexes.

Exercise – to use an option to buy or sell the underlying security or index.

Extrapolation – where one infers unknown information by projecting known information. It is used with great accuracy in mathematics and much worse accuracy in financial and economic forecasting.

Fixed Annuity – a contract issued by an insurance company guaranteeing a minimum interest rate with the crediting of excess interest determined by the performance of the insurer's general account. Index annuities are fixed annuities.

Floor – the minimum participation rate or minimum cap that could be applied at future renewals.

Free Withdrawals – withdrawals that are free of surrender charges, however loss of excess interest or premature distribution penalties could apply.

Guaranteed Lifetime Withdrawal Benefit (GLWB, lifetime benefit rider) – removes uncertainty over the amount and length of the payments the annuity owner receives; it offers the same protection against living too long that annuitization does, while still offering access to the annuity's cash value.

Immediate Annuity – income payments will (and must) commence within one year of purchase.

Index – the underlying external benchmark which the crediting of excess interest is based; a measure of the prices of a group of securities.

Indexing – matching the performance of a specified group of annuities. Indexing does not attempt to beat the market, but to be the market.

Longevity Annuity – A truly deferred annuity that is annuitized at an advanced age to produce a life income if the annuity owner is still alive, but expires without value if the annuity owner dies before the annuitization date.

Market Index Securities – a security promising a guarantee of principal if held to a 5 or 7 year maturity with upside index potential (see term yield spread index annuities).

Market Risk – the possibility to lose past gains or even principal. The original principal and credited interest of an index annuity are not subject to market risk. Even if the index declines the annuity owner would receive no less than their original principal back if they decided to cash in the policy at the end of the surrender period. Unlike a security, index annuities guarantee the original premium and the premium is backed by the insurance company that issued it.

Market Value Adjustment (MVA) – changes in the interest environment are taken into account if the annuity is cashed in before the end of the surrender charge period. What this can mean is if interest rates have risen since the annuity was issued, the penalties for cashing out could be higher than the schedule stated in the policy, and if rates have fallen since issued the penalties could be lower or even zero

Maturity Date – the maturity date is the longest one can keep annuity interest deferred before it must be taken out or annuitized. Maturity dates usually occur when the annuitant celebrates their 80th to 90th birthday.

Methodology (crediting method, crediting structure) – the way index movement becomes interest crediting is calculated. There are currently 40 different methods used to determine how index movement becomes interest credited.

Minimum Guaranteed Return (minimum interest rate) – the minimum interest guarantee. If *the annuity guaranteed 3% a year based on 100% of the premium. This means that at the end of a seven year term the minimum guaranteed return would be $1.23 for each $1 of premium. If the external index increased so that the index annuity interest crediting method resulted in a 30 cent interest gain for the entire period the annuity contract would credit 30 cents- not 30 cents plus 23 cents.* If the calculated index gain was zero for a year, the typical index annuity would not credit the minimum guarantee of 3% for that specific year, the contract would record 0% interest. Most index annuities compute the minimum guarantee on 90% of premium.

Monthly Cap Forward-Not Back – calculates gains and losses of the index on the monthly basis, adds up the monthly figures, and the final number is your interest for the period; the period's interest can never be less than zero. The maximum monthly gain recognized is subject to a cap, but monthly losses are not subject to a cap.

Option – a contract which conveys to its buyer the right, but not the obligation, to buy or sell something at a specified price on or before a given date; after this given date the option ceases to exist. Insurers typically buy options to provide the index linkage for the excess interest potential. Options may be American styled whereby they may be exercised at anytime prior to the given date, or they may have to be exercised only during a specified window. Options that may only be exercised during a specified period are European styled options.

Owner – the individual or entity that owns all rights to the annuity contract.

Price/Earnings or P/E Ratio – tells how many years' worth of earnings a share of stock is selling.

Participation Floor – a crediting factor minimum guarantee.

Participation Rate – the percentage of positive index movement credited to the annuity. *If the index methodology determined that the index increased 10% and the index annuity participated in 60% of the increase, it would be said that the contract has a 60% participation rate.* Participation

rates may also be expressed as asset fees or yield spreads.
Point-to-Point – a crediting method measuring index movement from an absolute initial point to the absolute end point for a period. An index had a period starting value of 100 and a period ending value of 120. A point-to-point method would record a positive index movement of 20 [120-100] or a 20% positive movement [(120-100)/100]. Point-to-point usually refers to annual periods, however the phrase is also used instead of term end point to refer to multiple year periods.

Principal Protection Funds – a security using a split-investment concept involving bonds and equities.

Private Annuity – a contract for income between two individuals.

Put Option (also see call option) – gives the buyer the right to sell an underlying security or index at a specified price on or before a given date.

Rainbow Method – uses a "look-back" where the best-performing indices of the crediting period are weighted more heavily than those that performed less well.

Refund Feature – a guarantee that, if the annuitant dies before receiving either a specified number of payments, the beneficiary will receive either the remaining number of guaranteed payments or the remaining principal

Return Floor – another way of saying minimum guaranteed return.

Rule of 72 – formula for determining approximately how many years it takes a sum to double at a given rate. 72 is divided by the return percentage and the answer is approximately the time it takes money to double at that rate.

Simple Interest (also see compound interest) – interest is only earned on the original principal.

Spousal Continuation Option – if the annuity owner names the spouse as primary beneficiary, that surviving spouse can, at the owner's death, treat the annuity as though the surviving spouse/ beneficiary was the original purchaser and continue the annuity

Standard & Poor's 500® (S&P 500®) – most widely used index annuity external index. The index does not include reinvested dividends of the underlying stocks

Strike Price (also see option, exercise price) – the specified share price or index value at which the shares or interest may be bought or sold. If the strike price of a call option is less than the current market price of the underlying security the call is said to be in-the-money. Conversely, if the strike price of a call option is greater than the current market price it is out-of-the-money and would not be exercised.

Surrender Charge (surrender penalty) – a charge imposed for withdrawing funds or terminating the annuity contract usually within a specified number of years. The charge is usually expressed as a declining percentage of the total contract value.

Surrender Value (cash value, contract value) – the minimum amount the annuity owner receives if the contract is surrendered.

Term Average Highest Anniversary – a crediting method where a rolling annual average of monthly index values is calculated and the highest averaged anniversary value used as an end point. It is <u>not</u> a high water mark methodology.

Term End Point – crediting methods measuring index movements over a greater timeframe than a year or two; the opposite of an annual reset method. Also referred to as a term point-to-point method. *Say that the index value was at 100 on the first day of the period. If the calculated index value were at 150 at the end of the period the positive index movement would be 50% (150-100/100). The company would credit a percentage of this movement as excess interest.* Index movement is calculated and interest credited at the end of the term and interim movements during the period are ignored.

Term High Point (High Water Mark) – a type of term end point structure that uses the highest anniversary index level as the end point. *Say that the index value was at 100 on the first day of the period, reached a value of 160 at the end of a contract year during the period, and ended the period at 150. A term high point method would use the 160 value - the highest contract anniversary point reached during the period, as the end point and the gross index gain would be 60% (160-100/100).* The company would then apply a participation rate to the gain. No true high water mark methods are currently used.

Term Yield Spread – a type of term end point structure which calculates the total index gain for a period, computes the annual compound rate of return, or internal rate of return, deducts a yield spread from the annual rate of return, and then recalculates the total index gain for the period based on the net annual rate. *Say that an index increased from 100 to 200 by the end of a nine year period. This is the equivalent of an 8% compound annual interest rate. If the annuity had a 2% term yield spread this would be deducted from the annual interest rate (8%-2%) and the net rate would be credited to the contract (6%) for each of the nine years.* Total index gain may also be computed by using the highest anniversary index level as the end point.

Variable Annuity – a contract issued by an insurance company offering separate accounts invested in a wide variety of stocks and/or bonds. The investment risk is borne by the annuity owner. Variable annuities are considered securities and require appropriate securities registration.

Vesting – typically used with term high point methods a portion of any gain is locked in each year and this vested portion is available for withdrawal.

Composite Investment Grade Bond Yields
1960 - 2010

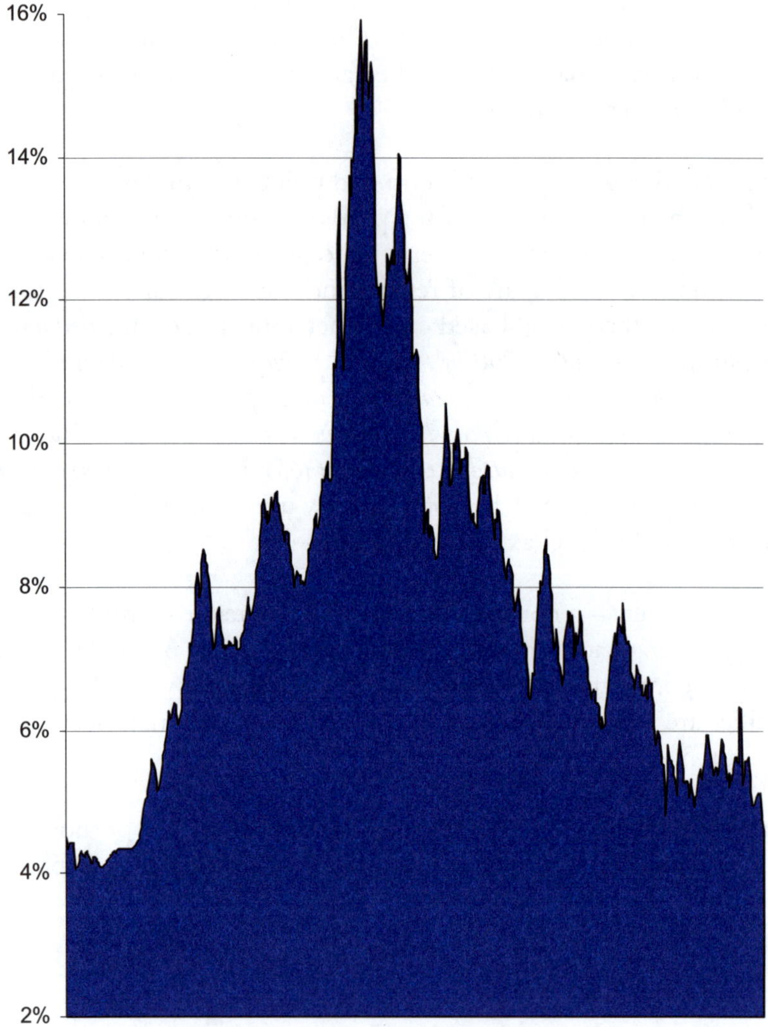

1/3 each 10 Yr US Treasury, AAA Corp, BAA Corp
Source: Board of Governors of the Federal Reserve System

6-Month Certificate of Deposit: Secondary Market Rate 1965 - 2010

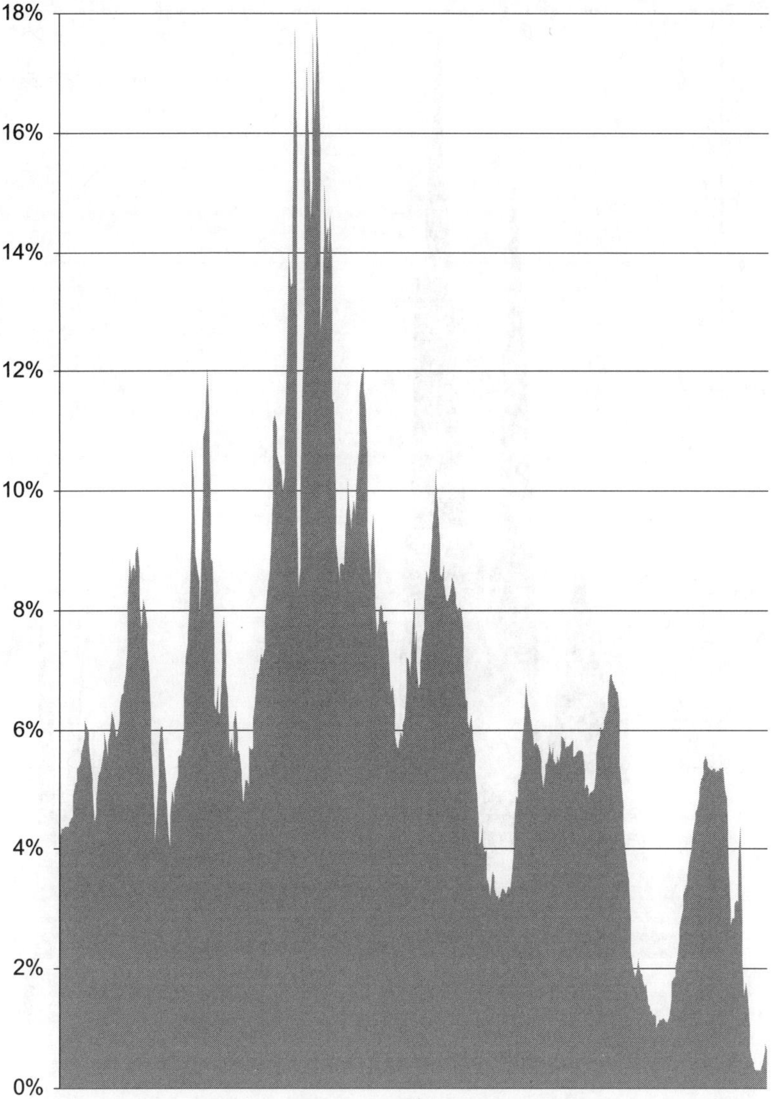

Source: Board of Governors of the Federal Reserve System

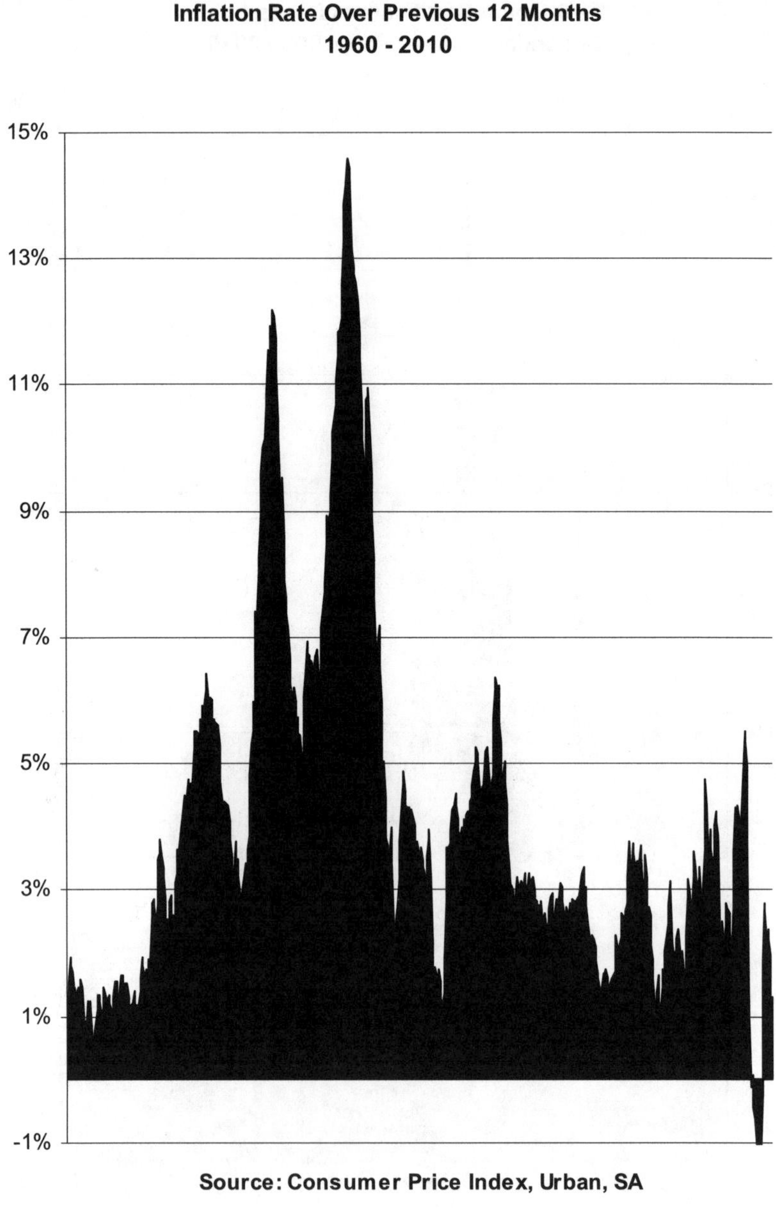
Inflation Rate Over Previous 12 Months
1960 - 2010
15%
13%
11%
9%
7%
5%
3%
1%
-1%
Source: Consumer Price Index, Urban, SA

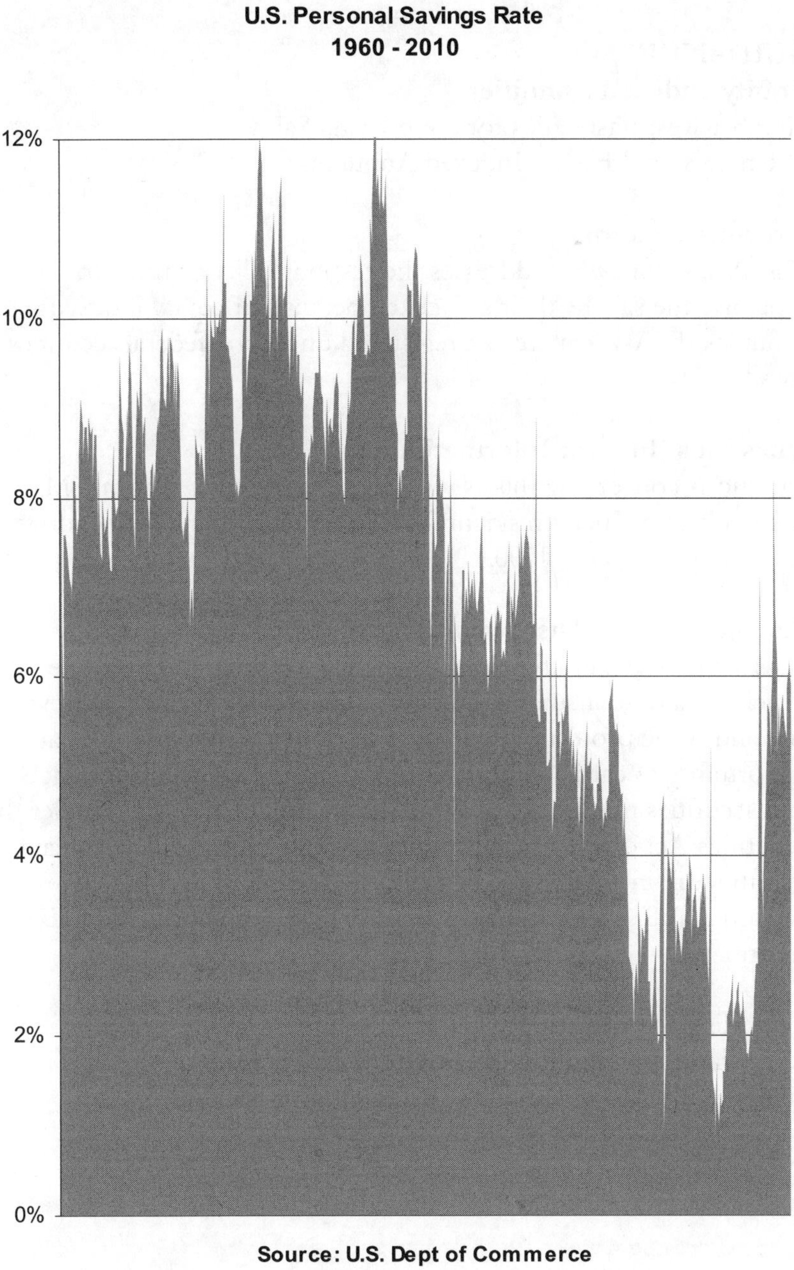
U.S. Personal Savings Rate
1960 - 2010
12%
10%
8%
6%
4%
2%
0%
Source: U.S. Dept of Commerce

Notice to Members 05-50

GUIDANCE
Equity-Indexed Annuities
Member Responsibilities for Supervising Sales of Unregistered Equity-Indexed Annuities

Executive Summary
This *Notice to Members* addresses the responsibility of firms to supervise the sale by their associated persons of equity-indexed annuities (EIAs) that are not registered under the federal securities laws.[1]

Questions/Further Information
Questions concerning this *Notice* may be directed to Thomas M. Selman, Senior Vice President, Investment Companies/Corporate Financing, (240) 386-4500.

Background and Discussion
Equity-indexed annuities are financial instruments in which the issuer, usually an insurance company, guarantees a stated interest rate and some protection from loss of principal, and provides an opportunity to earn additional interest based on the performance of a securities market index. Some EIAs are not registered under the Securities Act of 1933 (the Securities Act) based on a determination that they are insurance products that fall within that statute's Section 3(a)(8) exemption and therefore are not considered to be securities.[2]

According to one recently published estimate, in 2004 sales of equity-indexed annuities increased over 50 percent, from $14 billion in 2003 to an estimated $22 billion.[3]

1. Investor Protection Issues Presented by Equity-Indexed Annuities

EIAs are complex investments. Many EIAs permit investors to participate in only a stated percentage of an increase in an index. Many of these investments also impose a "cap rate" that represents the maximum annual account value percentage increase allowed to investors. Unregistered EIAs typically do not provide for investor participation in the dividends accumulated on the securities represented by the index.[4] EIAs have other features that contribute to their complexity such as minimum guarantees and fees and expenses, including surrender charges, premium bonuses, and multiple premium payment arrangements. In addition, investors may assume mistakenly that EIAs provide the same returns as an index mutual fund.

NASD is concerned about the manner in which associated persons are marketing and selling unregistered EIAs, and the absence of adequate supervision of these sales practices. We have seen sales material for unregistered EIAs that do not fully describe the features and risks of the product. For example, we have seen the following claims:

- "What if the market goes down and you would lose nothing?
- The market goes up-you gain!"
- "A Win/Win Investment Vehicle!"
- "How Your Retirement Funds Can Have: Security of Principal, Higher Than CD Rates of Interest, Opportunity for Growth (No Losses)"
- "Pick up where Social Security leaves off with NEW tax-deferred annuities…featuring… 2 indexed accounts linked to a popular stock market index."
- If you're looking for upside potential and no market downside look no further than [name of EIA]. This fixed annuity… enables you to make the most of S&P 500 Index gains…"
- "Growth Potential *without* Market Risk."

We understand that some associated persons who also act as insurance agents might be using this type of sales material in their insurance sales capacity. NASD is concerned that the unsupervised use of such sales material could confuse or mislead investors. If sales pieces containing these statements were deemed to be broker-dealer communications with the public, then they would be subject to the NASD advertising rules, and would have to provide a balanced description of the features and risks of the product.

Moreover, because of the product's complexity, some associated persons might have difficulty understanding all of the features of the product and determining the extent to which those features meet the needs of the customer. While unregistered EIAs may be appropriate for some retail investors, they are not suitable for all investors. For example, possible surrender charges and the combination of caps and participation rates associated with a particular product are factors that must be considered in any suitability determination.

2. The Uncertain Status of Unregistered Equity-Indexed Annuities

The question of whether a particular EIA is an insurance product or a security is complicated and depends upon the particular facts and circumstances concerning the instrument offered or sold. NASD does not seek to resolve that issue in this *Notice*; nor is this *Notice* intended to describe those circumstances in which an EIA might be deemed to be a security. However, a brief summary of the applicable provisions of the federal securities laws may be useful.

Section 2(a)(1) of the Securities Act broadly defines "security" to include such financial instruments as evidence of indebtedness, participation in profit-sharing agreements, and investment contracts. Section 3(a)(8) generally exempts from the Securities Act any security that is an "insurance or endowment policy or annuity contract or optional annuity contract, issued by a corporation subject to the supervision of the insurance commissioner, bank commissioner, or any agency or officer performing like functions, of any State or Territory of the United States or the District of Columbia."

In 1986, the Commission adopted Rule 151, a "safe harbor" under the Securities Act, which clarifies when certain annuity contracts are exempted securities under Section 3(a)(8). The fundamental construct of Rule 151 is derived from prior judicial interpretations of Section 3(a)(8). Consequently, the Commission has stated that the rationale underlying the conditions set forth in the rule are, along with applicable judicial interpretations, relevant to any Section 3(a)(8) analysis.[5]

In order for the Rule 151 safe harbor to apply:

- the product must be issued by an insurer that is subject to state insurance regulation;
- the insurer must assume investment risk, as provided in paragraph (b) of the rule; and
- the product may not be marketed primarily as an investment.

As noted above, the status of any particular EIA under the safe harbor (or under Section 3(a)(8)) will depend on the facts and circumstances. In 1997 the Commission issued a concept release requesting comment regarding EIAs.

3. Supervision under Rule 3030 and Rule 3040

Many firms assume that EIAs that are not registered under the Securities Act are insurance products and not securities. These firms treat the sale of unregistered EIAs by associated persons in their capacity as insurance agents as an outside business activity under Rule 3030, beyond the mandated purview of the firm's supervision. Rule 3030 does not require that the firm supervise or even approve an outside business activity, although a firm may choose to deny or limit the ability of associated persons to engage in the activity. Rule 3030 simply requires that an associated person promptly notify the firm in writing that he is engaging in a business activity outside the scope of his relationship with the firm.

However, if a particular EIA were a security, and an associated person sold the EIA outside the regular scope of his employment with the firm, Rule 3040 requires that the firm treat the sale as a private securities transaction and supervise the sale in accordance with the provisions of that rule. The associated person must notify the firm in writing before participating in a private securities transaction. If the associated person will receive compensation for the transaction, the firm must provide written approval of his participation in the transaction. If the firm does approve the participation, it must record the transaction on its books and records and supervise the associated person's participation in the transaction as if the transaction were executed on behalf of the firm.

A broker-dealer runs certain risks in applying Rule 3030 to the sale of an unregistered EIA on the assumption that the product is not a security. It is often unclear whether a particular EIA qualifies for the exemption under Section 3(a)(8), since the analysis is made on a case-by-case basis and may turn on the particular features and marketing materials associated with the product. As a result, if a particular EIA did not qualify for the exemption, a firm might incorrectly treat the EIA transaction as an outside business activity under Rule 3030 rather than a private securities transaction under Rule 3040 and thereby fail to supervise sales of the product as required by NASD rules.

Perhaps for these reasons, some firms require that associated persons obtain firm approval to sell exempt insurance products. Other firms require that their associated persons obtain more specific approval to sell unregistered EIAs. Still other firms maintain a list of approved EIAs and prohibit the sale of all others.

4. Supervisory Measures

Due to the uncertainty as to whether a particular unregistered EIA may be a security, as well as the potential regulatory violations and investor protection issues that would arise by the marketing and sale of unregistered EIAs that are deemed to be securities, firms must adopt special procedures under Rule 3030 with respect to these products. In particular, firms must require that their associated persons promptly notify the firm in writing when they intend to sell unregistered EIAs. Moreover, all recommendations to liquidate or surrender a registered security such as a mutual fund, variable annuity, or variable life contract must be suitable, including where such liquidations or surrender are for the purpose of funding the purchase of an unregistered EIA.

As discussed above, NASD is not taking a position on whether a particular EIA is a security, nor are we attempting to describe the circumstances in which an EIA would be deemed a security. However, the uncertainty of this matter has led some firms to treat an associated person's sale of an unregistered EIA outside the regular course or scope of his employment with the firm, as a private securities transaction. These firms supervise the sale according to Rule 3040 procedures. Firms are well advised to consider whether they should take a similar approach. Firms should consider maintaining a list of acceptable unregistered EIAs and prohibiting their associated persons from selling any other unregistered EIA, unless the associated person notifies the firm in writing that he intends to recommend an unregistered EIA that is not on the firm's list, and receives the firm's written confirmation that the sale of the unregistered EIA is acceptable.

Firms are encouraged to consider whether other supervisory procedures also might help protect the firm's customers. For example, a firm could require that all sales of unregistered EIAs occur through the firm. If an associated person is selling the unregistered EIA through the firm, the firm must supervise the marketing material, suitability analysis, and other sales practices associated with the recommendation of unregistered EIAs in the same manner that it supervises the sale of securities.

Firms also must provide any associated person selling any unregistered EIA through the firm with the proper training to understand the EIA's features and the extent to which the EIA meets the needs of a particular customer. The fact that an associated person holds a license as an insurance agent may not adequately qualify him to understand the features of an EIA or the extent to which an EIA meets the needs of a particular customer.

Of course, in this as in all other areas, NASD expects every associated person to comply with the procedures adopted by his firm.

Endnotes

1 The sale of an EIA registered under the federal securities laws is subject to the full panoply of regulation applicable to the sale of any security.

The principles articulated in this *Notice* apply to EIAs that are sold by associated persons of a broker-dealer, whether the EIA has been manufactured by an insurance company that is affiliated with the broker-dealer or by an unaffiliated insurance company.

2 The Securities and Exchange Commission (the Commission) has previously stated that Congress intended any insurance contract falling within Section 3(a)(8) to be excluded from all provisions of the Securities Act notwithstanding the language of the Act indicating that Section 3(a)(8) is an exemption from registration but not the antifraud provisions. *See* Definition of "Annuity Contract or Optional Annuity Contract," Securities Act Release No. 6558 (Nov. 21, 1984), 49 Fed. Reg. 46750, 46753 (Nov. 28, 1984).

3 "A Do-It-Yourself Kit for Investors: Build Your Own Equity-Indexed Annuity," *The Wall Street Journal* (January 26, 2005).

4 The index return may be calculated in a variety of ways, such as the "annual reset" method, under which the index starting point is reset each contract year; the "point-to-point" method, under which the change in the index from the start of a term is compared to the index at the end of the term; and the "annual high-water mark with look-back" method, which is a variation on the point-to-point method except that it compares the index starting point to the highest anniversary value during the term.

5 Securities Act Release No. 6645, 35 SEC Docket 952 (May 29, 1986) (adopting Rule 151) ("Adopting Release").

6 Request for Comment on Equity-Indexed Products, Securities Act Release No. 7438; File No. S7-22-97 (August 20, 1997). At least one court has ruled on the question of whether an EIA is a security. The court granted a motion to dismiss based upon the finding that the EIA, which was the subject of litigation, in that case was exempt

from the federal securities laws. *See Malone v. Addision Insurance Marketing*, 225 F. Supp. 2d 743 (W.D. Ky. 2002).

3030. Outside Business Activities of an Associated Person

No person associated with a member in any registered capacity shall be employed by, or accept compensation from, any other person as a result of any business activity, other than a passive investment, outside the scope of his relationship with his employer firm, unless he has provided prompt written notice to the member. Such notice shall be in the form required by the member. Activities subject to the requirements of Rule 3040 shall be exempted from this requirement.

Regulatory Notice 09-25 May 2009 Suitability and "Know Your Customer" Proposed Consolidated FINRA Rules Governing Suitability and Know-Your-Customer Obligations

ATTACHMENT A

* * * * *

Text of Proposed New FINRA Rules

* * * * *

2000. DUTIES AND CONFLICTS

* * * * *

2100. TRANSACTIONSWITH CUSTOMERS [GENERAL STANDARDS]

* * * * *

2110. Recommendations
2111. Suitability

(a) A member or an associated person must have a reasonable basis to believe that a recommended transaction or investment strategy involving a security or securities is suitable for the customer, based on the facts known by the member or associated person or disclosed by the customer in response to the member's or associated person's reasonable efforts to obtain information concerning the customer's age, other investments, financial situation and needs, tax status, investment objectives, investment experience, investment time horizon, liquidity needs, risk tolerance, and any other information the member or associated person considers to be reasonable in making recommendations.

(b) A member or associated person fulfills the customer-specific suitability obligation for an institutional account, as defined in NASD Rule 3110(c)(4), if (1) the institutional customer affirmatively indicates that it is willing to forego the protection of the customer-specific obligation of the suitability rule and (2) the member or associated person has a reasonable basis to believe that the institutional customer is (A) capable of evaluating investment risks independently, both in general and with regard to particular transactions and investment strategies involving a security or securities and (B) exercising independent judgment in evaluating the member's or associated person's recommendations. Where an institutional customer has delegated decision-making authority to an agent, such as an investment advisor or a bank trust department, these factors shall be applied to the agent.

IRC, 2005-CODE-VOL, SEC. 72. ANNUITIES; CERTAIN PROCEEDS OF ENDOWMENT AND LIFE INSURANCE CONTRACTS.

SEC. 72. ANNUITIES; CERTAIN PROCEEDS OF ENDOWMENT AND LIFE INSURANCE CONTRACTS.

72(a) GENERAL RULE FOR ANNUITIES. –
Except as otherwise provided in this chapter, gross income includes any amount received as an annuity (whether for a period certain or during one or more lives) under an annuity, endowment, or life insurance contract.

72(b) EXCLUSION RATIO. –

72(b)(1) IN GENERAL. –
Gross income does not include that part of any amount received as an annuity under an annuity, endowment, or life insurance contract which bears the same ratio to such amount as the investment in the contract (as of the annuity starting date) bears to the expected return under the contract (as of such date).

72(b)(2) EXCLUSION LIMITED TO INVESTMENT. –
The portion of any amount received as an annuity which is excluded from gross income under paragraph (1) shall not exceed the unrecovered investment in the contract immediately before the receipt of such amount.

72(e) AMOUNTS NOT RECEIVED AS ANNUITIES. –
72(e)(1) APPLICATION OF SUBSECTION. –

72(e)(1)(A) IN GENERAL. – This subsection shall apply to any amount which –

72(e)(1)(A)(i) is received under an annuity, endowment, or life insurance contract, and

72(e)(1)(A)(ii) is not received as an annuity, if no provision of this subtitle (other than this subsection) applies with respect to such amount.

72(e)(1)(B) DIVIDENDS. – For purposes of this section, any amount received which is in the nature of a dividend or similar distribution shall be treated as an amount not received as an annuity.

72(e)(2) GENERAL RULE.
Any amount to which this subsection applies –

72(e)(2)(A) if received on or after the annuity starting date, shall be included in gross income, or

72(e)(2)(B) if received before the annuity starting date –

72(e)(2)(B)(i) shall be included in gross income to the extent allocable to income on the contract, and

72(e)(2)(B)(ii) shall not be included in gross income to the extent allocable to the investment in the contract.

72(e)(3) ALLOCATION OF AMOUNTS TO INCOME AND INVESTMENT. For purposes of paragraph (2)(B) –

72(e)(3)(A) ALLOCATION TO INCOME. – Any amount to which this subsection applies shall be treated as allocable to income on the contract to the extent that such amount does not exceed the excess (if any) of –

72(e)(3)(A)(i) the cash value of the contract (determined without regard to any surrender charge) immediately before the amount is received, over

72(e)(3)(A)(ii) the investment in the contract at such time.

72(e)(3)(B) ALLOCATION TO INVESTMENT. – Any amount to which this subsection applies shall be treated as allocable to investment in the contract to the extent that such amount is not allocated to income under subparagraph (A).

72(e)(4) SPECIAL RULES FOR APPLICATION OF PARAGRAPH (2)(B). For purposes of paragraph (2)(B) –

72(e)(4)(A) LOANS TREATED AS DISTRIBUTIONS. – If, during any taxable year, an individual –

72(e)(4)(A)(i) receives (directly or indirectly) any amount as a loan under any contract to which this subsection applies, or

72(e)(4)(A)(ii) assigns or pledges (or agrees to assign or pledge) any portion of the value of any such contract, such amount or portion shall be treated as received under the contract as an amount not received as an annuity. The preceding sentence shall not apply for purposes of determining investment in the contract, except that the investment in the contract shall be increased by any amount included in gross income by reason of the amount treated as received under the preceding sentence.

72(e)(4)(B) TREATMENT OF POLICYHOLDER DIVIDENDS. – Any amount described in paragraph (1)(B) shall not be included in gross income under paragraph (2)(B)(i) to the extent such amount is retained by the insurer as a premium or other consideration paid for the contract.

72(e)(4)(C) TREATMENT OF TRANSFERS WITHOUT ADEQUATE CONSIDERATION. –

72(e)(4)(C)(i) IN GENERAL. – If an individual who holds an annuity contract transfers it without full and adequate consideration, such individual shall be treated as receiving an amount equal to the excess of –

72(e)(4)(C)(i)(I) the cash surrender value of such contract at the time of transfer, over

72(e)(4)(C)(i)(II) the investment in such contract at such time, under the contract as an amount not received as an annuity.

72(e)(4)(C)(iii) ADJUSTMENT TO INVESTMENT IN CONTRACT OF TRANSFEREE. – If under clause (i) an amount is included in the gross income of the transferor of an annuity contract, the investment in the contract of the transferee in such contract shall be increased by the amount so included.

72(e)(5) RETENTION OF EXISTING RULES IN CERTAIN CASES. –

72(e)(5)(A) IN GENERAL. – In any case to which this paragraph applies –

72(e)(5)(A)(i) paragraphs (2)(B) and (4)(A) shall not apply, and

72(e)(5)(A)(ii) if paragraph (2)(A) does not apply,

the amount shall be included in gross income, but only to the extent it exceeds the investment in the contract.

72(e)(5)(B) EXISTING CONTRACTS. – This paragraph shall apply to contracts entered into before August 14, 1982. Any amount allocable to investment in the contract after August 13, 1982, shall be treated as from a contract entered into after such date.

72(e)(5)(C) CERTAIN LIFE INSURANCE AND ENDOWMENT CONTRACTS. – Except as provided in paragraph (10) and except to the extent prescribed by the Secretary by regulations, this paragraph shall apply to any amount not received as an annuity which is received under a life insurance or endowment contract.

72(e)(5)(D) CONTRACTS UNDER QUALIFIED PLANS. – Except as provided in paragraph (8), this paragraph shall apply to any amount received –

72(e)(5)(D)(ii) from a contract –

72(e)(5)(D)(ii)(I) purchased by a trust described in clause (i),

72(e)(5)(D)(iii) from an individual retirement account or an individual retirement annuity.

72(e)(5)(E) FULL REFUNDS, SURRENDERS, REDEMPTIONS, AND MATURITIES. – This paragraph shall apply to –

72(e)(5)(E)(i) any amount received, whether in a single sum or otherwise, under a contract in full discharge of the obligation under the contract which is in the nature of a refund of the consideration paid for the contract, and

72(e)(5)(E)(ii) any amount received under a contract on its complete surrender, redemption, or maturity.

In the case of any amount to which the preceding sentence applies, the rule of paragraph (2)(A) shall not apply.

72(e)(6) INVESTMENT IN THE CONTRACT. – For purposes of this subsection, the investment in the contract as of any date is –

72(e)(6)(A) the aggregate amount of premiums or other consideration paid for the contract before such date, minus

72(e)(6)(B) the aggregate amount received under the contract before such date, to the extent that such amount was excludable from gross income under this subtitle or prior income tax laws.

72(e)(11) ANTI-ABUSE RULES –

72(e)(11)(A) IN GENERAL. – For purposes of determining the amount includible in gross income under this subsection –

72(e)(11)(A)(i) all modified endowment contracts issued by the same company to the same policyholder during any calendar year shall be treated as 1 modified endowment contract, and

72(e)(11)(A)(ii) all annuity contracts issued by the same company to the same policyholder during any calendar year shall be treated as 1 annuity contract.

The preceding sentence shall not apply to any contract described in paragraph (5)(D).

72(e)(11)(B) REGULATORY AUTHORITY. --The Secretary may by regulations prescribe such additional rules as may be necessary or appropriate to prevent avoidance of the purposes of this subsection through serial purchases of contracts or otherwise.

72(h) OPTION TO RECEIVE ANNUITY IN LIEU OF LUMP SUM. If –

72(h)(1) a contract provides for payment of a lump sum in full discharge of an obligation under the contract, subject to an option to receive an annuity in lieu of such lump sum;

72(h)(2) the option is exercised within 60 days after the day on which such lump sum first became payable; and

72(h)(3) part or all of such lump sum would (but for this subsection) be includible in gross income by reason of subsection (e) (1),

then, for purposes of this subtitle, no part of such lump sum shall be considered as includible in gross income at the time such lump sum first became payable.

72(q) 10-PERCENT PENALTY FOR PREMATURE DISTRIBUTIONS FROM ANNUITY CONTRACTS. –

72(q)(1) IMPOSITION OF PENALTY. –
If any taxpayer receives any amount under an annuity contract, the taxpayer's tax under this chapter for the taxable year in which such amount is received shall be increased by an amount equal to 10 percent of the portion of such amount which is includible in gross income.

72(q)(2) SUBSECTION NOT TO APPLY TO CERTAIN DISTRIBUTIONS. –
Paragraph (1) shall not apply to any distribution –

72(q)(2)(A) made on or after the date on which the taxpayer attains age 591/2 ,

72(q)(2)(B) made on or after the death of the holder (or, where the holder is not an individual, the death of the primary annuitant (as defined in subsection (s)(6)(B))),

72(q)(2)(C) attributable to the taxpayer's becoming disabled within the meaning of subsection (m)(7),

72(q)(2)(D) which is a part of a series of substantially equal periodic payments (not less frequently than annually) made for the life (or life expectancy) of the taxpayer or the joint lives (or joint life expectancies) of such taxpayer and his designated beneficiary,

72(q)(2)(E) from a plan, contract, account, trust, or annuity described in subsection (e)(5)(D),

72(q)(2)(F) allocable to investment in the contract before August 14, 1982,

72(q)(2)(H) to which subsection (t) applies (without regard to paragraph (2) thereof),

72(q)(2)(J) which is purchased by an employer upon the termination of a plan

72(q)(3) CHANGE IN SUBSTANTIALLY EQUAL PAYMENTS.
If –

72(q)(3)(A) paragraph (1) does not apply to a distribution by reason of paragraph (2)(D), and

72(q)(3)(B) the series of payments under such paragraph are subsequently modified (other than by reason of death or disability) --

72(q)(3)(B)(i) before the close of the 5-year period beginning on the date of the first payment and after the taxpayer attains age 591/2 , or

72(q)(3)(B)(ii) before the taxpayer attains age 591/2 ,

the taxpayer's tax for the 1st taxable year in which such modification occurs shall be increased by an amount, determined under regulations, equal to the tax which (but for paragraph (2)(D)) would have been imposed, plus interest for the deferral period (within the meaning of subsection (t)(4)(B)).

72(s) REQUIRED DISTRIBUTIONS WHERE HOLDER DIES BEFORE ENTIRE INTEREST IS DISTRIBUTED. –

72(s)(1) IN GENERAL. –
A contract shall not be treated as an annuity contract for purposes of this title unless it provides that –

72(s)(1)(A) if any holder of such contract dies on or after the annuity starting date and before the entire interest in such contract has been distributed, the remaining portion of such interest will be distributed at least as rapidly as under the method of distributions being used as of the date of his death, and

72(s)(1)(B) if any holder of such contract dies before the annuity starting date, the entire interest in such contract will be distributed within 5 years after the death of such holder.

72(s)(2) EXCEPTION FOR CERTAIN AMOUNTS PAYABLE OVER LIFE OF BENEFICIARY. – If –

72(s)(2)(A) any portion of the holder's interest is payable to (or for the benefit of) a designated beneficiary,

72(s)(2)(B) such portion will be distributed (in accordance with regulations) over the life of such designated beneficiary (or over a period not extending beyond the life expectancy of such beneficiary), and

72(s)(2)(C) such distributions begin not later than 1 year after the date of the holder's death or such later date as the Secretary may by regulations prescribe,

then for purposes of paragraph (1), the portion referred to in subparagraph (A) shall be treated as distributed on the day on which such distributions begin.

72(s)(3) SPECIAL RULE WHERE SURVIVING SPOUSE BENEFICIARY. –
If the designated beneficiary referred to in paragraph (2)(A) is the surviving spouse of the holder of the contract, paragraphs (1) and (2) shall be applied by treating such spouse as the holder of such contract.

72(s)(4) DESIGNATED BENEFICIARY. –
For purposes of this subsection, the term "designated beneficiary" means any individual designated a beneficiary by the holder of the contract.

72(s)(6) SPECIAL RULE WHERE HOLDER IS CORPORATION OR OTHER NON-INDIVIDUAL. –

72(s)(6)(A) IN GENERAL. – For purposes of this subsection, if the holder of the contract is not an individual, the primary annuitant shall be treated as the holder of the contract.

72(s)(6)(B) PRIMARY ANNUITANT. – For purposes of subparagraph (A), the term "primary annuitant" means the individual, the events in the life of whom are of primary importance in affecting the timing or amount of the payout under the contract.

72(s)(7) TREATMENT OF CHANGES IN PRIMARY ANNUITANT WHERE HOLDER OF CONTRACT IS NOT AN INDIVIDUAL. –
For purposes of this subsection, in the case of a holder of an annuity contract which is not an individual, if there is a change in a primary annuitant (as defined in paragraph (6)(B)), such change shall be treated as the death of the holder.

72(u) TREATMENT OF ANNUITY CONTRACTS NOT HELD BY NATURAL PERSONS. –

72(u)(1) IN GENERAL. --
If any annuity contract is held by a person who is not a natural person –

72(u)(1)(A) such contract shall not be treated as an annuity contract for purposes of this subtitle (other than subchapter L) and

72(u)(1)(B) the income on the contract for any taxable year of the policyholder shall be treated as ordinary income received or accrued by the owner during such taxable year.

For purposes of this paragraph, holding by a trust or other entity as an agent for a natural person shall not be taken into account.

72(u)(2) INCOME ON THE CONTRACT. –

72(u)(2)(A) IN GENERAL. – For purposes of paragraph (1), the term "income on the contract" means, with respect to any taxable year of the policyholder, the excess of –

72(u)(2)(A)(i) the sum of the net surrender value of the contract as of the close of the taxable year plus all distributions under the contract received during the taxable year or any prior taxable year, reduced by

72(u)(2)(A)(ii) the sum of the amount of net premiums under the contract for the taxable year and prior taxable years and amounts includible in gross income for prior taxable years with respect to such contract under this subsection.

Where necessary to prevent the avoidance of this subsection, the Secretary may substitute "fair market value of the contract" for "net surrender value of the contract" each place it appears in the preceding sentence.
72(u)(2)(B) NET PREMIUMS. --For purposes of this paragraph, the term "net premiums" means the amount of premiums paid under the contract reduced by any policyholder dividends.

72(u)(3) EXCEPTIONS. –
This subsection shall not apply to any annuity contract which --

72(u)(3)(A) is acquired by the estate of a decedent by reason of the death of the decedent,

72(u)(3)(E) is an immediate annuity.

72(u)(4) IMMEDIATE ANNUITY. –
For purposes of this subsection, the term "immediate annuity" means an annuity –

72(u)(4)(A) which is purchased with a single premium or annuity consideration,

72(u)(4)(B) the annuity starting date (as defined in subsection (c)(4)) of which commences no later than 1 year from the date of the purchase of the annuity, and

72(u)(4)(C) which provides for a series of substantially equal periodic payments (to be made not less frequently than annually) during the annuity period.

Index

Charts